Our Greatest Allies

RESPECT, RELATIONSHIP AND INTERVENTION
A CHILD'S JOURNEY

By
Maude Le Roux, OTR/L
Lauren O'Malley

aBM

Our Greatest Allies

Published by:
A Book's Mind
PO Box 272847
Fort Collins, CO 80527
www.abooksmind.com

ISBN 978-0-9883288-3-9

Our Greatest Allies

When a family has a child with an identified condition—whether diabetes, Down Syndrome, or autism—there is a very real danger that the child will be labeled and then treated like an object that is broken and needs to be fixed. A diabetic, a Down's child, an autistic. The disease takes precedence over the child's humanity. Whole medical and therapeutic systems of care confirm that the child "is" their condition. The family, in their desperate need to help their child, buys into the "therapies," and all efforts of the family are directed to "cure," "fix," or help the child "recover" or "reach his or her full potential." Too often the result is burnt-out caregivers, neglected siblings, and a marriage strained to breaking. In my developmental and behavioral pediatrics practice, I have seen it so many times.

But how does a family not do everything possible without feeling guilty? How can a child be helped in a way that does not treat him like a label, but respects his intrinsic motivation and deepest needs by understanding his biological and psychological complexity? How can a family survive intact as they search for and find the best ways to be helpful to their child? Read *Our Greatest Allies* and find out.

This tenderly written book is like having two wise and experienced companions accompany you on that universal "long and winding road" that begins with grief for the loss of the child you wished for, and ends when you have fallen in love with the child you have. Told in alternating chapters by Matty's mom, Lauren O'Malley, and Matty's occupational therapist, Maude Le Roux, OTR, this insightful and helpful case study covers the critical first six years in Matty's life.

As I read I wondered: How is this working mother of five children going to pull this off? Lauren is a very good writer who, in her chapters, is able to articulate her internal process as she takes those inevitable steps down the road—the first suspicion, then knowing something was not right, waiting for a diagnosis, getting a diagnosis, starting intervention, searching for the best intervention, and finally finding her allies. Parents who read this book will be heartened by Lauren's ability to be open and honest in the face of grief, anger, confusion, disappointment, and uncertainty—and still make strong decisions based on her gut level perceptions of what Matty needs, what she needs, and what her large and complex family needs. As Lauren says, "need trumps guilt!"

This is a nail-biter of a book. It is not clear in the beginning how Matty O'Malley will fare given the severity of his condition. Matty and his allies face a series of critical decisions that are filled with uncertainty even for the very experienced Maude. And it won't ruin the suspense to say that Matty does well. The real suspense is in how, at each critical juncture, his family and team helped him to do well. As Lauren exclaims toward the end of the book, "Oh how our children would thrive if we could create a culture of process rather than our infatuation with product.... When you cultivate a child's connection to purpose and process, learning and growth flourish naturally."

So this book is also about a set of interventions that really worked for Matty and his family. Maude Le Roux, who eventually becomes the team leader (and a great ally) for the O'Malley family, summarizes the plan this way, "The only solution to meet the true needs of the child is to look at him from all vantage points of a developmental perspective, and with a unified team approach, consider the place where the child needs us to start building his developmental support."

Based on the pioneering work of child psychiatrist Stanley Greenspan, MD, this book is a testament to a developmental, individualized, and relationship based (DIR®) model that honors and respects the child's uniqueness.

Maude's clearly written chapters describe this playful yet powerful developmental approach in detail. We learn about the importance of respecting the child's feeling life, while honoring his need to "keep the world the same" or risk causing him profound anxiety. We learn about the sensory profile of the child and how, by understanding his unique way of sensory processing, we can help the child integrate sensations to make sense of the world. Maude's description of "sensory processing" is one of the best I've ever read. She's even convinced me of the value of Tomatis® Sound training.

We learn that by establishing a secure sensory-perceptual base, we can then help a child make sense of the world. This leads to the most important of functional abilities—connecting with others through gesture, routines, and ultimately words. Each of Maude's chapters builds on the previous one until, by the end of the book, the reader has been schooled on how to organically apply a set of therapeutic principles to a particular child. In this regard, *Our Greatest Allies* will be of real interest to professionals as well as parents.

Let me end with a new word I learned from Matty's mom: lagniappe (pronounced LAN-yep). It means "a small gift," usually given by a storeowner as something extra beyond what was purchased—a little luxury, a little taste. When we honor our child's uniqueness and accept him for exactly who he is, we paradoxically help him make the most progress he can. We have solved the original dilemma of how to help him without turning him into a project or object. We become less anxious; we enjoy just being with our child; we experience the gift of everyday life. We give ourselves and our child a little lagniappe. So relax, find a comfy place to read, open the first pages of *Our Greatest Allies*, have a little taste. You're going to like it. You're going to learn a lot.

Rick Solomon MD
Medical Director
The Ann Arbor Center for
Developmental and Behavioral Pediatrics

Acknowledgments

Words cannot express our gratitude to the many people who have touched Matty's life and helped us bring his story you. We humbly thank our families, mentors, and the incredible teams that have huddled around Matty along his road to who he has become.

- ➢ To our husbands, how can we ever thank you for your endless patience in giving us the time to make this book be the best it could be.

- ➢ To Matty's amazing sisters, Grandma, and that special someone who has been a godsend to my children for more than a decade, I am forever thankful for you— Lauren.

- ➢ We thank the brilliant mentors of the programs we were able to leverage for Matty's success. Though Dr. Stanley Greenspan, Dr. Jean Ayers, and Dr. Alfred Tomatis have now passed from us, they are held dear as they remain the inspiration for seeing children differently, viewing them in a holistic way, and embracing their individual differences with the respect they deserve. Without their groundbreaking work, we would not have the "whole child" understanding that has allowed us to scaffold the process of growth in Matty.

- ➢ To Karen, thank you for your talent and grace. With unspoken humility, your instinct and creativity took Matty to new heights, allowing him to soar.

➢ We thank the team at *A Total Approach* that works together every day, diligently applying different principles of human understanding to the ultimate goal of bettering the lives of children and the families who love them.

➢ To the many teachers, therapists, and educational assistants who, over the years, have formed a radius of respect around Matty... I am deeply indebted to you. Though your chapters were not all described in this story, your dedication and kindness are appreciated beyond words—Lauren.

➢ To Natalie Randazzo, many thanks for your time and talent in creating the illustrations.

➢ With endless gratitude, we thank Matty for leading us on this journey. You taught us to remain true to your process of development, and we thank you for gracing us with the insight and courage to do so every step of the way.

➢ Lastly, we thank God for creating us in such a special way, so we may learn and share our journey... and help others along the way.

Table of Contents

Chapter 1 – Matty O'Malley......................................1
Lauren O'Malley had five children in just over five years. When Matty was born, things seemed only slightly and temporarily off-track. One Christmas portrait changed everything. One image that led to one word… a word that redefined their journey; but would not redefine him.

Chapter 2 – The Child… Not the Diagnosis..........................21
Maude Le Roux explains how to harness a child's full potential through a developmental approach to therapeutic intervention, especially for the treatment of autism. She explains how we assist in developing a "whole child" by respecting his sensory profile and tapping into his intrinsic motivation to learn and grow.

Chapter 3 – Early Intervention… Setting Sail
with No Clear Direction..57
Matty was certainly not like his sisters as he neared two. He wasn't pointing, wasn't imitating, and he was not at all like other two-year-olds. Early Intervention took several different paths before Lauren would learn what met Matty's real needs.

Chapter 4 – Understanding Sensory Processing....................83
"Aha" moments abound as Maude explains sensory processing and the systems that drive a child's physiological, intellectual, and social-emotional development. This fascinating discussion schools the reader in understanding how a child's sensory systems and developmental capacities impact his "behavior" and potential for growth.

Chapter 5 – Floortime™ and Schooltime...
a Whole New Ballgame 127

Lauren opens a new door to Floortime therapy, learning the value of play and a child's connection to meaning and purpose in learning. As Matty struggles in preschool, Lauren wonders if it's just not in the cards for him. Finally, she dials the number of an occupational therapist she's heard about. Her name is Maude Le Roux.

Chapter 6 – A Deep Dive into Matt's
Sensory Processing Systems 149

Maude meets Matt for the first time when she takes a comprehensive look at his sensory processing systems. The detailed evaluation describes each sensory system and how it impacts Matt's ability to function in his home and school environments.

Chapter 7 – The Student Body...
the Anatomy of Classroom Performance 163

Learning from Maude's evaluation of Matty, Lauren connects the dots in understanding how the body sets the stage for all learning and development. As Lauren begins to understand more about the value of the DIR model, Maude is brought in to consult on Matty's school program.

Chapter 8 – Developing the Child
through Relating and Understanding 183

As with her sensory processing chapter, Maude takes you on a deep dive of the Developmental, Individual Differences, Relationship (DIR) model. With an understanding of a child's sensory profile, the DIR model is a framework for building the social, emotional, and intellectual capacities that drive learning and development.

Chapter 9 – One Step off the Twister® Mat...
One Giant Leap for Development 223
At four years old, Matty seems to be making progress, but he suddenly gets stuck. Wanting to play on a Twister mat day after day leaves Lauren and his Floortime therapist anxious and unsure, but Maude is steadfast in respecting his need to remain "on the mat." Little did they know what developmental momentum that mat would generate.

Chapter 10 – Gaining Ground through Sound 239
Matt's therapeutic direction takes a new turn as he completes Tomatis Sound training. Even Maude was skeptical at first, but as she explains the science of Tomatis and how it was built upon what is indisputably known about the brain, more connections emerge. Soon after, Matt's progress catapults in new directions.

Chapter 11 – Cultivating Emotional
Growth and Self-Concept...263
Lauren and Matty hold hands for more than a year as they chart their way through the choppy waters of negative emotions and establishing Matty's self-concept. Kindergarten is a tumultuous time, but they both come out stronger. Matty was now able to soar.

Chapter 12 – The Child Makes the Journey Happen............293
Maude reflects on Matt's journey and his progress through a single approach... an approach of dignity.

Chapter 13 – Our Greatest Allies 303
Lauren describes her journey through the breadcrumb trail of allies she and Matt have found along the way. Thanks to Maude, it was a path paved with the respect, understanding, and relationships that Matt and other children like him so rightly deserve.

"I realized that this was just one word, just one moment—but it was a moment that would change me, not Matty."

Chapter 1

Matty O'Malley

Matthew Michael O'Malley, the fourth of my five children, was born on the same day as his sister only one year older. Irish twins by a mere thirteen hours. Matty has one of those names that sort of blends into a single word... mattyomalley. At home we call him Matty or Bud, but outside our family, "Hey Matty O'Malley" is a familiar greeting everywhere he goes. Born on a Wednesday, we were home by Friday morning after striking deals with my OB/Gyn and Matty's pediatrician. They would allow us to go home early only if I agreed to have a visiting nurse check in on us on Monday. We shook on it and we were home before noon on Friday.

Being my fourth child in four years, there was no nursing going on. In fact, there wasn't any liquid formula, boiling water, or even warming bottles going on. There were only bleary-eyed eyeball measurements of powdered formula poured into bottles of tepid tap water. All those perfect parents of two would be aghast, but for anyone who has braved being outnumbered by three or more, no further explanation is required. That's life when you spend every waking minute of every day bouncing from child to child, need to need. Each day begins and ends with crying. You live every day like a pinball getting plunged into action, shooting out of bed at the first cry and bouncing aimlessly from need to need until the day ends.

In retrospect, having five children in five years does seem a little crazy, but at the time I was pretty unfazed by it. I'm a fairly laid-back, grounded, roll with the punches kind of person. I come from a large family and really have no other frame of reference for what family is. I've never been overly driven by others' opinions about how many children I should have or how far apart I should have them. I'm just a simple, practical person.

People laugh at my annual labor stories, especially when I tell them how I drove myself to the hospital to have my last two babies. Face it, once you get to the hospital, you sit there and stare at the TV or the walls for twelve hours. There was no time for that. I had other children at home and it made no sense to either pay for childcare or inconvenience family to babysit when my husband was perfectly capable of watching the kids and I was perfectly capable of driving a few miles between contractions. When I had Matty, I simply drove to the hospital, waddled up to the labor and delivery floor, and actually ended up in the same delivery room with the same nurse I'd had when my daughter was born a year earlier. My husband came to the hospital as the time drew near—and the rest is a blur. When you have five labor and delivery experiences, they do tend to blend together; but of all my deliveries, Matty was actually the least eventful. I had a good epidural, no C-section, and no complications. Except for his big O'Malley noggin, his entrance into the world and short stay in the hospital were, fortunately, status quo.

Less than forty-eight hours old, Matty spent his first Friday evening at home, swaddled in his car seat on the kitchen table as we celebrated his sister's first birthday, which I missed two days earlier. Even from his first days of life, Matty was assimilated into our family without grand fanfare, not even being able to relish in his own day of birth, sharing his birthday with his sister from the moment he was born. But at the risk of sounding insensitive, I truly believe that being brought up in a larger family environment has been one of the gifts that has given Matty, in the end, a greater foundation for adapting in school, in society, and life in general.

Not just a "Sloppy Joe"

Turns out, the deal I struck with my doctor would be Matty's first stroke of Irish luck and my first indication that he might be heading down a different path than his sisters. Keeping my end of the bargain to come home on Friday, we had a Monday morning appointment with a visiting nurse. An hour-long appointment for her to check in on Matty. Really? I had three other children. I was well-versed in feeding, changing, and swaddling infants. "This was going to be a total waste of time," I thought, but I had agreed and she was coming whether I liked it or not. After checking the usual vitals, she asked, "How's he eating?" I remember telling her that after having three girls, I was already seeing the differences in having a boy. I explained how Matty seemed to be a sloppy eater. To get two ounces of formula into him, I would prepare three ounces, knowing that one would probably run down his neck. The nurse happened to be a neonatal intensive care nurse who specialized in infant feeding. I don't remember her name and I doubt she would remember her visit with me, but she was the first person to teach me about *sensory awareness*.

"He might not just be a messy eater," she explained, "he may be struggling because he doesn't have the *awareness* of the nipple or the *control* of the muscles in and around his mouth to be able to suck effectively." She explained the suck, swallow, breathe reflex and all that goes into being able to suck from a nipple (awareness of the nipple, muscle control in the lips, cheeks, and tongue, and the timing of breathing). At first I thought she was just trying to justify her visit, laying a lot of jargon on me so she would have something to fill out on the home-visit form she was probably required to complete. But after explaining why Matty couldn't suck efficiently, she taught me how to hold him more upright and provide gentle support under his chin, and how to hold the bottle at an angle that gave him better awareness of the nipple. He immediately downed two ounces and fell into a nice deep full-belly formula coma. I was amazed. With this new technique for feeding him, Matty started eating like a pro.

For Matty's first month, I'm sure my *hover meter* would have probably registered lower than the off-the-charts attention other mothers can give their infants. I just didn't have the time to linger over him, dwelling on his every moment. Distracted by the needs of three older sisters, there was simply no way I could spend hours and hours rocking him in a glider as he slept in my arms. I didn't have a glider, and even if I did, I would rarely have had the opportunity to sit and rock. Others needed to be fed and changed, and laundry was perpetual. He wasn't fussy or colicky, and after he started eating better, he didn't demand much attention. It's not that he yearned for attention he didn't get, nor did he appear uninterested in the attention he did get. He simply got as much as I could give him and he seemed to be satisfied with that.

"Seeing" the Situation Differently

I'm a pretty intuitive person and I tend to trust my gut. Often, I'll see something and that one image speaks volumes to me. It's these visual moments that make me stop and think, and help me draw connections and perspective. My first visually intuitive memory of Matty came when he was just a few weeks old. One day he was in his bouncy seat on the kitchen table, and as I walked into the kitchen, Matty about ten feet away, it struck me. There he was looking completely relaxed in his lazy boy of infant chairs, alert yet calm, with his head tilted slightly to the left. I didn't expect he should be holding his head up perfectly straight, but what hit me was that I wasn't even seeing a gradual increase in his neck strength. I was seeing the same exact visual image I had seen for the past weeks. Nothing had changed. Perhaps blessed by the annual experience of watching infant development day in and day out, I knew I should be seeing changes almost daily. But there he was again with his head cocked to the side, always to the same side and always at the same angle.

I took Matty to the pediatrician and explained that he wasn't beginning to hold his head up as straight or as quickly as his sisters had. The doctor shared my concern, suggested that Matty needed occupational therapy (OT), and I drove home with a diagnosis. *Torticollis*—my ticket to OT. I couldn't pronounce Torticollis, but I didn't need to. In one fifteen-minute appointment, I had my first lesson on how to get the key to open the door of intervention. A diagnosis.

So off to OT we went. Matty went to therapy from six weeks to four months of age. I learned from the therapist that his head tilted to the left because the muscles on the left side of his neck were contracted, while the muscles on the right side of his neck were not strong enough to keep his head up and straight. In my mind, I pictured the muscles on the left as a thick, tight vacuum cleaner belt and the muscles on the right as a thin, flimsy rubber band. So all we needed to do was stretch the vacuum cleaner belt and strengthen the rubber band, right? Easier said than done.

We would go to OT at a local rehab facility three times a week, and on off days I would somehow find the time to do exercises with him at home. Fortunately, after working through a few months of therapy, Matty's neck muscles seemed adequately stretched and strengthened and we were able to start decreasing his therapy visits. His journey may have started a little off track, but with intervention I assumed we were right back on the beaten path. The timing also worked out well because I would soon be going back to work and it would have been real difficult to continue to take him to his OT appointments given my work schedule.

"Mom at Work"

Being pregnant over seven straight years does have its advantages. I never had to throw out unused diapers, my "baby bucks" coupons never had a chance to expire, and I *owned* that expectant mother parking spot at the supermarket. This made my almost daily dash into the grocery store on my way home from work just a little easier. Throughout those years of pregnancies and having children I continued to work, but returning to work after Matty was born was the only time I remember questioning why on earth I did so. With four children, childcare would cost a fortune and I didn't make a fortune. I wasn't unhappy being a mother; as crazy as it was, I enjoyed most of it. But I was undoubtedly drawn by the prospect of returning to work, even just part-time, and I had to ask myself why. Was I a mother or was I a worker? I had four children ages four, three, one, and four months and I was thinking about returning to work. I'm sure people thought I was crazy for one reason or another. Co-workers thought I was crazy for having so many kids and mom-friends thought I was crazy for going back to work. But I never thought I was crazy. For a short time I thought about not returning, but somehow it didn't take too long for me to get clarity on why I wanted and needed to.

Working gives me access to the few things I value much more than money or career. First, it gives me time to be alone and inside my own head, my favorite place to be. Clearing the family lists out of my head gives me space to see things in the broader sense, to put things in perspective. It also gives me physical distance from my house and family. It is a place where my contributions are valued and understood and my work is respected. Understanding and respect—two imperatives that would soon drive the whole of my perspective on parenting, were the two things I needed for my own happiness, and were the main reasons why I chose to continue working.

I had to make a decision and as I had always done, I followed my gut. When it came down to it, work carved out a place in my life where I was appreciated and recognized for my contributions. Even though my part-time salary barely covered the cost of childcare, the feeling of being valued and respected was priceless to me. So when Matty was four months old, I started making arrangements for childcare, and back to work I went a month later. On more than one occasion I returned to work already pregnant. This was one of those times. The next year went by in a flash and eight months later, when Matty was thirteen months old, his younger sister was born.

During Matty's first year, other than the feeding and Torticollis issues, I saw nothing overly alarming in terms of his growth, yet he was consistently a little later in reaching milestones than his sisters—at least the milestones I knew to look for. He was later in pushing up on his arms and rolling over, but I attributed that to a strength deficit from the Torticollis. He sat up at seven months where his sisters sat at six. He crawled a little later and walked at thirteen months compared to twelve months for his sisters. Matty was a pretty quiet baby, not much of a babbler like his sisters were; and with my attention diverted and divided among three other children and an infant, his quietness didn't raise any suspicions in me. He was my only boy and I assumed it was normal for boys to do things later than girls. Nothing jumped off the pages of his book of development to bite me on the nose until he was about twenty months old. What I didn't know, but would soon learn, was that Matty wasn't just quiet... he was silent.

A Distant Portrait

I will never forget another visual image that is to this day seared into my memory. It was our family Christmas portrait taken when Matty was twenty months old. I remember taking the picture out of the Sears envelope, delighted by the smiles of my daughters, but troubled by what I saw in Matty. His face was expressionless, the corner of his lips turned down, his eyes staring beyond the moment. He was completely distant and disconnected from the experience. A typical twenty-month-old would be engaged in some way, either positively or negatively, either smiling or screaming—but what I saw was neither of these. He looked detached and withdrawn. In seeing Matty in that portrait, my heart and gut sunk to the floor. He was telling me something and my gut told me I had to listen.

That day I called my neighbor who was a preschool special education teacher and asked her to stop by. I didn't share my feelings about the Christmas picture; I think I just wanted someone to tell me I was concerned over nothing. I just wanted to hear her say that what she saw in Matty was a typically developing little boy, and allow me to convince myself that what I saw in the picture was nothing more than an awkward staring moment. I wanted to be told that I was overreacting and had no reason to worry. I wanted my instincts to be wrong.

When my neighbor stopped by she asked a lot of questions, mostly about milestones. When did he do the typical sitting, crawling, standing, and walking? Did he coo and babble as an infant? Did he say "ball," or "baby," or "bye-bye," or any words at all? She went further to inquire about other subtleties of development that I now know to be so important, but at the time had no idea he wasn't really hitting. Pointing, for example.

"If Matt wants something, how does he let you know?" she asked. I remember realizing that I never really thought about that before.

"If he wants a pretzel, what does he do? Does he get your attention and point to the bag of pretzels on the counter?" Well, no.

"Does he raise his arm or gesture in any way? Does he respond to your gestures? If you point to something, does he look at you and then look around the room to try to find what you're pointing at?"

I had to think about it. Although he wasn't too verbal at the time, I had to really think about what he did to communicate with me. Would he find me, take my hand, lead me into the kitchen, gesture for me to pick him up, and point to the pretzels he wanted? No. If I happen to be holding him in the kitchen and there was a cookie on the counter, would he reach out toward the cookie and verbalize something, even a grunt? Not that I could remember. I was completely taken back because I really couldn't put my finger on any specific way he communicated with me.

I suddenly felt a rush of all those things that would send a lie detector test off the charts. My heart started racing a little faster, I felt my cheeks start to flush, and I briefly disengaged from the conversation, all while trying to seem unfazed by the questioning.

"I think he sort of raises his arm in the direction of what he wants," I lied.

"Does he extend his finger at all or simply raise his arm," she asked.

At that moment I realized my answers should be yes. They weren't.

What's the Point?

As soon as she left, I shut the door and ran upstairs to fold the laundry. Folding laundry is my favorite of all mundane household chores. Our laundry room is on the second floor of our house and I always sit on my bed to fold. It's quiet and I'm usually alone. It's when I think, and sometimes when I cry. Sorting and folding, thinking and questioning. Why did it seem to be so important that Matty was pointing? What's the big deal about pointing? Only a day before my head was in a place where the prospect of any kind of issue with Matty would be something minor, something temporary, something like Torticollis. The uneasiness I felt when I saw the Christmas picture was now pointing, pardon the pun, in a more alarming direction. The thought of something that wasn't only temporary was too frightening to even consider. But now I wasn't so sure. I sensed more than casual concern about pointing and gesturing, and the number of "No's" I uttered in response to my neighbor's questions had me deeply worried. What if this was something more serious? More permanent?

My neighbor asked if she could come back the next day to play with Matty a little. She returned this time with some paperwork and seemed to be conducting a more formal visit. I could tell she was gauging Matty's ability to respond to one- and two-step requests when she asked him to "please give me the ball," which he did, followed by "can you please pick up the car and hand it to mommy?" Matty walked in the direction of the car but didn't pick it up. "Does he babble and make sounds such as 'm', 'd', 'b'?" she asked. "Does he use any nouns or combine two words? Does he imitate simple gestures?" And she again asked about pointing. "Does he point to his toes or his belly if asked to identify them? Does he actually extend his index finger or does he just raise his arm?"

Many questions, all with the same gut wrenching answer. No. She was kind and compassionate in her way of suggesting that maybe I should give my pediatrician a call to discuss it. She also left me with the phone number of my local Early Intervention (EI) program in case I ended up needing it, which didn't bother me as much as knowing she brought it with her. Whatever she'd seen the day before was that blatant, that worrisome. Were there other signs that I was too busy to see, or worse yet, chose to ignore? How could I have missed something about my child that was so obvious to her?

The Christmas picture stirred a fear in my gut that I didn't want to admit. I found myself gripped by the uneasiness of what I sensed my neighbor suspected. I just wanted it to go away. I went to sleep each night just wanting to wake up to find Matty pointing and engaging and babbling the day away. In the days and weeks that followed that didn't happen. I did piles of laundry and had countless self-conversations. Is all this worry really necessary? Maybe he's just a late bloomer. Maybe the Christmas picture was a fluke. And pointing? Maybe he's just a kid who doesn't like to point. Maybe he's just a mellow kid who isn't very demanding and has no deep inclination to boss people around. It'll all come eventually and I may look back on all this needless worry and laugh. Am I just being that parent who worries about every little bump and bruise… and complete lack of communication?

Nuances of Development 101

I didn't know how to process the possibility of what this could be. I wanted to believe it would all work itself out in the end and that Matty could just keep toddling along on his merry way. With all the needs I was responsible for, I didn't have the strength or energy to stop and deal with any more. Do I need to pursue this now? Or if I wait will it eventually work itself out somehow? In my head I was stuck. Washing and worrying, I folded and feared what this situation would shape up to be. I didn't know exactly what I would be dealing with, but whatever it was, my cup was already full. I couldn't handle one more drop.

Load after load was spent dwelling in anger and self-blame, wondering how I could have been so blind to the fact that my child wasn't expressing himself. Maybe it was covered in one of those *How to Be the Best Parent in the World* books I never read. Maybe if I wasn't working I would have had the time to read one of those books and I would have known what to look for. Then I would have known he wasn't just a quiet, easy-going child and I would have seen there was something amiss long ago. How could I have failed my child so miserably to not even be able to recognize he was not meeting such a critical milestone?

Matty was twenty months old and was not verbal, but more importantly, Matty was not *communicating*. He wasn't just a passive kid who went with the flow of our crazy household. He was a child who was not communicating at all—through speech or expressions or gestures. This realization was very profound for me. Was Matty pointing? No. How would he tell me he wanted to get out of his crib? He didn't. I would peek into his room every day and there he would be, sitting quietly, never a peep out of him to tell me he wanted to be picked up.

Although I didn't realize it at the time, I was learning the value of communicating *intent*. This was my first lesson in the nuances of development. It was not simply a speech or language issue, it was a communication void. Pointing is not just a non-verbal way of getting what you want. It's deeper than that. Pointing is the catalyst for engagement. It's the proof that "I have a plan... I want that cookie and I'm going to find a way to engage you because I know you are my only means of getting that cookie." The actual act of extending the index finger to engage another to show desire or intent is one of the most subtle yet critical aspects of early development. I wish I knew this then.

Looking back, I was fortunate to have had endless laundry to do and countless diapers to change. Perhaps one of the benefits of having children so close in age is learning that doing your best just has to be good enough. There is no other option. *Need trumps guilt.* It's a blessing I've learned to appreciate as one of the many gifts of a larger family. Time and energy completely consumed by others' needs leaves no place for guilt to thrive; and when need is calling the shots, you have no other choice than to let go of the guilt. When you have physically and emotionally given everything you have to simply meet the demands of each passing day, you're really liberated from the guilt that you haven't given enough. Being constantly consumed with everyone else's needs kept me from allowing my guilt to stew on the front burner while Matty's needs boiled over on the back. Whether I should have recognized the signs or called my neighbor sooner, I now appreciate my instinct for having called her at all.

On to Early Intervention

Armed with the phone number of my county's EI program, I set sail on a twelve-month journey on a vessel that could have been aptly named the *Hurry up and Wait*. My child needed help *now* and I now knew it. What I didn't know was what kind of help he needed and where to get it. As much as I didn't want to, I knew I needed to get things going sooner rather than later. I rallied some strength and braced myself for a challenge, but had no idea just how numbing the next year would turn out to be.

I called to get the EI ball rolling and was somewhat surprised at the level of responsiveness, and how easily and relatively quickly the process moved. Although there were several steps to go through, they were all adequately explained and laid out with appointment dates over the coming weeks. While traversing the EI intake process, I also stayed busy working my way through a web of conversations with parents and service providers of other children in our school district. Matty wasn't even two yet and I couldn't believe I was starting to have conversations about his *preschool readiness*.

"Early Intervention works," I was told. "The earlier you get him help, the better off he'll be in the long run."

I was told Matty needed help and services *now*, and I had no reason not to believe it to be true.

Weeks were passing by and the time was helping me put things in perspective. Going through the process to start EI services, it soon became apparent that Matty would likely get far less and perhaps not even the right services until I had a diagnosis in hand. Until then, the service offering would be minimal. The only possibility of leveraging more EI services was to have a diagnosis indicating the need for broader intervention. The more I spoke to other parents, the more I realized that we would also probably have to get Matty additional services on our own—but I didn't know where to begin. At the time I didn't know exactly what we were dealing with; I only knew that Matty wasn't communicating and he needed help. The best way to help him was to get him the services he needed, but how do you find those services when you don't even know what they are or who can provide them?

We saw our pediatrician who immediately gave me a referral for an opinion on the communication delay, but feedback from EI and the dialogue I'd been having with other parents soon changed my purpose for getting in to see a developmental pediatrician. My primary goal was no longer to consult on the issue at hand; it had now become a means to an end. Matty needed services, and like my experience with getting him OT for Torticollis, a diagnosis would again be the ticket. I certainly would listen to and value the doctor's opinion, but it was equally important to get a diagnosis and get it as soon as possible so we could start the appropriate services. The only route to getting a diagnosis was to get into a developmental pediatrician's office; not a simple feat as I would soon learn.

"Your Next Appointment is When?"

No longer in a plummet, my focus was now split between the evaluations needed to begin EI services and trying to get an appointment with a developmental pediatrician. This is where disillusionment quickly set in. Everywhere you turn, the system espouses how you need to hurry up and intervene; oh wait, we neglected to mention—the system doesn't hurry. I was soon aware that on this issue, the medical community wasn't going to be doing anything STAT. Of about ten developmental pediatricians in my area, not one had less than a nine month wait for an appointment, and the process of just getting an appointment was exasperating. You call to make an appointment and *the procedure* was immediately administered by the receptionist like a painful injection. After being grilled about the severity of the situation, every doctor's office seemed to read from the same script.

"We will send you a packet to complete including a full medical history and behavioral questionnaire. After we receive your packet back, it will go through a process to be reviewed by the doctor. If the doctor feels it's necessary to see the child, our scheduling secretary will contact you to set up an appointment."

"When is your next available appointment?" I would ask.

"We're scheduling new patient appointments twelve months from now."

One year to wait.

Anger

As any parent who has dealt with the enormity of trying to help their child in the face of helplessness knows, the most difficult emotion to harness or dispel is anger. It's hard to find a place for the frustration of constantly searching and never finding. Not really knowing exactly what you're looking for, but knowing full well that precious days are slipping by until you find it. I am a person of average intelligence and I know I have the capacity to enable an action plan to help my child. I am the mother of five children, for goodness sake; I should have the capacity to deal with the fact that one of my children needs help.

But I wasn't able to discern a clear course of action. I couldn't get the appropriate type or level of services Matty needed without a diagnosis, and the possibility of getting a diagnosis was, at best, nine months away. The anger of knowing I had the capacity to implement a plan of action was painfully compounded by the frustration of the medical community talking out of both sides of its mouth. The medical establishment's espousal of early intervention was hard to swallow as it allowed children to wait up to eighteen months to see a developmental pediatrician. It was like trying to floor the accelerator while someone else was slamming on the brake. Infuriating.

Networking

I began my siege just after the New Year, starting with referrals from my pediatrician and fanning out from there until my list of developmental pediatricians was at least ten deep. I had my *A-list* of top docs espoused as the best in the area, and I had my *B-list* of docs who had good credentials, but whom I simply knew nothing about. I pursued them all.

"We'll send you a packet to complete. After we receive it back, it will go through a review process and if your son meets the criteria to schedule an appointment, we'll call you."

The mailbox was checked daily and packets were returned the same day I received them. Then I'd wait some more. Days turning into weeks and weeks into months, crucial development ticking away. You need services to intervene, you need a diagnosis to get services, you need to get an appointment to get a diagnosis, and you seem to need Divine Intervention to land an appointment with a developmental pediatrician. I called anyone I knew with even remote ties to the medical community, hoping someone would happen to know someone who could finagle a way to get an appointment faster.

Finally in May, a full five months into my mission, a friend's sister-in-law was able to help me get in to see a developmental pediatrician. Trees were in bloom, birds were singing, and we were on our way to the appointment. For months, the services Matty needed had been held hostage by this diagnosis—and now the day was here. I had all those weeks to brace myself emotionally, but in truth, I didn't. I didn't have the time, and I think I'm forever blessed by that. I was too preoccupied with diaper changes, potty training, and the EI process. The reality of what it could all mean never really settled with me beyond getting the services Matty needed at the time, although I did fear what it could do to our family. Could we be joining the ranks of so many other families, struggling with similar *A-list* diagnoses—many ripped apart by the likes of Alzheimer's, addiction, and anorexia?

One Word

Driving through the parking garage, I had one of those weird, surreal experiences that will always remain with me, and has become a constant source of strength for me. Have you ever been reading something and you come across a word you certainly know, you've known it forever, but all of a sudden it looks wrong? It's the same word you've known all your life, but suddenly you're not sure if it's spelled correctly and somehow it looks different to you? It's like a temporary short circuit in your brain that makes something completely familiar seem totally unfamiliar to you. I don't know if there's some kind of reverse-déjà vu name for that, but I recall having a similar sort of feeling in the parking garage that day.

After squeezing into an empty spot, I sat for a minute, trying to gather my paperwork, and my composure. I turned and looked at Matty. In those big eyes with eyelashes to die for, I saw such vulnerability, such dependence. I felt I was standing on a fault line that, when shaken by this diagnosis, could swallow up this innocent view of him forever. Would my sweet, gentle boy whom I loved so deeply suddenly be rewired in my mind as something different to me? Can one word be that powerful?

After a somewhat uneventful appointment, we left with what we came for. A single code on an insurance form. Leaving the office, I folded the form in half, in half again, and again, and again. The receptionist handed me a parking token that I quickly slid into my pocket as I juggled the papers and booklets of information the doctor had given me to help begin our new journey.

Time stood still as I started the drive home through a maze of exit arrows and parking levels. "It will be me who owns this diagnosis, not Matty," I thought, "this was just one word, just one moment—but it was a moment that would change me. Like that familiar word, I will not allow him to become unfamiliar to me. No single word can have the power to recast or devalue his existence. I won't allow it to."

As we waited in line at the parking garage exit, in searching for the token now lost among my vending machine change, I shoved that insurance form deep down into my pocket where it would remain in my mind for years to come.

The gate lowered in my rear view mirror. "This diagnosis is nothing but pocket change," I thought. And to this day I keep that diagnosis like pocket change in my mind. I always have it with me, always know it's there. But like spare change, one day I may reach into my pocket… only to find it's gone.

"Every course of treatment begins from the same place—a place of respect."

Chapter 2

The Child… Not the Diagnosis

Autism became real to me in 1996, when I first started my career in pediatrics in a West Virginia school district. I was struck by the beauty of these children and their absolute, unconditionally honest view of life. I wish I knew then what I know now; I know I could have made more of a difference. The diagnosis of autism has received much attention in recent years and many of my colleagues and other professionals have their own ideas and perspectives on how to treat children with this pervasive and perplexing neuro-biological disorder. I think of the many overwhelmed and overwrought parents and families who come to me, all with the same question, "Where do we go from here?"

To them my answer is always the same, "Right now, I don't know the exact place where we will be in the future, but I absolutely do know the place where we will start."

Every course of treatment begins from the same place—a place of respect. I have a deep respect for every child's developmental needs and right to self-integrity. I have equally profound respect for the needs of the family and the power of the parent's relationship with the child to be the catalyst for success. Each child's journey begins with a single sheet of white paper; a blank canvas with no preconceived ideas, no hidden agendas. It is simply a place to collect the notes and observations to paint a portrait of respect for the individual capacities of every child who allows me to peek inside his or her world. It is the place to define the qualities that make a child unique to himself, not different from the rest of the world. Standardized testing and methodologies have a place and we need them to help our perspective on treatment, but the most important foundation is to establish the communication and relationships that allow us to see the uniqueness of each child, and to consider that individuality in the treatment plan. The simplicity and delicacy of each fragile sheet of paper that begins my journey with every child reminds me to demand this of myself... respect first, facts later.

Honor the Child

Autism has a place on a continuum of diagnoses that share developmental and sensory processing challenges affecting the hierarchy of typical early development. The medical community classifies autism along a spectrum of disorders with similar symptoms, and thanks to the tremendous efforts of a coalition of autism organizations, most people now know that roughly "1 in 88 children has been identified with an autism spectrum disorder (ASD)." (Centers for Disease Control and Prevention (CDC)) This awareness is certainly to be applauded, but we must never allow a diagnosis to define the essence of who a child is or who he can become. To over-consider the diagnosis is to run the risk of placing a ceiling on a child's potential, and this is simply unfair to the child and the family. We must always remind ourselves that every child has the right to the same expectations in life as we do... to be safe and protected, to make sense of our environment and relationships, to understand what is expected, and to have the fullest resources to apply ourselves to the ever-changing demands of this thing called life. It is our obligation to honor the child and treat all children, diagnosis or no diagnosis, with the respect we demand in our own lives. They deserve no less.

Autism knows no social or global boundaries. I was born in South Africa and completed my college training in my home country before moving to the U.S. I have the privilege of returning to South Africa twice a year to train, mentor and assist other professionals. But whether in the U.S. or South Africa or anywhere else, the diagnosis of autism and the issues that arise from it are the same. No matter the continent or ethnicity, my European colleagues and professionals around the world are all speaking the same language in the earnest search for answers to this complex global phenomenon.

I respect the child and everything he brings to the table, even if all he can bring is a *behavior* that may reside outside our social comfort zone. Behavior to me is not a force to be extinguished or eliminated and I do not view self-stimulatory behavior (or *stimming*) as a diagnostic criteria. I see it as a way for an atypically developing child to satisfy a deep-seated sensory or emotional need that he cannot otherwise access in a typical way due to his lack of development. My goal is to journey to the center of the need to diminish it at its source.

With the exception of the broad brush of childhood development, in my work I rarely think about *children* as an entity. The concept is just too general. The landscape of individual differences in physiological, emotional, social, and environmental factors is so vast yet so unique to each child. The *child* must always be respected first, irrespective of the children around him. I believe strongly that each child wants to be known by us, but on his terms, as he may fail to understand our terms and expectations in his atypically developing world.

We must not allow a diagnosis to marginalize a child, although this happens far too often. If we want people to accept us for who we are, and we are definitely not perfect, we certainly should afford the same quality of life to these beautiful children who are trying to enter and share the same space with us. All interventions must be about the individual profile of the child, not the actual diagnosis. The responsibility is ours. *We* must learn how to get to know them and *we* are the ones who need to enter into their world, attempt to understand their reasoning, and figure out ways to allow them to trust us and join us in ours.

Harnessing a Child's Full Potential

It would be rare indeed to meet a parent who doesn't love or respect their child, although I have met parents who couldn't articulate what it was about their child that cultivated their love and respect. Parents too often let the *cannots* drive their perspective. Their thoughts linger heavily around thinking, "My child can't do this or isn't doing that." It is always such a rewarding activity to ask parents to simply watch their child for a week or two with no expectations. I ask them to just be an observer, to watch what their child is doing, and see what he is interested in, to note what he looks at or touches, to take in his non-verbal cues and see all the positive and beautiful things he brings to the table. The idea behind this exercise is to allow parents to see and feel a baseline of validation for their child. My first meetings with parents of a child with developmental delays are often filled with angst and tears of fear. But when parents slow down and really watch their child, they're often quite struck by what they see.

Truly seeing what a child does initiate as his or her own contribution creates the most visceral connection to respect. More often than not, my second meetings with parents are more tearful than the first. Only they're tears born out of liberation in finding a new place of genuine honor for their child. Parents realize that they are not the ones living inside the body of their child and that their child really does communicate what he needs if they can learn the language of how he expresses it. Parents are relieved to know that they don't always have to know what's best for their child, for it is the child who really knows what he needs in any given moment. We have to learn from the child what makes him feel good and why, as well as what makes him want to run away. To consider the child's experience first before we foster our expectations on him becomes a plan of give and take—following the child's lead, yet leading the child from one secure scaffold to the next. This genuine understanding brings parents to a whole new level of respect.

It is quite traumatizing for me to visit a treatment session or classroom and see how children are being *trained* to be what we as adults would like to see them be. What I see is an approach of "this is the way you should behave" or "this way is better for you because I am the therapist (or teacher) and this is what I want you to do." I use the word *traumatized* with intent. When you observe this type of training-based environment, the predictability of the child's response is distressing. Time after time, I see the child first respond with hesitation, then confusion, then quite frequently... *the negative behavior*. If a child is constantly being fed what adults would like for him to learn, it is very difficult for his ideas to be validated, and it is even more difficult for him to build self-esteem. Even more so, the child will have a difficult time creating trusting relationships, especially when well-meaning teachers or caregivers continuously thwart his agenda or ideas. From the child's perspective, the potential for such relationships merely becomes one to be tolerated, and for learning situations to become rote rather than integrative.

Learning is all about tackling the new and novel, and this involves risk. If a child feels unsafe, there will be no scaffold or place of comfort to build upon and his typical choice will be to avoid new learning. As the adults, we often create the need for a behavior plan by the very act of not acknowledging the child's needs; and because the child has a diagnosis, he frequently becomes the one to blame for the failure of our plan. Children are meant to feel safe, warm, and loved. As adults, we crave the same from our life partners and family members, and we know how we feel if we don't get what we need. When we are treated with respect in our relationships, these are the relationships we embrace and work hard to maintain, are they not? It is not difficult then to understand that the best way to harness a child's full potential and bring out the best in him is to create an atmosphere of warmth and respect, a place where he is grounded in the security of his relationships with teachers,

therapists, and caregivers, and feels safe to explore until he finds
the choice that meets *his needs*.

The Developmental Perspective

I subscribe to a **developmental approach** to viewing and
treating children, and I believe therapy for the treatment of
autism is best served from a developmental frame of reference.
Throughout our entire life, our brain, mind, thoughts, and
perspectives are shaped by our exposure to and experiences of
the world we live in—but no time is more precious than early
childhood. This is when we are rooted in how we process the
environment and how we make decisions about how we will
respond to the many ways we are touched by others and the
world in which we exist. The developmental perspective is based
on the concept that from intra-uterine life and throughout early
childhood, there are certain aspects of development that need
to be laid down as the foundation for building all subsequent
layers of development. The most basic foundation of early
development lies in our ability to first process information
through our senses. Next we develop the ability to organize and
integrate this information for functional use, and only then are
we able to execute function in an organized way.

Executive functions involve our ability to organize
ourselves, to multi-task, and to not give in to our impulses or have
emotional upsets in times of challenge. Executive functioning
also includes understanding the concept of time. Building the
necessary skills of executive functioning to become a lifelong
learner is dependent upon building blocks of very early life
experiences. Our foundational layers are built upon sensory
processing, and this lays down the scaffold upon which executive
functions can become an automatic part of how we live life. When
foundational layers are laid down successfully, we develop a
certain **automaticity** in our interaction with the world that needs
no further assistance from our cortical processes, our intellect.
This automaticity allows us to function efficiently without having

to pay undue mental effort as it resides in our subconscious behavior. During neurotypical development, certain aspects of our processing abilities are absorbed into this autopilot mode, freeing up more of our cognitive and emotional capacities to understand our experience of the world. Children who receive a spectrum diagnosis are often devoid of the intended meaning of daily activities because they are *stuck* in the first layers of not effectively processing incoming sensory information. With the resulting deficiencies in the area of executive functioning, they are then expected to perform tasks in a world they do not process efficiently, and therefore do not understand.

Early development depends on our sensory, motor, emotional, environmental, and relationship experiences. All of it matters and all of it together shapes who we are today and how we cope with our life experiences. If a child has a solid neuro-biological system but is deprived of early attachment to one or both parents, it could affect how he relates to all relationships in life. If a child lacks the ability to process information in a balanced way, it could affect all future learning experiences. The building blocks are crucial to all areas of executive function, which is why laying down the foundation to build the necessary developmental skills is so critical to any treatment program for a child with atypical development.

The Sensory Starting Line

In the beginning, it is all about sensory immersion and the development of relationships within the sensory environment. Developmentally speaking, a child certainly does not pop out of the womb saying, "Hey Mom, what's up?" Development begins in utero, starting with the central nervous system, and continues in the early years with motor and speech development. Today, much emphasis is put on the development of specific motor and language milestones such as walking and talking, but the quality of *sensory reception* and *adaptation* is often overlooked.

Infant Development is all about Sensory Immersion

True to the latest science, there is evidence of genes playing a role in the origin of autism, allowing for a predisposition in certain children; however, it is not yet clear what causes this predisposition to evolve into a diagnosis. What science does know is that this diagnosis involves the central nervous system and that the prime time for development of the central nervous system is in the first five to seven years of life. Intra-uterine development and the first months of life are strongly dependent on the development of the central nervous system, which depends on the taking in and organization of sensory information.

The first essences of relationships are closely bonded with the processing of sensory information. The developing baby in the womb can already clearly *hear* his mother's voice and others surrounding her in the third trimester of pregnancy. By the time a baby is born, his *tactile* system is ready to accept the warm embraces of his parents and to learn how to suckle and snuggle in the safe comfort of his mother's arms. When *vision* starts clearing a couple of days after birth, the baby is intently watching his mother's face, searching it, trying to take it in. As they share mutual visual exchanges, the language of "motherese" gives the baby the sounds of language to explore as his system starts to get ready for the process of language that could occur as early as nine months of age.

Beyond establishing the security of relationships, these experiences are the sensory underpinnings of global childhood development.

Adaptation refers to the ability of the central nervous system to adapt to the sensory experiences of the environment. The earliest aspects of development rely heavily upon a baby's ability to adapt to the extra-uterine environment. When babies are easily agitated and have difficulty calming, they're described as being fussy or colicky and parents are mostly told they will grow out of it. The fact is, for many children, being a fussy baby is perfectly okay if the child has the capacity to build on his foundational developmental resources to cope with and *adapt* to the environment in a flexible manner. But many atypically developing children lack the solid developmental foundation for adaptation. When this is later recognized, parents often realize their child could have benefitted from closer scrutiny during those very early months of life.

Until the sensory building blocks are thoroughly investigated and developmentally determined, we simply will not know what the child's potential will be. We have to know the origin from which a child may have developed a faulty connection that continues to need ongoing coping, especially as each year brings higher expectations and the need for coping becomes stronger. This is why we frequently hear of children who only started to show symptoms, melt downs, or aversive behavior in later years rather than at the very onset of the difficulty. We also know that functional areas overlap during certain stages of development to form a firmer foundation, allowing a child to become more secure and increasingly more efficient in how he functions in the environment. Each time a child reaches a new growth spurt in his life, he may temporarily let go of a previously learned capacity until the next capacity is strengthened and he can now use both functions together. For example, it is not uncommon to see a child who has some language ability go through a period of time where he *turns off* his language capacities to focus all his energy on mastering another task such as motor development, only to pick up language again later with an increased ability to talk and move simultaneously. Regardless of the diagnosis, we have to look back in a child's development to find the closest possible place *where development went astray*, as this is where to begin therapeutic intervention.

In a developmental approach, all factors of development should be considered. Gross motor development impacts fine motor development. Motor planning development impacts problem-solving and social thinking. Emotional development is affected by fight, fright, and flight responses. These are but a few of the complexities that combine to impact the choices made by a child in a given moment. If an atypically developing child's early experience caused him discomfort, future experiences will be evaluated as carrying the same risk and he will raise barriers of avoidance to those experiences going forward. For each child this can appear in many forms and intensities. Not only do these walls prevent a specific activity from being completed, they also rob the child of any tangential learning experience he could have benefitted from in that moment. We must always assume the potential for change, as we simply do not know a child's true executive and cognitive function until sensory and developmental building block issues are normalized to the highest extent possible.

Though Puzzling... Jigsaw Intervention is Not the Answer

Science tells us, and professionals agree, that children with these developmental profiles have difficulty integrating developmental capacities and putting things together to support streamlined development. Yet for many intervention programs, the solution is to prescribe a set of disjointed interventions, send a child to different therapists for different reasons, many times having no communication between the different modalities, and then expect the child to put it all together himself.

A child with a profile of disjointed development cannot be expected to gain what he needs from this jigsaw intervention approach. The better solution to meet the true needs of the child is to look at him from all vantage points of a developmental perspective, and, with a unified team approach, consider the place where the child needs us to start building his developmental support.

Two Views of the Brain

Occupational therapy refers to top-down approaches and bottom-up approaches as a way of describing how the brain and nervous system growth will be impacted by treatment. Grossly speaking, the top system of the brain, the **cortical system**, is the place where a child's cognitive functions come to full fruition. The layers below the cortical system are called the **subcortical** system and are central to the processing of incoming information from our senses. Information coming in through the senses is transported by twelve cranial nerves on each side of the brain. These nerves work together with exquisite timing and synchronization to process and interpreted information to affect a functional outcome.

This perspective on development, where capacities build upon each other like bricks in a foundation, is a bottom-up perspective. The developmental perspective goes hand-in-hand with a bottom-up approach, because that's how human development occurs. When the pieces of development are not laid down to provide the level of automaticity a child needs for cognitive growth, it would be better to target intervention at the underlying bottom processes and let the developmental process do its work from there.

Approaching intervention from a bottom-up perspective means that an intervention team works together to ensure the foundational bricks are all available and aligned with each other to the greatest possible extent to form a solid base for the higher order learning that takes place at the top of the brain. In a top-down approach a child is expected to use his cortical (cognitive) system, i.e. his intellect, to understand what is being taught with only secondary appreciation for how the subcortical system of the brain affects learning.

Consider a child learning to read. In order for a child to develop the skill of reading, the interaction between the auditory and visual systems must be within split-second timing in order to gain automaticity over the sound-symbol association. Though both bottom-up and top-down approaches are used in occupational therapy, the top-down approach would not be the place to initiate a new treatment plan for a child with reading difficulties.

A top-down approach would focus on teaching words over and over, and may even seem successful at first; but what you are really achieving is memorization as a coping strategy rather than the ease and fluidity of reading that is possible for children with effective processing systems. If the cranial nerves supporting the visual and auditory system are ineffective in processing information, the top-down approach does nothing to improve the processing that reading is so dependent upon. The bottom-up approach would focus on bringing the processing speed and timing to their highest level of efficiency, allowing a natural progression of reading skills to build from a stronger foundation.

Coping Illuminates Real Needs

Children are amazing in their ability to cope within their circumstances, even though their coping might seem inefficient or may not be as socially acceptable as we would have it. The truth is our brain is a wonderfully made system, always looking out for a way to get a task completed (or avoided) in the face of adversity. One example can be seen in a child's need for movement. Our **vestibular system** is our movement system and children move to satisfy this system. If a child is unable to use his vestibular system efficiently, yet is feeling the need in his body to have access to this system, he has learned that if he does rapid finger play, he can stimulate his vestibular centers through his visual system and derive some satisfaction from it. Some hyper children have figured out that if they can maintain some form of movement, they can enable their listening system to be more effective in the face of auditory challenges. Other children have figured out that if they don't look directly at a teacher or speaker, they can heighten their auditory system to listen more effectively. These are all children who are coping. They are finding the most effective ways to satiate a subcortical need while trying to enlist their cognitive systems. We can get very far in pinpointing areas of weakness by simply observing these coping strategies and analyzing the need for them.

Subcortical Needs Rule

As adults who can reason effectively, we can understand how it feels to be a prisoner to a basic biological need such as the urge to go to the restroom. These autonomic functions form part of our subcortical system and are executed from the base of the brain as our first line of defense for survival. Again, subcortical needs must be met before cognitive functions can be enlisted effectively. Let's take a common example to explain some of what this could implicate.

Say you are attending a seminar and an hour or so after you have finished your morning cup of coffee, a dialogue starts occurring between your bladder and your subcortical brain. It begins as a quiet whisper and you may be somewhat aware it's happening, but you can fairly easily tune it out and remain focused. Yet as time goes by the need becomes more urgent, and if the need is not met, the brain becomes increasingly less able to ignore the messages as they start to override the focus and control you need for the activity you are engaged in. That is, your ability to focus decreases quite rapidly as the subcortical need increases. There may be other people present in the room with you, yet no one is aware you are experiencing this little war of engagement vs. urgency of need.

This is a physical example for adults but is quite akin to the little wars that rage in our children with developmental needs as they fight to override one system with another. They cognitively understand what is expected of them, but their primal needs have an urgency to be relieved. Unfortunately, the actions some children take to meet their subcortical needs are viewed as *behavior* because we don't understand what's at the root of what we're seeing. These needs can include the need for movement, the need to invoke the body's calming responses through activities such as crashing and jumping, or the need to simply look away from an activity, appearing distracted and looking as if the child has lost attention to the task.

If no one in the school environment has an understanding of what lies beneath the actions a child is exhibiting, and since there is a behavior plan in place, the child obtains a negative consequence for not paying attention and possibly distracting other children. The child may have no way of communicating what is happening or may not think to communicate his needs, as he has no idea that his body may be interpreting signals differently than the other children in the classroom. If we, as neurotypical adults, don't expect each other to suppress our autonomic needs in a given situation, we should be careful to not expect more of developing children than we would be able to cope with ourselves.

Social-Emotional Development Triggers Intrinsic Motivation

A developmental approach is all-inclusive. It must consider physiological development *and* cognitive intellectual development *and* social-emotional development, all in parallel. It's surprising to say, but given all the rapid advancement in science and technology of the last fifty years, the pace of accepting social-emotional goals in treatment plans for children with developmental delays lags far behind. The good news... momentum is brewing. Dr. Candice Pert's research and writing *(Molecules of Emotion)* carefully describes the role of emotions on the physical system of the body. It's a phenomenon we've all seen. Happier children will take more learning risks, be more alert, and simply appear more erect in posture. We've also seen how negative emotions are often the triggers for setbacks, meltdowns, and avoiding the very learning situations that are so important to embrace.

To exclude the emotional component of a treatment plan is to think that we do not derive meaning from learning through emotional content. It is, quite frankly, a common-sense imperative that we consider social-emotional development as a strong component of any treatment plan. Hopefully, schools will soon begin to recognize the validity of social-emotional developmental growth in the academic setting. It took years for individualized education programs (IEPs) to add social skills training, but hopefully it won't take as long to see emotional growth incorporated into development plans as well. It only makes sense. If the child is emotionally involved in a positive way, the very important concept of intrinsic motivation is triggered. **Intrinsic motivation** is simply a child's inner drive to develop and grow. When you trigger intrinsic motivation you gain integrative learning and do not need the repetition that is often viewed as necessary, particularly for children with special needs.

Communication First

A child with developmental delays often presents with speech and language delays. If there's one area where I hope we can hasten the pace of understanding to affect intervention planning, it's in the distinction between *speech/language* and *communication*. Once we begin to expect speech in a child, we tend to lose focus on the many other ways he communicates. Babies have the intent to imitate and respond to their mother's overtures from the earliest times in the first year of life. Humans are created to be social beings and this starts way before we actually speak. Non-verbal language is said to be 90 percent of communication today with only 10 percent being the spoken word. It is understandable that parents and caregivers want to hear their children speak, but the actual formation of speech sounds is partly an output device. As we begin to speak, we must first take in information from a social partner, then plan and organize a response before the actual words can be said in a sequence that makes sense to the listener. So much happens between two people when conveying a message before a word is ever spoken, or without speech even occurring. An interesting exercise is to mute your favorite TV show and see if you can discern the gist of the story. In all likelihood you can, even though the addition of language would provide more depth and meaning.

As far as development is concerned, we all know communication happens far earlier than speech. Cries, smiles, and gestures are the tools at an infant's disposal and parents instinctively know how to interpret these cues. If non-verbal communication is good enough for neurotypical development, it should also be good enough for our children experiencing developmental challenges. I have often seen that as we work on a child's communicative intent and focus more on circles of communication and reciprocation, both verbal and non-verbal, the child becomes more motivated to use the spoken word. On a similar note, therapists and caregivers have believed for many years that providing a child with an assistive technology device for speech would inhibit the motivation to use actual speech. This might be true if it were the only therapeutic intervention being used, but I have seen many children eventually choose to disregard their assistive device in favor of speech to communicate in moments of true engagement simply because the device is too inconvenient to use or is inaccessible at the time.

If a team has worked on communication from a developmental approach on a consistent basis, the motivation to communicate more effectively is an instinct a child gravitates to naturally. We need to use whatever tools we have to gain the ultimate goal of speech for each child, but the primary focus must be on the development of communication as the basis for the motivation to speak. This certainly does not mean we stop working on oral motor skill or the acquisition of language; it simply means that our focus of creating change should be on *communication first* as the catalyst for speech development.

Neuroplasticity... The Brain Remains Plastic throughout Life

Much is being said in the news and books about early intervention. It is true that the sooner we can get our child into the right therapies the better. The early years of central nervous system development are the prime time for change. Our priority must be to start at the most basic level of early development, strengthen the weaknesses as much as we can, and then move on to higher developmental functions. It is a steady process, never pushing too hard, but always persisting in challenging the child into new areas of learning. Early intervention is wonderful, but the right intervention at any age is the key to attaining the most favorable outcomes.

It is never too late. Human development begins in the womb and continues until our final heartbeat lays us to rest. There is no magic age when therapy ceases to have an impact; it all depends on an individual's profile. It does take more intensity and more time, but I have seen many older children make effective changes and develop more skill when the right interventions are used, preferably with the bottom-up approach.

The nineties gave us an important key in terms of science when it was proven that our brain remains capable of making new neuronal connections throughout our entire life (the principle of neuroplasticity). Therapists have known this for much longer than it took for research to prove it. Such is the case for many good interventions. The need for scientific research and proof is valid—it just takes time. But the longer a person or child lives with a weakness in the central nervous system, the more entrenched he becomes in coping with it, accommodating for it, and adapting to it.

Behavior "is" Communication

It's rather a linguistic oddity that the word *behavior*, in its typical social usage today, refers to *negative actions* with respect to accepted standards; yet by typical dictionary definition, no negative words are used to explain the meaning of the word.

To me, behavior is simply a means of communication for many children. No child has ever been born with the ability to decide to become a behavior problem; and for many children, behavior is purely a science of survival. It is a rare occasion indeed to see a child who was not born with the desire to please and be pleased by parents and caregivers. When this desire is suppressed by a child's need to meet an overriding intrinsic need, it frequently brings about an aberrant response to the environment. This could be in the form of strong fight, fright, and flight reactions during which the child appears incapable or undesirous of pleasing others; hence, we frequently encounter behavior plans designed to extinguish these behaviors.

Our primary function in life is to keep ourselves safe—physically and emotionally. Children with developmental delays are no different. We cannot expect a child to understand his subliminal needs and use his cognitive capacities to override those needs in order to meet our requirement to extinguish a behavior; and it is my clinical and professional obligation to ascertain to my best ability what would be causing these behaviors to occur.

When we see behavior as a communication, doors open to a whole new world of understanding. When we believe that the child innately wants to have a warm and comforting relationship, we will see that belief play out in the child's response to us. If we view a child through a window of understanding, not judgment, then we can objectively assess why he may need to move or look away while we talk to him. We understand it might not be that he *wants* to look away, but that looking away is *needed* in order for him to maintain his listening focus.

The physiology of our bodies requires us to use our different sensory systems to support us in maintaining function. Perhaps when a child needs to move rather than stop and look at you, it is because he is not sufficiently supported by his incoming processing systems to maintain the level of engagement needed.

He simply cannot take in what is being said without getting the support he needs from other processing systems such as his movement system. But because we have a human need to be responded to, we feel he is not acting according to expectations, and therefore preface our statements with a number of repetitions of "look at me." We fail to understand that when a child overrides his need to support his subcortical processing systems (in this case through movement), and we demand what we believe he needs to do in order to focus his attention (look at us), we accomplish little more than undermining his overall ability to listen and process what we are communicating in the first place. It's when we start to understand that "look at me" is more about us than the child that we begin to understand behavior as communication.

Behavior Plans Reflect "Our" Goals...Not the Child's

So many behavior plans are *our* goals rather than the child's goals. Too many intervention plans are built on assumptions of how the child is supposed to look, behave, or feel. It's somewhat unfortunate that the word *behavior* and its presumed negative implication tends to pigeonhole our perspective into a realm of reward and consequences. This narrow perspective drives behavior plans which are expected to follow suit and measurably support positive change. But when there is little to no understanding that sensory, and/or emotional needs drive certain behaviors, we frequently see behavior plans that provide a favorite sensory activity as a *reward* for good behavior.

To the many morning coffee lovers out there, it simply would not make sense if you were told you could have your cup of coffee only after you were awake and alert. This is what it is like for children who have behavior plans where the reward is to meet their need. In developmental theory, this is not just putting the cart before the horse, it's punishing the horse for being behind the cart in the first place. In contrast, I have seen so many children begin to blossom from simply being validated for what they really need. If we are able to satisfy the sensory need before a required task, we might not have the behavior to begin with. I have witnessed multiple times when, for the first time, a genuine connection is made between a mother and a child simply because Mom recognized and met her child's true need. It is simply joyous. It is a moment of complete intimacy and engagement that every parent wishes for and is quite beautiful to behold.

I am reminded of my own childhood when my loving and well-meaning mother forced me to eat cold cauliflower for three hours while my dessert was looking at me across the table. I knew what I wanted, but was the distaste and nausea I had to experience really worth the outcome? I didn't really learn to eat cauliflower. I learned to do what someone else decided should be important to me. I didn't enjoy the cauliflower, I didn't learn to develop a taste for cauliflower, and I still don't like cauliflower. All that remains for me is the negative memory. Though my analogy pales in comparison to the needs of the children I treat, the feelings and learned outcome are similar.

Rewarding Relationships

I do not assert that there is no place for reward. It would be great if extrinsic rewards were replaced with the experience of having a close and engaging relationship with someone. The sooner we can stimulate a child's attention in valuing a relationship rather than a physical object or food, the more ground can be laid to really attack the theory of mind issue. **Theory of mind** is explained as seeing ourselves and others as separate entities, ascribing beliefs and desires to ourselves, and understanding that others have beliefs different from us. The theory of mind principle is based upon the fact that it is difficult for a child with a developmental delay, such as is found in autism, to develop a sense of perspective over the thoughts of others. The child may think that his thoughts would be the same as the other person's, or would simply not be able to stand in someone else's shoes to understand what is being communicated.

This empathetic ability is derived from having trusting and engaging relationships through which individuality can begin to be embraced. A child with a developmental delay relishes the connection found in relationships just as much, and even more so than some typical children. If a typically developing child does something right, do we rush to find the M&Ms? Or do we simply hold our arms out to give them a hug while sharing a big smile of pleasure with our very smart child? This is a pristinely emotional relationship reward. The earlier this type of relationship can be harnessed and cultivated, the more secure a child will feel in taking the risks that will ultimately empower his learning.

It's Human Nature

In his book *The Neurobehavioral and Social-Emotional Development of Children*, Dr. Ed Tronick writes about the early sharing and communicative intent of babies. We achieve this important relationship through play, which is every child's most important time of learning. A neurotypical child wants to please his parents and teachers. He does not want people to not accept him; he wants to achieve. All of these rewards are intrinsically built into human nature. Of course, I do not suggest the global elimination of all extrinsic motivators. Like everything, moderation is key; but the closer we stay true to basic human nature and typical development, the closer we will get to knowing the right next step for each developing child, neurotypical or not. It may take longer initially, but it is a process built on safety, security, and trust.

A child with a diagnosis on the autism spectrum has an even greater need to feel the value of safe relationships than neurotypical peers, as his innate developmental and communicative abilities are often negatively impacted by his neuro-biological profile and the challenges he has to face in every situation of his environment.

Intrinsic Learning

If learning truly meets a child's needs, you will not have to teach that same learning again. It is true that children learn from repetition, but the acknowledgement of the emotional reward within that repetition should not be understated. When we watch typical children play, they repeat new learning often— or so it appears. If you watch closely, you can see the subtlety of slight changes with each repetition. Say a neurotypical child is learning to eat with a spoon. Sitting in her high chair, she may first drop her spoon accidentally. Mom dutifully picks it up, cleans it, and places it back in her tiny little hand. The child then begins to purposefully drop the spoon again and again. Each time she does it, she is not prompted; it is a natural, spontaneous response, a decision of her own making. With every repetition she is learning something new and reaping emotional reward. She could be listening to the sound it makes, gauging how long it takes before it reaches the ground, seeing what side of the spoon faces up when it lands, or figuring out how hard she needs to throw it to make a louder noise. And finally, Mommy's favorite, seeing how many times it takes to make Mommy really mad.

The point is, the child is learning and taking in from the environment through her own spontaneous volition and initiation. She is driven by her own intrinsic motivation. Her sensory development in the repetition of the activity caused exploration in multiple directions with varying qualities, and she was the one wanting to learn from it. It is this intrinsic drive that causes her central nervous system to fire and create the learning she can then recall when needed at a later time. Learning is not etched in the developing mind through endless, senseless repetition as this type of learning is not self-initiated, non-intrinsic, and very frequently simply does not make sense to the child. Impactful and integrated learning is built on the intrinsic motivation to accomplish, to gain, to see what happens next.

Rote Learning is Not Learning

Children with developmental delays, especially those on
the autism spectrum, frequently have an extraordinary capacity
for storing long-term memories. Most people generally assume
this ability is a unique neurological construct, but over the years
we have come to realize that this capacity to memorize may be
more of a coping strategy than an automatic product of innate
functioning of the brain. One strong possibility is that this
ability originates in each child's developmental adaptation to the
environment. If a child's central nervous system is not providing
integrated and modulated feedback about the environment,
the child will want to avoid new experiences and situations.
Sameness becomes the order of the day, every day, as a primary
source of protection from the environment. If everything can
stay the same, the child has the potential to avoid as much
anxiety over unexpected change as possible. This is one of the
many reasons why kids with developmental delays don't like
transitions and avoid novel activities and new venues.

If a child's central nervous system cannot be relied upon to
provide him with adequate information, he is going to have to
find a compensation for this difficulty. A child will literally store
up a memory bank of how certain places or situations *felt like* in
the past, and rely on those memories to rule over his immediate
judgment with regard to processing new and novel experiences.
This makes it incredibly difficult to scaffold new learning, yet
new and novel experiences are exactly what the central nervous
system needs in order to develop.

The answer is certainly not to play into this strength and use
a child's memory to accomplish rote learning. Rote learning is
attached to the memory bank; in many cases it needs a prompt to
be elicited and carries little meaning for the child. This is non-
intrinsic. What good does it do if a child can count to 100, but
cannot count three doors down the hallway to get to a bathroom?
Intrinsic learning is built on what the child is motivated to do,

not on what we as adults feel he should be learning at a certain age.

Finding the Child's Intrinsic Motivation to Learn

I have many memories of my own related to connecting to a child's motivation to engage in new learning. I remember working with a child diagnosed on the autism spectrum in my center one day. We were both lying on our backs facing the ceiling. He had a piece of string that he was finger-playing with and I was imitating him. I could have asked him to sit up and do some therapy activity with me, but this was his preference. To the outsider, I'm sure I looked like I was lazy and not doing my job very well. But for me, I was working hard in my mind contemplating what it would take for him to turn to me, to recognize me as being there with him, and even more—to elicit him wanting to be with me.

We did this silent finger-play for thirty minutes; I paralleled him and he kept going. I paced him exactly at his pace, wanting to be as much in sync with him as I possibly could. He slowly started altering what he was doing, waiting for me to imitate him. I dutifully did just that. I was soaring with this acknowledgment of me! This little game, now initiated by him, went on for a while, and then he turned his face toward me with a smile from ear to ear. It was such a breakthrough experience for me—a moment when I first started to realize what I share with you today. Every child wants to be recognized at his or her own level and place of safety before he will travel a mile with you. And he did. We accomplished all kinds of learning together. He simply needed to know and trust that I was not going to expect more of him than he thought he could give.

If we understand that all children want to learn and connect with others, we should equally understand their need to have a strong primary capacity for self-protection. They are the experts on how they are experiencing a moment, and most of the time, nothing matters to them beyond the here and now. They live life in real time, feeling they must protect each moment at all cost. If we respect this, we can get far.

The Hidden Potential in Every Child

We've learned so much from adults diagnosed with autism. Sue Rubin tells one story in her documentary, *Autism is a World*, about her own autism experience. She talks of herself as being "mentally retarded" until the age of eleven, but has managed with assistance to obtain a college degree.

Her behavior during the entire documentary looks quite different from expected age behavior and could so easily be judged as being mentally incapacitated. This is not to say that intellectual deficiencies cannot co-exist with an autism diagnosis, but to assume so only serves to put a ceiling on expectations for any child who is less able to return communication.

Another prominent example is Ron Davis, who tells his great story in his book, *The Gift of Dyslexia*. Mr. Davis was also diagnosed with autism in his earlier years and is now the director of an institute for training and assisting children with dyslexia. These are two wonderful public stories, though there are many more we do not always hear about. In practice I see hidden potential everyday with the children I treat by always assuming intelligence and patiently working our way up the developmental ladder.

Learning through Play and Intrinsic Motivation

If a child has a compromised capacity to integrate and process information through his central nervous system, he will put up every defense in his book to protect himself from new and novel stimuli that he does not intuitively know how to process. This shield of inward focus obstructs the motivation for intrinsic learning. How then can a child so inherently guarded move closer to the experiences of learning intrinsically?

The answer is through *play*, no matter the age. It is through play and following a child's lead that we can effectively harness a child's interest and gently scaffold it into expanding to new areas of learning. In watching a child play, there are limitless opportunities for learning, enhancing sequencing abilities, practicing problem-solving, and generalizing skills. The ultimate aim in early childhood is for a child to choose to play exuberantly with peers and learn as much as possible from these interactions rather than from direct teaching by adults. By using techniques that enhance a child's already strong memory skills, you are not touching the very important complex pieces of brain development that go with having an idea, initiating that idea, planning and sequencing it, and seeing it play out in a rewarding way in front of your eyes. Play does all of this and more.

It really does not make sense that school systems are moving more toward curriculum and structured learning at younger and younger ages, seeing play as a frivolous passing of time. Children are wired to learn through play, and the early years of development are a crucial foundation for later learning. It pains me to see those years and all that development and foundation for learning brushed aside. Play adds much value to the developmental process as it is also a vehicle through which a child processes social and emotional feedback. A child brings in past experiences from the school or home environment and acts them out in the safety of play situations until full integration of learning is reached, and then adds further nuances to increase the learning even more. Success drives intrinsic motivation, and through play we can build the success needed to inspire a child to participate in further learning. Through trusting relationships, a child will build the need to care about what others think, aim to please those he cares about so deeply, and ultimately move beyond himself.

Let's Not Make a Habit of It

Another important factor to consider is *habituation*. For the central nervous system to fire and create the synapses it needs to develop, it needs new and novel stimuli. If you arrive at your office today and someone is using a hammer right above you on the roof, you sit down with certain dread wondering how you are going to make it through the day. Yet after a few minutes you are surprised to find yourself engrossed in your work. You still register the worker and the banging, but your central nervous system has filtered out the repetitive noise as non-important. Your central nervous system has *habituated* to the input and is no longer registering it as new or novel. Now this is probably a good thing for an adult needing to do a job, but it is not good for a child to habituate to the input of repetitive teaching.

From a sensory processing perspective, repeated non-novel experiences do not increase learning as much as the repetitive experience dictates. After the first repetitions of exactly the same stimuli, a child is more involved in rote learning than being actively involved in taking in new information. I have seen many one-and-done experiences when a single exposure to new learning was all a child needed, and time and time again, I have seen children spontaneously initiate new learning simply because an activity from a prior session meant something to them and they wanted to build on their experience. Simply put, intrinsic motivation is the key to new learning.

Fluid Intelligence is What Really Matters

A *Newsweek* article titled "The Puzzle of Hidden Ability," by Sharon Begley, senior health and science correspondent at Reuters, reports on an intelligence study led by Laurent Mottron and Michelle Dawson of Rivière-des-Prairies Hospital in Montreal as follows: *"For the study, children took two IQ tests. In the more widely used Wechsler, [the children] tried to arrange and complete pictures, do simple arithmetic, demonstrate vocabulary comprehension, and answer questions, such as what to do if you find a wallet on the street—almost all in response to a stranger's questions. In the Raven's Progressive Matrices test, [the children received] brief instructions, then went off on their own to analyze three-by-three arrays of geometric designs, with one missing, and choose (from six or eight possibilities) the design that belonged in the empty place.*

The disparity in scores was striking. One autistic child's Wechsler result meant he was mentally retarded (an IQ below 70); his Raven's put him in the 94th percentile. Overall, the [children with autism] (all had full-blown autism, not Asperger's) scored around the 30th percentile on the Wechsler, which corresponds to 'low average' IQ. But they averaged in the 56th percentile on the Raven's. Not a single autistic child scored in the 'high intelligence' range on the Wechsler; on the Raven's, one-third did. Healthy children showed no such disparity."

"The Wechsler measures crystallized intelligence—what you've learned. The Raven's measures 'fluid intelligence'—the ability to learn, process information, ignore distractions, solve problems and reason—and so is arguably a truer measure of intelligence," says psychologist Steven Stemler of Wesleyan University.

I truly hope science will reveal more about the capacities of these compromised children to broaden our collective understanding of their abilities and individual differences, and teach us how to find more ways to enhance their learning.

Humbly Entering a Child's Space... Without Threatening It

I have been involved in monthly training groups of teachers in school districts over the past years. I believe it has been a positive experience for everyone involved, but there were times when I've had to tighten my jaw to keep it from dropping at some of the things I've heard. On one occasion, a speech language pathologist shared that a very prominent doctor in our area told her that the difference between a child diagnosed with autism and a child diagnosed with Asperger Syndrome is that the child diagnosed with autism has no investment in relationships. These words were piercing. I clearly remember furiously thinking how to be supportive of another professional with great standing, yet how to completely abolish any notion of this idea at the same time. It is simply not true.

There is no human being who does not answer to nature's cry to be involved in a meaningful relationship unless functional capacities are completely diminished. We can get through to any child if we try to find out who he is, and humbly enter his space without threatening it. We must always remember that we are his guest in his space. We all know adults who don't have a very clear idea of what personal space is and know the feeling of retreating until we feel trapped in the corner of a room. We should consider this fleeing feeling when building lesson and treatment plans for children with these difficulties.

The desire for relationships is always there and should be assumed as automatically as we should assume intelligence. It's amazing that with all the current information available, there still remains the thought process that because a child is unable to provide feedback, he must have no thoughts. This incorrect and noxious assumption has led to many more destructive interventions than I care to ever witness again—meltdowns that should never have happened, and unnecessary behavior plans crafted in response to behaviors far removed from the origin of the problem. It is truly a gut punch for me to see how often a behavior becomes the child's problem when, in fact, we are responsible for setting up the situation by not recognizing what the child was trying to communicate in the first place.

In so many cases, we want to teach curriculum, writing, and speech with no thought of developing the relationships that can connect a child to his motivation and capacities for learning. We simply expect a child to overcome these obstacles because we have goals and objectives that need to be reached. If you invest in a relationship that a child trusts he will move mountains for you. The path to get there might not follow your expected plan, and he might not get there on your timeline, but he *will* get there.

Parents and the Value of Parenting

No child is an island in a treatment program. The sound commitment and perspective of parents goes far in focusing on the right treatment at the right time to harvest a child's innate capacities. But parents need communication and support, especially when several professionals offer different and sometimes contradictory direction on what to do and what not to do. Parents must quickly learn what they never wanted to know in the first place, and frequently find themselves trapped in a directionless maze. They often have homework from teachers and speech language, occupational, and physical therapists, not to mention the consideration of different diets, nutrition, and biomedical interventions. In this information age, it is very difficult for parents to find their child's road of therapeutic intervention in the mesh beliefs, theories, and interventions available today.

We, as a collective body of professionals, need to partner together from our different vantage points to make it easier—but we do not do this. Parents are stressed. They bear the ultimate responsibility of their child's future with sometimes minimal assistance in getting there. Parents often know something is wrong well before any doctor or professional tells them, but then have difficulty knowing when and where to start an intervention route. It is a daunting task to decide whose ideas to follow. I remember one distraught father's description. "I feel I'm in a free-fall with twenty pull cords hanging from my parachute... "

But amidst the confusing swirl of the infosphere, one fact has proven itself time and time again. The best place of peace for parents is in their ability to connect with their own child. No recommendation or technique matters as much as having a responsive child who can say, "I love you." Families are too soon weakened by the all-consuming chain of visits to doctors and therapists offices in search of the right mix of interventions. Parents need a new model. They need meaningful home programs that fit in with their schedules and are easy in structure, yet flexible in choices. They need medical partners to help them understand the whys and hows so they can reinvest that knowledge into the best approach for their child and their family.

The central nervous system needs frequent firing to keep making connections, and once-a-week therapy is simply not enough to bridge the gap of the developmental delay over the course of time. When parents complement professional intervention by completing home programs, the success of the once a week clinical therapy session increases tremendously. But it's a fine line and a careful balance. *Parent* is both a noun and a verb. Parents must be respected for who they are and also what they do. They parent. The demands of a home program should never turn them into surrogate therapists or teachers. Parents should be able build and manage their family as a nucleus and be the source of nurturing their child so desperately needs. Expecting parents to take on too much responsibility by acting as a therapist or teacher only serves to dilute the role of parenting for the entire family, and we must consider this in planning home programs.

"Instinct is the Nose of the Mind"–*Madame de Girardin*

In thinking about parents and parent involvement, many thoughts come to mind. Parents are the ultimate experts on their child and so many parents admit during consultations that they knew something was wrong way before a professional acknowledged it. They have a gut instinct about their child that I have come to deeply respect and admire. This is not to say that any parent should become a bloodhound determined to sniff out every anomaly, and it certainly does not make each and every inquiry a valid one, but my experience has proven that spending time in careful exploration of parents' instincts and observations yields many important details that can lead to more targeted and timely intervention.

Intervention programs are consuming. Entire families and often extended families can get absorbed into the crusade. I have seen many parents separate or divorce because of the upset to the balance of the family and the pull of responsibility for a child with special needs. I have stood in amazement during home visits when the house appears to be a whirlwind of therapists and teachers coming and going. What has happened to the privacy, intimacy, and camaraderie of being a family? Is there a point where more simply does not equate higher rates of improvement? Is getting more therapy hours from relative strangers really going to be more effective than playful family time where brothers and sisters feel involved in the needs of the family and there is time enough for everybody? These are open questions that will have different answers for every family, but they are necessary questions for families to be asking themselves.

Many parents struggle with the decision to leave their job to devote more time and energy to the special needs of their child. This is a personal decision unique to every parent; there are no hard-and-fast rules about what is best for the family or the child. It is important for parents to satisfy themselves as only they know their own styles and reward systems. For some parents it will be better to remain in a job they derive satisfaction from, as it makes them more fulfilled and this shines through in every moment spent with their child. For other parents, it might not be the best idea to stay in a job solely to make more money to be able to provide more. For them, the guilt of not having enough time may add to their anxiety and could inhibit the quality of the time they do spend their child. In either case and in every situation, the tone of a parent's energy is a vital force in a program's momentum.

Parents carry so much responsibility and may benefit from having some counseling sessions for themselves. They frequently neglect to indulge themselves because the demand for funding multiple therapies for their child is too great. But it is necessary to negotiate a balance in the lives of families and it is the professional's burden to assist families in this way. A parent's emotional health is very important to the growth of a child, and a parent who feels replenished and re-energized after a validation session has so much more to give to the rest of the family. Some professionals are reluctant to become *family therapists*, and I don't suggest we all should; but we must always respect the need, take the time, and allow the door of discussion to remain open in the best interest of the child.

Expectations

Finally, we need to talk about expectations. When it comes to treating children with special developmental needs, there has been no single cure, no cookie-cutter recipe, and no quick fix. This is a fact. When we expect too much too soon, children feel our anxiety and respond defensively with a reaction of avoidance, hindering the very growth we would like to see. At this point, intervention has to be about *process*—the process of development.

With a natural developmental approach to intervention, professionals support parents in learning how to scaffold their child into higher places of learning. When a therapeutic plan is based in development, we do not expect major changes with each new intervention. Rather, we choose therapies with a focus on the next milestones as part of the natural developmental continuum. Sometimes this causes a *"Wow!"* in the changes we see; other times the gradual climb is more the order of the day. But when we set our focus on the next developmental milestone, parents are more at peace in waiting for change. In time, the joy of seeing a child do more than expected will make all the waiting worthwhile. What I have found with this approach is that the wait does not necessitate slower progress. In fact, it actually speeds up the progress as the child's learning is intrinsic, integrative, and becomes inherently molded into his everyday experiences.

Discipline and Boundaries

The special needs child needs to live by the same rules as other children in the family, and it is important that he be responsible for chores, even if he makes the smallest contribution. Though we all have a special love and affinity for children with special needs, it is very important that they have the same opportunities for growth and problem-solving that neurotypical children in the family have, as they really need the practice to grow and improve in function.

I have seen so many parents become the extension of their child, doing things for the child that perhaps could have held some potential for learning even if the child completes but one step toward the goal. We know why we have this inclination. Much of it is out of love and also guilt. This special child did not ask to be dealt these cards of developmental difficulties. We know they have to overcome much in order to prosper, and therefore we want to nurture them and protect them even more. As loving and understandable as this is, we should also consider how much this attention may be robbing them of the experiences they need to learn and grow.

No One Has a Clue

To the mothers and fathers of special needs children who give of themselves unconditionally and unselfishly to their families every day—I am in awe. I have profound personal respect for you, the many parents I have come to know through the privilege of treating your children, and the many more I don't know, but respect no less. You possess unparalleled commitment and understanding unlike many relationships in our society.

Your willing spirit and the depth of your love never cease to amaze me. You gracefully balance the needs of family, typical children, and your beautiful child with special needs. No one has a clue what you live. At the very least you're a mom, dad, nurse, housekeeper, chef, banker, teacher, therapist, and advocate on any given day. Beyond this, you're the absolute center of your special child's universe. The many roles you play could fill a small room, yet I know you often feel alone in every crowd. You persevere with profound courage while the rest of the world remains oblivious to your isolation, your depth, your fear. I see it every day. You are the true fabric of the many families so dependent upon your fortitude to survive.

I may have an occupation that I am trained to do, but it is from my experience in genuinely connecting with children and working with families, that I hope this writing brings more balance and harmony to even a single child or family.

"...what Matty needed was not a program that offered more hours of service, but more service to his true needs."

Chapter 3

Early Intervention… Setting Sail with No Clear Direction

Pictures really do speak louder than words. When my kids were younger I would take them to Sears for an annual Christmas portrait. Taking five kids under the age of six to the mall for a picture perfect portrait can make for some fun memories. One year when my youngest was eighteen months old, she was not in the mood to sit still and smile for the camera. She spent the entire sitting treating us to the most ear-piercing, tonsil-bearing screams she could muster. Of course, Matty was not a big fan of blood-curdling screaming six inches from his ear, so he melted down in his own way, harmonizing to her shrieks while striking an arched back pose with his head in the lap of his sister seated behind him. Everyone in the room just had to laugh at the whole scene—three sitting patiently, two screaming bloody murder, and one frazzled photographer. After about ten minutes and twenty shots, we decided not to torture them anymore and called it a wrap. I couldn't help but think that if Norman Rockwell was going to do a day-in-the-life portrait of the O'Malleys, this would be it. We actually ordered one of the pictures as our Christmas card … tonsils, tears and all… and signed it with the perfect holiday greeting… *"From our Home to Yours!"* We sent it out to friends and family and everyone had a nice chuckle. They'd all been there.

I always took the kids to the same studio and chose the same fireplace background for our portrait every year. I joked that if I kept sending a Christmas card with my kids sitting in front of the same beautifully decorated mantle year after year, maybe people would start to think it was actually my house. But I was always much better at getting the portraits taken than getting them displayed on our walls. Only once did I actually get one of them hung, and when the family room was painted five years ago, that portrait came down and was stacked on top of other school pictures on our hutch. It hasn't been re-hung since, but I do look at them from time to time. Looking back, I'm glad I did the portraits this way, in front of the same setting every twelve months. You can really see a beautiful progression of teeth lost, bangs grown, and the slimming of chubby cheeks.

In a way, Matty communicated to me through those portraits. His demeanor spoke volumes in reflecting his journey—even when he could not yet utter a word. If I used one word to describe how Matty looked in each of our annual Christmas portraits, it would be these: when he was eight months old, he looked *confused*; at twenty months, he looked *disconnected*; and as each year passed, he looked *distressed* at three, *timid* at four, *anxious* at five, *engaged* at six, and finally, *happy* at seven years of age. His journey from being confused and disconnected to engaged and happy may have been off the beaten path of most children, but who cares.

As I look back I can draw connections to how the steps of my own journey paralleled the Matty I see in those portraits. When he looked confused, I began to wonder; when he looked disconnected, I sought help; and when he looked distressed, I learned why. When he was timid I stayed close; when he was anxious, I held his hand; when he was engaged I followed him; and when he was happy, I let him soar. My instincts told me then and my heart knows now that children are constantly communicating to us—we just have to listen with more than our ears.

Our journey began with my gut feeling about the portrait at Christmastime when Matty was twenty months old, but we didn't get to see a developmental pediatrician for a diagnosis until months later. It was frustrating to realize that the diagnosis-intervention paradox seemed to be so heavily weighted against the best interest of the child. If you wait for a diagnosis before beginning intervention, you risk losing precious time; but if you intervene without a diagnosis, you risk putting the wrong interventions in place. Flashing back to when I first learned that Matty had, at the very least, a speech and communication difficulty, it was daunting to think I'd be watching the clock tick for nine-to-twelve months while waiting to see a specialist. At the time I was struggling to even wrap my head around the need for intervention and was frightened by the thought of having no idea how long it would take to get an appointment. We began EI services immediately that January, and fortunately we ended up being able to see a developmental pediatrician in May, shortly after Matty's second birthday.

Not So Terrible Two

One thing I've learned from having five children is that the *terrible twos* is a total farce. Not that kids aren't ill-tempered and self-righteous at that age; the sham is that it only lasts while they're two. The reality is that it begins at about eighteen months and can last until they're four (then starts all over again at twelve, but I won't go there). Matty was certainly not like his sisters as he neared two, and not at all like other two-year-olds. I remember how he just loved to spend time in his crib. He would wake up at 7:00 in the morning only to be irritable, and seemed to be in need of a nap again by 8:30. He was completely content spending time quietly looking out the window at the tree tops, watching the birds and planes fly by. People would comment, saying "he's so good staying up there in his room."

"It's not good," I would think, "he's almost two years old, being good should not be part of his agenda at all."

Matty wasn't pointing, wasn't imitating, and was not beginning to act like a two-year-old. He was habitual and repetitive. He loved to open and close doors and turn lights on and off. He shook everything and was oddly seduced by spinning wheels. When playing outside, every time a car went by, he would stop what he was doing to stare at the wheels going past. He loved buses and trucks with their big wheels and shiny round hubcaps. He was allured by all things round—wheels, balls, and coins, to name a few. When we would go for walks, Matty had to go out into the middle of the street and look at every manhole he passed. Between the manholes and wheels of passing cars, a quick walk soon turned into something that wasn't so quick.

The way he played was not at all like the play of his sisters. He would throw or walk through a pile of Legos® rather than build with them. He liked to lie on his tummy, left ear to the ground, and push a car back and forth while watching the wheels spin. He would push his wagon rather than pull it. He preferred to play alone and was never the initiator of play. He physically moved away from social opportunities, and often shut down or shut out his sisters when they tried to solicit him to join in their play.

His purpose, it seemed, was different than any of my other children; and his preferences, I would later learn, were not preferences at all. They were a means to meeting his physical needs disguised as an untypical way of interacting with toys, people, and the environment as a whole. I now know that when he was quiet and simply staring out the window, he was not just being a good little boy. He was visually focusing on the vertical lines of tree trunks and telephone poles to self-regulate, trying to the exclude the environment. When he was playing with the same thing over and over he was not exploring its properties, but was focusing on a familiar object in a way he could control rather than having to process something unfamiliar.

Yes, he was certainly different, but surprisingly, he wasn't the glowing anomaly it may sound. He fit well into our family routine and generally went with the flow of our crazy household.

When not making a racket running with push toys back and forth in the kitchen, he was quiet and unobtrusive. He shied away from playtime with his sisters, but relished any one-on-one time he could get with adults.

Early Intervention

Our EI home program began in January when Matty was one-year-nine-months old. The initial evaluation revealed speech and motor delays, and EI services would be provided by St. John's Center for Early Childhood Development. Matty would receive one hour of speech therapy and one hour of OT each week. The first speech therapist was ineffective and almost painful to experience. She would start every session by talking to me for the first half hour, explaining a newly adopted approach called *Floortime*. As I understood by the explanation, when using Floortime strategies you *follow the child's lead*. So I watched, week after week, as the therapist would simply follow my then barely verbal child around the house.

When Matty walked by a truck, she would crawl behind him and say, "Matt, do you want to play with the truck?" Matty kept walking. Then he'd pass by a ball and the therapist would say, "Matt, do you want to play with the ball?" Matty kept going. And so this would go on for the second half hour of the session, always leaving that last few minutes to make sure I knew Matty hadn't really made progress and that I understood what I should focus on over the next week.

Matty didn't like that therapist right from day one. He always seemed to be conspicuously absent while we chatted before the sessions. When it was finally time for the session to start, she would call his name in a condescending tone any adult would find offensive. Never once did Matty respond. Every single time I had to go find him and bring him into the family room. I would sit him down in the middle of the floor and he would immediately try to escape, or at the very least, he would turn away so he wasn't directly facing her. Not once do I remember Matty uttering a syllable during those sessions.

Our OT on the other hand was a much different story. She was gentle and warm and always arrived with different types of equipment for fun activities. She too would spend a few minutes each session talking to me, but I looked forward to my chats with her. She taught me about **sensory integration**, or **SI**. I learned about **deep-pressure** and how the body naturally seeks deep-pressure input as a way to calm. "It's called the **proprioceptive system**," she said, "the calming system of the body." I learned that there are different ways the body can get proprioceptive (deep-pressure) input, the most obvious was to literally put pressure all over the body; another way is by getting impact through the joints.

Everyone seeks deep-pressure—both children and adults. Maybe that's why little boys love to jump and crash, why older boys love contact sports, and why adults love jogging and massages. "The impact of jumping and crashing," she explained, "provides deep-pressure input, which inherently calms an overexcited nervous system." You can even get **oral deep-pressure** input, which may be why babies love binkies and thumbs, kids love chewing on shirt sleeves, and adults overeat, smoke, and chew gum. Once I understood the function of the proprioceptive system, and why and how we all seek out this type of input to calm ourselves, it really made sense to me.

A Calm Brain and Body

The OT would always start her sessions with sensory activities to get Matty regulated. In SI terms, **regulation** is the brain's ability to organize the sensory information we encounter in the environment. To remain focused on a task, our brain and body must constantly regulate itself to the changing demands of the environment. If a child doesn't have a strong capacity to organize and integrate the flow of information coming in, and his proprioceptive system is not able to calm the brain and body, his ability to attend to a task is compromised. But when the proprioceptive system gets what it seeks, which is typically deep-pressure input, the calming response is elicited and organization and attention abilities begin to normalize.

It didn't take long to see this in action. The therapist would bring a large therapy ball and have Matty lie on the ground while she rolled it all over him. He loved it. It took a few days for Matty to learn to jump, but once he did he couldn't get enough of jumping on the bed. When it was time for OT, Matty would run upstairs to jump and crash on the bed for twenty minutes before beginning other activities. At first I thought it would be a counter-productive waste of time to encourage stimulating jumping and crashing as a warm-up for activities requiring a lot of focus. But the difference in Matty was immediate. Giving him deep-pressure input proved to have a very beneficial, consistent, and predictable outcome of better regulation. I soon saw it was not time wasted—it was time invested.

We bought one of those small trampolines that had a safety bar for him to hold onto while jumping, and when he jumped, he jumped hard. I remember the intensity in his face as he jumped. He wasn't just jumping up and down to experience the feeling of being airborne—he was jumping with purpose. He would make the most of every jump, jamming his feet down with each bounce to get the deepest impact. He would even start off by jumping with his legs straight and knees locked to get the most input through his joints. When he was able to get regulated, he was much more focused and had a higher threshold for frustration, not just during the remaining OT session, but for a couple of hours afterward. After the first month or two of our EI services, I was really disappointed with the progress of the speech therapy, but fortunately I was seeing a difference in Matty during his OT sessions.

What's the Real Need… and the Right Course of Action?

In addition to getting Matty's EI program going, I was also introduced to a type of therapy called **Applied Behavioral Analysis**, or **ABA**. Being so focused on trying to get an appointment with a developmental pediatrician and working with St. John's to get Matty's EI program started, I didn't have the bandwidth to really research ABA. I may have read a few overviews or articles, but admittedly, I didn't do nearly as much research as the other parents I was meeting. I do recall being told by more than one person that "ABA works; the data supports it."

ABA, they said, "is very intensive but it works," and that "data has proven it has significantly improved the lives of many, many children."

At that point we didn't yet have a diagnosis. I knew Matty had a communication deficit, but I didn't know enough to articulate any specific issues beyond that. I sensed they were there, but I didn't have a succinct way to package them in my head. At the time, I only knew Matty was less like his sisters and more like the children I'd heard about who were getting ABA; and if ABA was working for those children, why wouldn't it work for him?

As I networked with parents and therapists, I was shocked at the number of hours other families were investing in ABA (twenty hours per week was common). I didn't know the totality of Matty's issues and I was torn about whether to make that much of an investment based on what little I knew at that time. On one hand, you want to do anything you can to help your child, and ABA seemed like the approach everyone was using. But on the other hand, I hadn't yet seen a developmental pediatrician to confirm anything beyond the communication issues. If I had been able to see a specialist of some sort—a developmental pediatrician, a neurologist, or some professional who could validate the need and approve of my course of action—I would have been more comfortable in making the decision to invest in an ABA program. I didn't have that level of comfort. I knew my son needed help and I wouldn't deny him anything in the world, but what was the real need? And who could say this was the most appropriate course of action to meet that need? I really didn't know the extent of the problem and I didn't know the extent of his needs, but I felt like I was racing against the clock. I was torn. I felt an undercurrent of apprehension, yet I was anxious to get Matty started on a program. Early intervention meant just that—you intervene early.

My doubts eventually took a backseat to the overwhelming feeling that I could never live with the regret of lost opportunity, so in early spring we started a private ABA program in addition to Matty's EI services provided by St. John's. The ABA program was not part of the EI program and would be paid for by us. In ABA circles, our program would have likely been considered a starter program, seven hours of ABA in our home each week. Seven hours seemed like peanuts compared to the programs other parents had going in their homes, but I was reluctant to invest more until I had a sound feeling in my gut that it was the right course of action.

Getting Started with ABA

In getting set up to begin ABA, we prepared a room in our house that was a perfect environment. We called it "the classroom." It was a room with sloped ceilings and a dormer window. The sloped ceiling actually made it a quiet and cozy space to work. We set up a few small bookshelves to hold the materials the therapists would be using for the sessions. We made curtains out of white pillow cases and hung them on the bookcases to cover the toys and books that might be a distraction. We divided the room into separate areas, the main area having a single table and chair with bookcases on each side. The other areas were like centers with different types of toys and materials to work on specific activities. Because of the slope of the roof, when Matty sat at the table his head was only about a foot from the ceiling. I think he liked that.

After the classroom was all prepared, I met with the ABA team to schedule the sessions and learn more about how the program would work. It was then I realized how little I knew. What I did know was that it was based on teaching new skills through significant repetition. If a child could not identify body parts, you would repeat a request to touch eyes, ears, nose, and mouth until the skill was attained. It seemed a lot like memorizing times tables; you just keep doing it and doing it until it becomes second nature. But as I learned more, I remember feeling a little uneasy about the language of ABA—words like drill, compliance, reinforcers, and skill mastery. The words seemed so militaristic, so dominating, so robotic. I learned about Discrete Trial, a method of breaking skills down into the smallest *discrete steps* and teaching each step intensively through repetition. When a child complies with a request, and once the child executes the request three to five times in a row for three consecutive sessions, the skill is considered *mastered*. I was uncomfortable at first, but like the acronyms of a new job, I soon became quite versed in throwing the terms around in context.

I learned that ABA uses *reinforcers*. A reinforcer can be anything a child chooses, such as candy, a toy, more computer time, or anything that helps connect a positive reward for a desired behavior. I was a little taken back by such a behavioral reward system, but I guess it's not called Applied *"Behavioral"* Analysis for nothing. Before beginning the program we talked about what kind of reinforcers would be best for Matty. "Do we *have* to use reinforcers?" I asked, "Because I can't really think of anything Matty wants *that much*. Can we just wait and see if he'll respond without reinforcers?" We had a wonderfully compassionate and open-minded ABA team that truly wanted to make a difference in the lives of children, and they agreed to start ABA without using reinforcers. We would start first with imitating and labeling vocabulary. Matty cooperated and enjoyed the sessions right off the bat. He was happy, and ABA seemed to fit the bill for the first few months.

A Typical Day of ABA

We were now four months into our journey and Matty would soon turn two. We were pretty settled into a program of one hour each of speech and OT, and seven hours per week of ABA. Speech and OT were provided by St. John's and we were paying for the ABA hours out of our own pocket—all this during the months when I was preoccupied with trying to get an appointment with a developmental pediatrician. Matty was not a *behavioral* child. He didn't exhibit aggressive or negative behaviors and was generally pretty good natured. Therapists would comment that they liked working with Matty because he really tried and wasn't inclined toward behavioral reactions. I'm glad we started the program without reinforcers, as he was always cooperative and tried his best without the need for reward. He would happily go up to the classroom when the therapists came to the door. We were thrilled to see his cooperation and smooth transition into the program.

As we moved further along in Matty's ABA program, I saw how they really weren't kidding when they said ABA was based on lots of data. We had a book that logged and tracked everything the therapists did. They worked off drill sheets listing drills to be worked, such as block imitation, puzzles, expressive and receptive language drills, drawing, play, and self-help. A typical drill sheet would list about thirty drills with a plus or minus column to the right of each drill. If Matty completed a task successfully, a plus was recorded. I believe most ABA programs consider three consecutive pluses a mastered skill. I don't remember why, but our rule was five consecutive times rather than three to ensure mastery. There was also an area at the end of the drill sheet for the therapist to make comments on the day's progress.

"Do this," the therapist would say, followed by stomping her feet. Matty would stomp.

"Do this," the therapist would open and shut her hands. Matty would open and shut his hands.

After three more similar drills, Matty would get all pluses for gross motor imitation. Next it's playing with trains.

"Put train on track," plus.

"Put driver on train," Matty picks up a lion—minus.

"Choo choo..." said the therapist. Matty didn't respond—minus.

"Up hill," plus.

"Down hill," plus.

"Stop train," added the therapist. Matty kept going—minus.

"Everybody off," minus.

Notes in therapist comment section: *"More work needed on train play. Use one train only, red train. Put people on train, not animals."*

I wasn't really sure why it mattered whether people or animals were driving the train, as I had three little girls who would not only have had a lion drive a train, they would have taken their sock off and had the sock drive the train with the barrettes from their hair as the passengers. But even though some of the drills struck me as overly anal, I let it go. Matty was starting to make progress in terms of speech. His vocabulary was increasing and he loved to sing songs.

In the beginning, I would run upstairs after the therapist left to look at the drill sheet to see how he did. I desperately wanted to see all pluses and rave reviews in the comments section. Some days I saw what I was looking for; other days I didn't. My mood became tethered to those drill sheets. Up and down, good day and bad day. One day I found myself sitting on my bed folding towels, upset because Matty hadn't gotten a plus for a specific drill. He had mastered the skill two weeks earlier but didn't do it that day. Was he still able to do it? Would he have to go back to square one and prove his mastery again? Or worse, was he regressing?

It was then I realized I had to stop looking at the drill sheets every day or I was going to drive myself nuts. I was expecting each day to be better than the day before and that's simply unrealistic. I had to gain altitude. I had to get out of the weeds, climb back to 40,000 feet, and look at the whole picture. It had been a few months; he'd made progress and I had no reason to believe that wouldn't continue. I had lost perspective and was tangled in the minutia. From that day on I looked at the drill sheets maybe once a week, then every other week, and, finally, I barely looked at them at all. And you know what? Matty kept making progress. Lesson learned.

Lackluster Speech Progress

At a meeting with our case manager at St. John's , I brought up the lackluster progress of the speech therapy and explained how we were supplementing EI services with ABA therapy. Up to that point, I had never mentioned our privately funded ABA program to the EI case manager. I'm not sure why, but I think I may have been afraid that as a social program, Early Intervention would determine us ineligible for all services if it was documented that we could afford our own private services. A few people told me that a child couldn't be denied services for that reason, so I took a chance and asked whether ABA could be written into Matty's service plan to replace the speech therapy. I shared that there was no connection between Matty and the speech therapist.

"It just seems as though he tunes the speech therapist out," I said reluctantly, and went on to explain how Matty would run up to the classroom when the OT or the ABA therapists arrived, and how the speech therapist would try to solicit words I knew Matty knew, but he would just say nothing. "The speech sessions are beginning to seem like a waste of time," I added, "and ABA seems to be making more progress in speech than the speech therapy. So I thought perhaps we can convert my hour of speech therapy into an hour of ABA therapy."

It was a little uncomfortable to explain how the therapist wasn't very effective, but I did it. Much to my surprise, after deeper discussion, I walked out of the meeting with not one, but three hours of ABA written into Matty's EI program. His current ABA therapists were gracious enough to go through the paperwork to have St. John's pay them directly, so things were looking good. It wasn't a full-blown, twenty-hour per week ABA program, but it was a start, and it would be three hours less that we would be supplementing each week.

A Fork in the Road

Matty turned two in the spring, and as summer began we were cruising with one hour of OT and seven hours of ABA per week. Rolling the ABA program into the EI program started to bring all of Matty's services together more cohesively, and that was a good thing. It gave the program synergy. Matty was doing well in the ABA sessions, enhancing his receptive and expressive language as well as his fine and gross motor skills. He continued to be cooperative and really seemed to take comfort in the structure of the sessions. He had bonded with the therapists and knew what to expect with each session; but it was in his sessions with the OT where Matty really shined. They would start those sessions with lots of jumping and crashing and Matty loved it. I was starting to see two different Mattys: a regulated Matty who was better able to engage and generally deal with the environment, and an unregulated Matty who spent more time avoiding the environment than participating in it. Matty didn't just jump and crash because that's what little boys love to do; he *needed* to jump and crash. He was simply a different child after he got enough of the proprioceptive input he needed.

During the summer I learned of another EI service provider called Charter House that was providing up to twenty hours per week of in-home ABA therapy. If this was true, it would be like hitting the ABA lottery. Although Charter House was forty-five minutes away, I immediately called to see if there was a possibility to make the switch. "You mean I had to battle to get three hours from St. John's, and by simply changing providers, you'll give him up to twenty hours?" I asked.

The program director told me the ABA therapy could continue in my home with Matty's current therapists, but she was quick to explain that it was strictly a discrete trial program and they paid less than my therapists charged. But even though Charter House paid a lower rate, and even if we supplemented the difference to make the therapists whole, it still wouldn't cost us any more than what we were currently paying. By making this change, we could effectively increase Matty's hours to fifteen-to-twenty per week without increasing our out-of-pocket costs at all.

Matty seemed to be doing well with his current ABA therapists and he loved the OT therapist, but by changing to Charter House, he could only get ABA. No speech and no OT. I checked back with the pediatric rehabilitation facility where Matty had earlier gone for OT, and found that they had a therapist who specialized in SI, which was appealing since sensory work had started to become as much of a focus as ABA. And bingo, my medical insurance would cover the sessions. So, by making the change to Charter House, we would be losing our current OT therapist who Matty really loved, but he would still be getting SI privately and we'd have a net gain of up to thirteen hours of ABA. I met with Matty's ABA therapists and they were willing to sign up with the new provider. It seemed like a no-brainer, right?

Again, my gut seemed to want to have a say in this. Changing to Charter House seemed like a win-win, but I was strangely reluctant to do it. We would be getting more hours, we would be keeping the wonderful ABA team Matty had bonded with, and we could get OT from a sensory OT. It seemed like we would be making what we had, well... better.

But two things were eating at me about the new program—the focus and the intensity. The program we would be going to was more rigid and less inclusive. Although the director seemed very open to hiring Matty's current therapists, she was very explicit about how the program would be run. It was a discrete trial program that seemed more like boot camp, with little room for nurturing or emotional growth. It offered ABA and that was it; other services were not included. Speech was not an option. OT was not an option. For those services we were on our own.

I liked the teaming we now had with Matty's services under the same provider. If we went with Charter House for ABA, OT and speech had to be handled separately, and that didn't sit well with me. Not so much because it would require greater effort on my part, but more because it was beginning to dawn on me that this program would be bringing us back to a more compartmentalized approach. I liked the momentum of our current program, and I think this was the undercurrent of my reluctance. I was starting to realize that a program of disconnected pockets of intervention was not the best way to address a child's needs on the whole.

One day I was sorting laundry, thinking about why I was gripped with such a sense of reluctance to switch to Charter House. Although I was going through the motions of pursuing it, I really didn't feel strongly that I wanted it to happen. I had heard over and over how early intervention was key, and how children who got lots of services early on were far more likely to lead significantly better lives than those who had not. The fear that I wasn't making the most of every minute was a huge factor in why I jumped into ABA in the first place. I had read articles about how intensive ABA programs were helping scores of children lead fuller lives, and I still have no reason or evidence to believe otherwise. But was it helping *my* child? There were also elements of ABA that I was beginning to more seriously question as they related to Matty. As I saw more and learned more about ABA, I began to wonder whether its principles were the ticket for him.

Drifting Away from ABA

The general principles of ABA seemed to be based on modifying the way a child interacts with the world, but how can you separate and treat only the *actions* without at least attempting to change what's causing the child to act or not act that way to begin with? As I saw how regulation changed the way Matty engaged with the world, I began to gain genuine respect for how the body sets the stage for how the mind interacts—a *body-mind* connection. ABA seemed to have a radar lock on behavior, independent from the body and mind in which it's rooted. In learning about Charter House's rigid ABA program I began to realize how far away from an authentic ABA approach we had drifted. What we had may have started out wanting to be an ABA program when it grew up, but its aspirations fell far short. It was never deep in discrete trial, we never used reinforcers, and it was not focused on behavior. As I learned what a *real* ABA program looked like, I was becoming less and less sure that a more intense ABA focus was right for Matty.

But this was like winning the services jackpot. Many families were painfully on the brink of financial and emotional bankruptcy to support a twenty-hour ABA program for their child. And here we were with an opportunity to net a thirteen-hour per week gain in therapy at a wash financially. But... twenty hours per week? Putting a toddler on-task for the equivalent of an adult part-time job seemed so, well, child-laborish. Matty had been doing well so far with our ABA-lite program, so would more necessarily mean he would all of a sudden be doing really well, or super well? Does *more* necessarily mean *better*? Or could more just be, well—more? Or maybe, could more even be worse? Yes, Matty was doing well with his current program, but it wasn't really a true ABA program. He was also doing well with OT. I was surely seeing a relationship between the sensory work the OT was doing and Matty's ability to engage in a more relaxed and connected way. But even with my doubts, I continued to go through the motions to make the change.

Through the summer and throughout my investigation into Charter House, I was also laying the groundwork to increase the ABA hours provided by St. John's. Regardless of whether we opted to switch, it made sense to at least try to reduce our financial outlay for the hours we were currently supplementing. In July we had a meeting with St. John's to reevaluate whether Matty's needs were being met by his current program. I used this meeting as an opportunity to make a case for increasing Matty's service hours. I was seven months into our voyage and was only now beginning to feel my sea legs.

I needed leverage, and this time I did my research. That meeting was certainly one of those times when I had to reach deep into my pocket and slap that diagnosis down on the table. I researched my state's Early Intervention Services guidelines and used every word of them to make the case for additional hours of service to meet Matty's needs. This helped justify an increase in service hours to two hours of OT and five hours of ABA, along with the continuation of ABA program management and team meetings, and a comprehensive speech assessment.

Exposure to Charter House's *real* ABA program was the eye opener I needed to help me realize one thing—Matty's intervention services must truly reflect his needs. Matty was inflexible and detached in the way he navigated through the environment. I now realized that, for Matty, the Charter House program would too be rigid and disconnected to other therapies in its intervention approach. To me, it was like trying to cure a nut allergy with a daily dose of peanuts. If the goal was to help Matty become more flexible and connected, then his program had to be agile and inclusive. His current program was flexible enough to move in any direction he needed it to move. He was showing us he needed a more sensory-based approach, and it was now obvious that deepening our connection to an approach focused solely on behavioral expectations was moving him in the opposite direction he needed to go. To stay true to Matty's real needs, the choice was clear.

I called Charter House and explained that we would not be continuing with the transition to their program. Although the decision to switch EI providers turned out to be fairly anticlimactic in the end, it was a very valuable personal learning experience for me. I learned that a more intense program was not at all what Matty needed. On the surface it appeared we were sacrificing a golden opportunity to make a net gain, but the reality was that what Matty needed was not a program that offered more hours of service, but more service to his true needs. Matty needed to feel safe in order to embrace the challenge to become less rigid. His relationship with the therapists and the predictability and flexibility of the sessions were his safe harbor, and it would only be from there that he could begin to sail in any direction he needed to go.

Learning More about Floortime

Throughout that summer, I met with an informal support group of moms who were in similar situations. We started meeting to swap our stories, all sharing the same familiar undertone—children and parents needing much more help and direction than EI, the medical community, and insurance companies were providing. One of the moms who had been supporting a pretty intensive ABA program told me about a therapist who came to her house a few times a week to do Floortime with her son. "He loves it," she said. "He lights up and runs down to the basement whenever the Floortime therapist comes to the door. He really seems to be making more natural progress in his play skills." She lit up with excitement as she told me about her son's progress.

At the time, I knew two things about Floortime: 1) it's a strategy based on *following the child's lead*; and 2) if it was what I saw the speech therapist trying to do with Matty—it was a total waste of time. I explained how the therapist followed Matty around the house saying, "Matty, do you want to play with this… ," "Matty, do you want to play with that… ," with Matty spending the entire session on the run. If that's what Floortime is, no thanks. If the premise of Floortime is to *follow a child's lead*, what's the point? To follow the lead of a child who seems to wander aimlessly seems counterintuitive to having any *goal* at all.

She listened to my Floortime not-so-success story, but fortunately the conversation didn't end there. Agreeing that what I experienced may have been a poorly executed attempt, she encouraged me not to abandon Floortime, but to consider learning more about it and the **DIR model**, which is the overarching model that encompasses the Floortime strategy and techniques. She explained that Floortime is not play in the absence of goals. Rather, done well and well-supervised, it is in fact deeply rooted in goals—*the child's goals*. Not our goals. It's an approach aimed at the root cause, the developmental missteps, and *missed steps,* I would later learn, rather than at the symptomatic behavior we want to sweep under the carpet and pretend never existed. As luck would have it, Karen, the Floortime therapist who had been working with this mom's son, also worked as a service provider in my school district. I asked for Karen's number, went home that evening and dialed the phone.

A Networking Windfall—Two More
Developmental Pediatricians

It was now nearing September, Matty was almost two and a half, and we were still newlyweds to our May diagnosis. We saw Matty's first developmental pediatrician only once. After stuffing that diagnosis in my pocket in May, I did not return. I wasn't foolish enough to think I could chart my own course, I just knew that pediatrician was not the person for me. Throughout the summer, I continued my quest to find another developmental pediatrician, someone I would hopefully feel a better connection to. Someone who could lead the way. Fortunately, eventually, all the networking finally paid off.

As it turned out, my husband's sister's husband's sister's husband's friend's wife (how's that for networking?) was a very well-respected developmental pediatrician at a children's hospital only forty-five minutes away. After a few September letters and phone calls later, I was able to get an October appointment. Coincidentally, all my earlier hard work to get an appointment at a different children's hospital in our area paid off as well, and we now had two appointments with developmental pediatricians within a week of each other.

In preparation for our appointments with the developmental pediatricians I prepared the following summary.

Social	
Eye Contact	Minimal with siblings and adults other than Mom or Dad.
Pointing	Does not regularly point.
Interaction	Does not seek out or enjoy social interactions with siblings or others.
Family Activities	Difficult to engage, likes to walk the perimeter of the yard.
Transitions	Does not cope well with unexpected transitions or when extended family comes to the house.
Speech	
Vocabulary	Limited vocabulary, not spontaneous, must be prompted.
Articulation	Often not clear for anyone other than family to understand him.
Inflection	Not much inflection in his voice and often sounds monotone.
Spontaneity	Does not show spontaneous exuberance.
Oral Motor Skills	Does not pucker, blow kisses and can't play tongue games.
Listening/Attention	
Responding to Name	Does not always look up and make immediate eye contact.
Following Directions	Follows one-step directions but not two or more steps.
Getting Attention	Does not call "Mommy," "Daddy" or siblings' name to gain attention.
Fine Motor Skills	
Draw/Color/Paint	Light pressure makes these activities unenjoyable.
Scissors	Difficulty squeezing.
Grip	Does not hold things with thumb and index finger.
Gross Motor Skills	
Ball Play	Difficulty throwing, catching, kicking ball.
Jumping	Can jump in place but not forward or backward.
Tricycle	Cannot pedal a tricycle.
Stairs	Sometimes has trouble going up/down stairs.
Walking	Likes to take long (3-4 miles) walks with Dad pulling a wagon with 10 pound weights.
Regulation	
Deep-pressure	Craves continuously. Asks for hugs and pillow hugs.
Crashing	Loves to jump and crash on bed and couch.
Movement	Loves to ride in car.
Play	
Cars	Loves to watch wheels spin.
Sandbox	Likes pushing his hands deep into the sandbox.
Pretend	Does not like to participate in pretend play.
Threshold	Cannot play independently for more than five minutes.

We saw both pediatricians and each ran their own battery of developmental tests. Both doctors agreed on the general category of diagnosis, but had varying opinions on the severity. Matty was more regulated for one of the appointments and that was ultimately reflected in the outcome. By that point, Matty had undergone three evaluations by developmental pediatricians, two speech evaluations, two OT evaluations, and two ABA assessments. After all these experiences, the sobering revelation for me was that all this examination resulted in little more than a collection of professional observations. They were evaluations of snapshots of Matty during several thirty-minute periods in his life. Yes, there were some diagnostic tools and always history from me, but there were no chemical tests, blood tests, X-Rays or MRIs to indicate or confirm the existence or severity of any diagnosis.

I started to realize that the diagnosis I so eagerly worked toward six months earlier would end up being somewhat more of a reflection of how Matty's sensory moons were aligned during a given appointment on a given day than any concrete diagnostic conclusion. I had waited a long time to see these doctors, half expecting one of them to assume control and relieve me from the responsibility of leading the charge. But I was starting to realize that all of the medical opinions and guidance were just that... opinion and guidance. Not fact, not leadership. I was starting to come to the realization that there would probably be no guardian angel leading me through this. I would certainly seek medical opinion; but in the end, it was becoming clear to me that I would be piloting this ship and I would be charting its course.

Going "Sensory"

As the leaves began to change, our not-so-ABA program continued to look less and less so. It was now clear that sensory challenges were a core part of who Matty was, so it only made sense to increase the sensory emphasis throughout his whole program. We introduced more sensory activities during his ABA sessions, adding joint compression and other deep-pressure activities to the beginning of each session and every half hour throughout. Therapists would document Matty's cues on sensory seeking activities as well as their sensory observations (i.e. "Matty did better with blowing the horn immediately after using the electric toothbrush today").

Deep-Pressure and Movement Go Hand-in-Hand

As I learned a little more about SI, I learned how movement went hand-in-hand with deep-pressure to help Matty get and stay regulated, and to enhance his ability to focus. I added a Sit 'n Spin toy in the classroom and tried to introduce more movement into his non-therapy hours by wrapping him up in a blanket and swinging him back and forth at night. He also spent a lot more time on our backyard swing.

We noticed that Matty was more verbal after swinging. The OT told me that this was not uncommon and that swinging is often used at the beginning of speech therapy to stimulate verbalization. I learned about an organization that donated money for the purchase of equipment for children in our area, and I applied for a platform swing and a cocoon swing that we hung right outside the classroom. They're still there and even now I find all my kids up there swinging from time to time.

I picked up a couple of small inflatable pools at a summer clearance sale; we made a ball pit out of one and a rice bath out of the other. The balls were a hand-me-down, so between the pools and the rice I spent less than $20. A small expense, but a huge investment in Matty's ability to be regulated. Matty just loved jumping into the ball pit, feeling relief from the impact through his joints when he landed and the tactile input of the balls all over his body. The same for the rice bath. He would bury his whole lower body in the rice as if at the beach. We would hide little animals and toys down deep in the rice and he loved searching elbow deep, feeling the pressure on as much of his arm as he could. We added a sensory basket with vibrating toys, textured hand toys, and an electric toothbrush, and definitely did a lot more finger painting with shaving cream.

I loved how Matty would come down for dinner after therapy smelling like Edge. With the changes to the EI program, we were now supplementing less ABA hours than before, so I also started taking Matty for private OT with the SI therapist I learned about over the summer.

Newton's Cradle

When the weather began to cool and we started spending more time indoors, I made it a point one week to really watch everything Matty did from a sensory perspective—it was enlightening. In family activities, Matty would always work his way to the periphery, more looking in than joining in. When my eyes caught his, he would look away, almost as if he was afraid I was going to put a stronger expectation on him to join us. When he sat on the floor, he would always sit leaning against something with his back supported and was not able to sit like a pretzel in the middle of any space. I frequently saw him sitting quietly, watching others carefully without them realizing it. Matty didn't initiate any communication with my other children and seemed, at best, to tolerate their overtures to him. When he wasn't avoiding the fray of activity, he would jump on the couch or push a heavy box of wooden blocks around on the family room carpet.

As I observed him, I saw that the poor child spent most of his waking energy in one of two states: 1) avoiding sensory input, and 2) seeking regulation against any input he couldn't avoid.

It made me think of those Newton's cradle pendulums that used to be a familiar site on office credenzas. Like the bouncing balls of Newton's cradle, Matty would perpetually bounce between avoiding sensory input and seeking regulatory input. For Matty, I could engrave the word *avoid* on one ball and *seek* on the other. The crashing of the *seek* ball would drive energy through his body, causing the *avoid* ball to engage. Then it would crash, causing the seek ball to engage. Seek, crash... avoid, crash. And so it would go, on and on—all day... every day.

"The reality is—there is no magic way to know how sensory processing affects your child's development other than to break it down and decompose it into the subtleties of your own child's profile.

What follows is a look at each sensory system and the related developmental capabilities that drive a child's potential for growth."

Chapter 4

Understanding Sensory Processing

Sensory Processing is the ability to take in, sort out, and give meaning to information from the world around us. Information is taken in through our senses (vision, hearing, touch, taste, smell, body position, movement, etc.) and travels to our brainstem where it is processed and organized. It is the neurological *perception* and *processing* of sensory information that transforms it into the feel of your clothes, the temperature of a room, or the sound of your child's voice.

Sensory processing is an automatic, instant, and unconscious process of normal development. All learning is dependent on our ability to take in, process, regulate, and integrate sensation from sensory experiences, and to further use that information to plan and organize behavior in everyday activities including academic learning. Sensory processing can impact global development including visual, auditory, and fine and gross motor development; and it can have consequential effects on listening, learning skills, sustained attention, behavior, social skills, peer relationships, sleep/wake cycles and eating habits.

Sensory processing lays down the fundamental structure for development. It is a subtle influence and somewhat of a gray area of development not as easily noted by pediatricians in the very early stages of the growth of a baby. Sensory processing has been a very difficult area to research, but has certainly stood the test of time since the notable Dr. Jean Ayres, occupational therapist and developmental psychologist, established the first foundations of this work nearly fifty years ago. As pediatricians and the education system begin to understand the influence of *sensory,* it is starting to play a larger part in medical and educational evaluations, yet it still happens that parents enter my office and explain that they have never heard of it.

Sensory processing is multifaceted for sure, and on the whole, parents have difficulty understanding how the different sensory processing systems interact with each other to influence development. Parents want to learn more, and many books are available that are very comprehensive in terms of the neuro-anatomy and the theory behind sensory processing. But most parents are not looking for in-depth clinical teaching; they are simply looking to grasp the connection between sensory processing and their own child's development.

The reality is—there is no magic way to know how sensory processing affects your child's development other than to break it down and decompose it into the subtleties of your own child's profile. What follows is a look at each sensory system and the related developmental capabilities that drive a child's potential for growth. By no means is this one discussion going to be exhaustive, but it may be helpful to have this understanding as a guideline when interpreting what your child's evaluation or behavior may possibly mean.

The Sensory Landscape

A good place to begin to understand a child from a sensory perspective is to start by understanding that there are two components to sensory processing: **sensory modulation** and **sensory integration**. Though we are looking at the same sensory processing systems, "sensory modulation is the ability to regulate and organize the amount and intensity of sensory input to sustain optimal attention. Poor modulation can be seen as distractibility, impulsiveness, increased or decreased activity level, disorganization, anxiety, behavioral outbursts, rigidity, difficulty with sustained attention, irregular sleep patterns, and poor self-concept. Sensory modulation difficulties are typically the cause of sensory seeking or sensory avoidance responses." (Winnie Dunn.) Sensory *seeking* behavior can be seen as a child not seeming to have the ability to sit still and needing to move all the time. Sensory *avoidance* behavior can be seen in a child who avoids movement or getting his hands messy with paint, and tends to limit these sensory experiences.

The terms **regulation** and **modulation** are frequently used interchangeably. When we look at modulation, we look at how each sensory system is enabling or disabling a child's ability to maintain optimum focus and arousal. Every person has a certain threshold for different sensations, but for each one of us there is a certain *just right* place where information is taken in at optimum speed, and attention is active and fluid. When a child or person is over-aroused, this threshold is reached too early, causing the central nervous system to be overactive. When a child or person is under-aroused, the threshold takes longer to reach and it causes the central nervous system *not to be awake enough*. When children struggle with a modulation difficulty they have an inability to use their central nervous system to bring them to that just right place. In a classroom environment, this causes a child to be pre-occupied with his central nervous system instead of paying full attention to learning. This difficulty could be at the root of what is responsible for many behaviors that appear to be random to teachers and parents.

The other aspect of sensory processing is **sensory integration (SI)**. SI is concerned with how the sensory systems discriminate (differentiate) sensations as well as how the senses interact with each other to achieve functional outcomes. With a healthy sensory system we know exactly where someone has touched us without even looking, and we also know exactly how hard or how softly we are touched. When we close our eyes we do not lose our sense of where we are in space and when we write with a pencil we know exactly how hard to press to get the correct feedback to make the pencil move. Our sensory systems are constantly working independently and in sync with each other to receive information and make it work for us to achieve functional outcomes. For healthy sensory integration to occur, one must first be able to effectively differentiate sensations coming in, and then be able to efficiently integrate them together. Most often we see children with a combination of modulation and integration difficulties, however sometimes a child presents with only sensory modulation or only sensory integration difficulties.

Sensory Systems and Developmental Capacities

To begin to understand *sensory* is to first understand that it extends beyond the five classic senses we are all familiar with. Certainly sight, hearing, touch, taste, and smell are at the core of how we interact with the environment, but there are additional senses and developmental capacities that, although not part of the traditional set, are no less important. Our sense of movement and body position, our core strength, and our ability to plan and sequence have a large role in the way we experience the world. This discussion will touch on how all of the senses and developmental capacities integrate with each other to define the way we ultimately react to and interact with the environment.

Vestibular–Proprioceptive System

The **vestibular system** provides our sense of movement, and one of its functions is to tell us where we are in space. The vestibular system is most likely the *central executive* of all the senses. We perceive where we are in space by the direction our head is facing; vestibular receptors in the inner ear detect our position in relation to gravity to let us know where we are. Together with the visual system the vestibular system directs our movement, and adding the auditory system, it maintains a vigilance of all the information in the space surrounding us. Together with the tactile deep-pressure system (somatosensory system), it provides us with an awareness of our bodies as we move through the space we are traveling in. The vestibular system allows us to differentiate between being upright, upside down, and lying down. It allows us to know whether we are moving or standing still, speeding up or slowing down. The vestibular system is the system most used in children who are seeking more information from their environment.

"Coping" with the Vestibular System

When a child seems to seek movement it is important to look beyond the vestibular system because the root cause is frequently not simply a difficulty in the vestibular system, but a difficulty in another system to which the child is seeking vestibular information as a coping strategy. This makes a great difference in where an intervention plan should be started. One difficulty specific to the vestibular system is called gravitational insecurity, which makes it difficult for the child to perceive where he is in space if he is on anything that is moving such as a swing or traveling on an escalator. This difficulty causes a child to always want to have his feet flat on the ground. There is also an opposite situation. In order for the vestibular system to get the most input, we have to hold our heads upside down. It's no wonder that we frequently see profiles of children who love to stand on their heads on the couch or even watch television upside down. Both of these situations are impacted by the vestibular system, though both for different reasons, calling for different approaches to intervention. In the case of gravitational insecurity we would want to build core strength and use a multisensory approach to gradually re-introduce movement into the body again. In the case of "the upside down" child, we would need to focus very strongly on connecting the child's need for vestibular input with the more calming proprioceptive system.

The proprioceptive system refers to the flow of information returned from our muscles and joints as we move through space.

It continuously provides feedback as to how we are moving, for example, one leg in front of the other, without us having to look down to see. The vestibular and proprioceptive systems are linked together in terms of movement and contribute to complex functions such as sustained upright posture, balance, bilateral motor coordination, emotional stability, the ability to sustain arousal, as well as the spatial perception of oneself, others, and the environment.

The Right Sensory Diet for Movement Seekers

Some children seem to constantly seek movement. It is very important to consider a thoughtful **sensory diet** for a vestibular seeker, since he might not necessarily need more vestibular action. Rather, what he may be seeking is vestibular input *with the resulting proprioceptive response*. We have all seen children who never seem to get enough of vestibular equipment, and if they could, they would jump on a trampoline or bounce on a ball all day. Consider the notion that they might be seeking the *connection* between the vestibular and proprioceptive systems, and are not satiated by the vestibular or proprioceptive input alone.

In discussing the vestibular system, I should also add a quick note with regard to balance. Balance is certainly influenced by the vestibular system as it directly relates to where we are in space. When going up and down steps and when we are on moving equipment such as a swing, we also have to consider the visual system. Depth perception is the ability of vision to gauge how far or near you are from a certain surface, such as guiding your steps down stairs. If both eyes are not working well together, the origin could be a depth perception difficulty imitating a vestibular difficulty. This becomes an important consideration in planning intervention as the latter situation (deficiency in ocular-motor control–depth perception) could very easily mimic a difficulty in the vestibular system and influence the treatment plan.

Postural Control

Vestibular function also greatly impacts postural control. **Postural control** is at the core of our foundation for being able to sit for extended periods of time in order to complete activities and to develop control of fine motor skills such as handwriting and higher level gross motor skills including balance. Effective postural control is achieved through the harmonious synchrony of **flexion** and **extension** postures in our bodies. For purposes of understanding, *flexion* is the bending of a joint, such as when you are sitting, your knees are flexed. *Extension* is the opposite of flexion, such as when you are standing, your knees are extended. There are three muscle systems that contribute to effective postural control—prone extension, antigravity flexion, and co-contraction.

Prone extension is our ability to maintain an extended position in prone against gravity. This is demonstrated by the ability to lay face down (prone position), and lift and keep both upper and lower extremities in the air (extension). Think of a Superman pose where a child lies on his belly, lifting his arms up and straight out while lifting his legs up off the ground. Another system is **antigravity flexion**. This pertains to the child's ability to maintain a supine position (lying face up) with his arms across his chest while his upper body is lifted up from gravity (similar to a crunch). Both of these systems have to work in harmony to achieve the third system of co-contraction. **Co-contraction** is the ability of the joints and muscles to flex and extend in an easy and fluent manner to support motor movements.

Postural Control

Extensor and flexor muscle systems must constantly balance each other (co-contraction) to maintain position.

Let's consider these three muscle systems at work. When a child is sitting at a school desk, good seated positioning is defined by feet firmly on the floor with knee, hip and elbows at 90 degree angles while the elbow is supported on the desk. In order to maintain this position for extended listening, the extensors and flexors must constantly balance each other. If one muscle system is weaker than the other, it is going to cause more strain on the stronger system to counterbalance. This may cause the child to instinctively move around and adjust his position to seek a better place of comfort. This antsy looking child could appear to be distractible or in need of some behavior modification, though very frequently this would be a wrong conclusion. In either case the child is losing focus, but only because his postural control system is causing him to move to find a more comfortable position and preventing him from paying full attention. Postural control could be an isolated difficulty in a child, though it frequently co-occurs in profiles of children struggling with sensory processing.

Somatosensory System (Tactile-Proprioceptive System)

The somatosensory system, also called the tactile-proprioceptive system, refers to our sense of touch with the sense organ being our skin. Touch sensations of pressure, vibration, movement, temperature and pain are received by receptors in the skin. The sense of touch also gives us information needed for visual perception, motor planning, body awareness, fine motor coordination, general motor actions, academic learning, emotional security and social skills.

The tactile system develops very early in utero, at about six weeks. It is an extremely important system after birth and contributes greatly to infant security, emotional attachment, growth and weight gain. The proprioceptive system also develops in utero and is fully developed at birth. It involves the perception of joint and body movements as well as positions of the body or body segments in space. The **somatosensory** system is the marriage of the tactile and proprioceptive systems, and is foundational to the development of praxis (motor planning). In order to plan our motor movements in a timely manner, we need to have a sense of our bodies, be aware of our trunk, limbs, and head in space, and also know from memory what the movement felt like before. The somatosensory system sets up this incredibly complicated ability.

We all rely on constant tactile stimulation to keep us organized and functioning efficiently. People who experience difficulty feeling when and where something touches their skin would be considered to be **under-reactive**, while those who are overly aware of anything touching their skin are considered **over-reactive**. Difficulty in accepting tactile stimuli can lead to difficulties in the ability to know one's position in space in relation to other people or objects, as well as a distorted ability to perceive one's own body awareness. It can also create difficulty in grading touch experiences imposed on the body, or with one's ability to know how hard or soft to touch something or someone.

Many children who gravitate to movement and deep-pressure types of activities are considered to have hyposensitive/under-reactive responses to vestibular-proprioceptive input. Likewise, children and adults who avoid movement or are bothered by light touch such as shirt tags are hypersensitive/over-reactive to this type of input. For individuals with over or under-reactive tactile-proprioceptive systems, much can be done to bring these systems into balance. Deep-pressure calms the tactile system and can come in endless forms. Massage, crashing, and weighted vests are but a few. Across the age spectrum, there are variations of tactile massage that can be greatly effective in bringing balance to the tactile-proprioceptive system. Many of these techniques can be easily taught to parents.

Some occupational therapists prescribe the use of weights (weighted vests, ankle/wrist, etc.) to help magnify the information sent from the muscles and joints to the central nervous system. Hand weights are a beneficial feedback tool for writing and drawing activities and ankle weights are sometimes used for short periods of time to assist with grounding and body awareness. Although the temporary use of some weights can be helpful, I am very careful about the use of weighted vests. If the child does not have efficient postural control, the weight could exacerbate a more drooped posture and add to the misalignment of postural joints, creating incorrect feedback messaging that would not be supportive of good development. Limiting the use of a weighted vest to twenty minutes is considered to be the optimal time for actual benefit as the central nervous system habituates to it, thus making prolonged use counterproductive.

You need continuous, efficient feedback from your tactile-proprioceptive system to maintain proper positioning. It must be noted that for any motor activity, it is important to pay attention to the correct positioning and alignment of the actual motor requirement. To develop efficient motor planning capacities, it is very important that the joints and muscles give the body the correct placement feedback in order for the action to be etched with automaticity. Therefore it is even more important to be concerned with *joint placement* and *initial positioning* than with the actual movement required. If the somatosensory system is not giving the body correct feedback as to how the movement feels in the joints, the potential for maladaptive and compensatory patterns of movement increases.

Deep-Pressure Protocol

I have seen a method called the Deep-Pressure Protocol (Pat and Julia Wilbarger, formerly known as the Wilbarger protocol) be highly effective, especially for children with hypersensitive tactile systems. Parents have seen overnight reactions with the use of this protocol, and I have also seen results after the protocol was completed in two to three weeks.

This method involves providing deep-pressure to the tactile system by brushing the skin using a specific type of brush, maintaining a rigorous schedule, and using a specific brush stroke technique and pressure. It is a fairly simple technique for family and school personnel to do, but it is a very specific protocol, which should not be attempted if you have not been trained by a trained therapist.

Visual Processing

Vision is quite a complex process. Development of skills within the visual system is dependent upon our prenatal and postnatal experiences. The vision system has many facets and can impact learning and development in a host of ways. Humans can visually detect information from the environment in a 180-degree radius, and this contributes to making vision an excellent conduit for learning.

One notion that immediately jumps to mind is the thought that some children with developmental delays are *visual learners*. Given our compensatory nature, to think of someone as a visual learner implies that this strength was developed because of an inherent deficiency elsewhere, such as an auditory weakness. If the auditory system is weaker than the apparent visual ability, it would make sense that a child would compensate with his visual system. Teachers are very adept at spotting their visual learners and are quite good at accommodating what they perceive to be this natural learning style. But when it comes to childhood development, we have to ask ourselves whether it makes sense to throw in the towel on one sense, assume its weakness is irreparable, and put all our eggs in the basket of the stronger sense. That is essentially what happens when we throw a child in the bucket of visual learners. When we continue to teach in a visual mode, we are strengthening the strength at the cost of weakening the weakness (the auditory system).

The Balance of Underlying Sensory Systems... one Hidden Key to Visual Difficulties

When considering visual difficulties, the vestibular system should also be considered. Children frequently use their visual systems to compensate for *not having to enlist movement.* Our goal should be to bring the different systems into balance with treatment plans that target the weakness. If a child does need a visual accommodation to learn from his immediate environment, it should be temporary with a plan to wean the accommodation as sensory integration work brings the auditory, vestibular, and visual systems into balance.

In neurotypical terms, we all have preferences. Each of us can probably easily consider ourselves as being either auditory, visual, or a tactile-kinesthetic learner (learning through touch and handling). We start from a fairly stable place of auditory and visual parity and develop a preference from there. But it is different for a child with developmental delays. We are not speaking from a place of balance—but imbalance. To optimize the learning process, treatment plans must focus on correcting this sensory disparity to the highest possible extent.

Visual Perception

Our vision system supports a large percentage of all learning and using our visual system in learning relies on much more than the mechanics of our eyes and optic nerve. Learning also relies on visual perception and incorporating what we see into motor activity. **Visual perception** is an integrative ability involving the understanding of what is seen and includes spatial relations (the distance between objects or yourself and an object), visual discrimination (the ability to discern visual difference from one picture or one object to another), figure-ground (the ability to perceive a house being in front of the woods and not vice versa), visual closure (the ability to know the full visual picture when only a part is visually available), and visual memory. Functionally, visual perception is: the ability to perceive objects adequately; recognize objects when seen in various orientations; differentiate one object among others in close and far proximity; identify an object when only part of it is seen; and know where an object is in relation to oneself and other objects.

Visual perception develops mostly in the child's visual experience of the space he is moving around in. A baby experiences a huge rush of visual perceptual experiences in three-dimensional space the moment he begins to crawl. What is *behind* the couch? What is *under* the table? What if I climb *over* that chair? These words constitute some of the lingual terms we use to define the 3-D space we live in. It is from this visual inquisitiveness that a child develops and strengthens visual perception. The motivation to get to a bright red shining object under the table across the room is what propels a baby to activate untrained sensori-motor systems in gearing for the action to crawl.

It is unfortunate that our children's time spent in the glorious world consumed by total 3-D exploration is being cut short by earlier and more vigorous demands of curriculum. The exploration of objects, relationships, and varying emotional themes has become a second-hand citizen in many of today's early learning environments. The moment we place a pencil and paper in the hands of a young one, he has to convert visual information from 3-D to 2-D. The truth is that many children might not be ready for this transition when it is presented and visual distortions could occur if their systems are not mature enough. Examples of such visual distortions could be that a stable object appears to be moving, seeing double, or seeing a shadow that does not exist. Some children develop a contrast sensitivity, where they find it very difficult to deal with aspects such as black and white print, looking at clothing with bright contrasting stripes, or carpets with bold geometric angles.

Our Mind's Eye

Another interesting aspect of visual perception is how we can visualize in our mind when no physical visual object is present. This is interesting in that we all bring our visual memories of visual images to bear when we are listening to someone or reading a story. We bring forth our own visual imagery to enhance the meaning of any situation. Have you ever wondered if the person sitting next to you at the movie theatre was seeing the movie the same way you were?

Children need their visual imagery to support their ability to maintain comprehension of what they are reading. In their mind's eye they need to maintain a visual picture of a story to draw upon in deriving understanding of what they are reading. There is much we do not know about visual perception. Our official test batteries are good in providing part of the answers, but are not yet sufficient on all measures of the enormous capacity of the visual perceptual system.

Visual-Motor Skills

Visual-motor skill consists of combining vision with a fine motor task such as copying from one surface to another while controlling writing. Visual-motor integration is the process of combining visual perception with a motor output (i.e. writing, copying, drawing shapes, or building with blocks). Visual-motor integration has a direct correlation to handwriting and is the motor outcome of what is seen or perceived to be seen. Eye-hand coordination is the precise visual guidance of goal-directed arm and hand movements such as the movement involved in throwing and catching a ball. It also involves depth perception, as we must be able to adjust our responses according to our judgment of how fast or slow a ball is moving and the distance it has traveled, while adequately projecting when and how to hold our hand ready to catch it.

Depth perception is very dependent on efficient coordination of eye movements along with how well the eyes work and move together in order to focus. Ocular motor control and eye teaming are evaluated through several characteristics.

- *Visual Pursuits* are the smooth tracking movement of the eyes as demonstrated in the eyes' ability to follow a target while the head remains in a stable position, such as visually following an airplane in the sky without moving the head (eye-head dissociation).

- *Saccades* are the eyes' ability to shift rapidly from one position to another when scanning spatial environments. Saccades are very important in reading because the eyes must move efficiently and fluidly across the line of words being read.

- *Convergence* is the eyes' ability to turn inward together to focus on an object close up. Functionally, if both eyes do not focus on a ball at the same time, a child cannot adequately judge where the ball is and will not be able to plan his response with good timing. For reading and writing, if both eyes are not converging at the same point on the page, a child will typically miss words or skip lines, and it's not entirely unusual for children to state that words *move* while they try to read and write.

In terms of visual processing we must consider reading and writing together, not as separate entities, and it behooves us to address these skills as an interdependent team. We must use our ability to process visual information for the sound symbol association needed for reading, as well as the ability to produce the same letter in writing with consistency in shape, form, size and spacing.

Even Light Sensitivity can Impact Visual Perception

Another less known facet of visual difficulties is the Irlen Syndrome (concept designed by Helen L. Irlen, MA, LMFT), a light hypersensitivity syndrome that not only impacts reading and writing, but also how an individual perceives the environment. Photophobia, or light sensitivity, is an intolerance of light. Sunlight, fluorescent lights, bright light, glare, and even headlights and lights at night can be bothersome. Discomfort may be reduced with Irlen Colored Filters.

There are a variety of symptoms that can be caused by sensitivity to light including eye strain, fatigue, nausea, dizziness, and anxiety. Lights may also be a trigger for headaches and migraines. Sometimes photophobia/light sensitivity is a symptom of a head injury (TBI), concussion, whip lash, or the result of underlying medical problems.

The problem seems to be an inability for the brain to adjust to various levels of brightness/color. This may cause children to have difficulty focusing under fluorescent lighting, looking at a shiny white board in the classroom, and even have difficulty coping with the contrast of black-and-white print in their reading material.

Auditory Processing

Auditory processing is a term to group tasks that support the brain's ability to recognize, coordinate, and interpret auditory information. Our auditory sense is the one sense that provides us with information 360 degrees around us, and it also has an integrative relationship with other sensory capacities, especially the vestibular system. No matter where our physical placement is in a room, whether we are standing still or moving, we can discern auditory information from all angles. The auditory system does not end with the mechanics of what we hear; it extends further into how we process what we hear. This is called **auditory processing**, which is what we do with what we hear. *Hearing* is discerning exactly what the ear can hear and is determined by the testing of an audiologist. *Listening* is using what you are hearing.

Auditory processing consists of many components including locating the source of sound, identifying patterns or rhythms of sounds, discriminating auditory information, separating foreground-background noise, and remembering what you hear (auditory memory and auditory sequential memory). When auditory signals are received, we attend to those signals by analyzing and storing them, and then retrieving information related to those signals from other areas of our brain. Understanding the message in the information derived from these signals most certainly relies on the use of information previously acquired and stored in the brain, but it is also highly dependent upon modulation and the integration of auditory system information with signals from the visual, vestibular and other sensory systems.

Have you ever wondered why so many children diagnosed on the spectrum of autism have a heightened sense of auditory awareness? If you think about the compensatory nature of our sensori-motor systems, this is altogether consistent. If one has no or limited sight, the brain compensates with better hearing. If a child has compromised motor systems and cannot efficiently motor plan his actions, he intrinsically knows he is unable to react with the timing and speed needed; therefore, he compensates with the heightening of other senses to understand his environment. For a child with diminished capacity to adapt his actions and reactions, it is vital for him to remain vigilant in his environment and using his auditory sense to its strongest levels of awareness is likely the most efficient compensatory response.

The problem with this coping mechanism is that it causes the auditory system to remain in high alert during times of crucial motor and language development, rendering it unavailable to experience and practice the more subtle nuances of sound at different frequencies. This can then affect sound processing and possibly language development as well. Although this is but a hypothesis at this time, in practice I have seen many cases of defensive (over-alert) auditory systems accompanied by deficient sensori-motor development.

From the perspective of the occupational therapist, the purpose of including the auditory system in an intervention program is to treat the entire body and mind from a global sensory processing perspective. In order for me to effectively treat sensory integration, it would be counterintuitive to neglect one system, especially when the auditory system overlays so strongly with the vestibular and visual systems. However, occupational therapists do not do the work of audiologists who specifically focus on audiometry. Some audiologists are also trained to diagnose Central Auditory Processing Disorder (CAPD). They apply a thorough battery of testing to determine the strengths and weaknesses of the auditory system and we frequently recommend families to them. Occupational therapists are more concerned with how the strengths and weaknesses in the auditory system are contributing to the overall sensory profile of a child and how this fits into an intervention program.

Support for the "Supporting Role"

Until relatively recently, interventions to improve the auditory system's *supportive role* were limited; but "sound therapies" are now being found to be quite effective in assisting this function. Sound therapies are aimed at using the auditory system as a conduit to other processing systems to enhance a child's overall sensory integrative experiences.

There are many professionals who do not endorse the field of sound therapy as a viable intervention and it is true that much more research is required. Auditory processing is at the center of much research as well, and continued study will go far in further validating the best methods, therapies, and courses of treatment for children with auditory and other sensory processing difficulties.

Movement Creates Auditory Momentum

Our twelve pairs of cranial nerves work together to carry information to and from the brain to support everyday functional living. One of these nerves is the **vestibulo-cochlear nerve,** which transports both auditory and vestibular (movement) information to the brainstem. It stands to reason, if this superhighway nerve handles two types of traffic, and if the nerve capacities are less than optimal, then both types of traffic could be impacted. That is, auditory attention and movement often go hand-in-hand. It also makes sense that when we consider balance or movement difficulties in a child, we should be considering his sense of audition as well.

Consider our child fidgeting at his desk, appearing to have a craving to move in his chair. More often than not the child understands the teacher's request to remain still in his seat, and really tries for a minute or two, only to resume his fidgety behavior again. It's not that the child *wants* to cause a behavior disruption, though it is often misconstrued in that way. Rather, the child *needs* to move in order to process the teacher's verbal information. When the child forces himself to override the need for movement, he curtails the momentum supporting auditory processing, and thus diminishes those auditory abilities. So the price for sitting still is to *not* be able to listen. From this perspective, many behaviors we see would not be seen as behaviors at all, but rather as coping strategies. We should respect the behavior as a *need* and focus our responsibility on finding ways to help the child meet the need rather than expect him to extinguish the behavior (i.e., remain seated while losing all focus on the learning material, but looking good while doing it). We need to think about what we are actually achieving.

On the flip side, we should also consider children who appear to be passive and very difficult to activate, but who are quite possibly so overwhelmed by the environment that they shut down or hyperfocus on tasks, completely shutting out environmental information. They simply make an active decision not to allow any more information in because their threshold for sensory information is reached far too early. This has important implications for educational and clinical programming. The more a child continues to avoid the experiences needed to mature the central nervous system, the harder it is in later years to break habitual pathways and the child's deeply rooted investment in staying safe. It is important to identify these difficulties in children as early as possible to support the healthiest development of the central nervous system.

Taste and Smell Processing/Oral Motor

Oral motor skills refer to the ability to carry out movements and other functions with the lips, tongue, cheeks, and muscles in the mouth area. Oral sensory processing is the ability to readily respond to touch and taste stimuli to the mouth. Oral motor skills are the foundation for feeding and speech articulation as well as facial expression. Difficulties in these areas can be the result of poor sensory discrimination and modulation in and around the oral structures, lack of motor control, decreased strength of oral muscles, and sensory sensitivities to textures or smells. Foundational oral motor skills include: proper lip closure; tongue lateralization (tongue movement right and left of center); mature chewing patterns; tactile discrimination and modulation within the mouth; postural stability; and respiratory control. Indicators of problems with foundational oral motor skills may include poor articulation, limited dietary preferences, messy eating habits, and drooling.

Most children and many adults seek to calm themselves through oral stimulation. Parents often complain that they are tired of looking at soaked collars or shirt sleeves as their children need to chew and chew. This chewing is most frequently related to a child going through a stressful time and needing to alleviate his system, quite the same as the baby being calmed by a binkie. Dr. T. Berry Brazelton's *Touch Points* talks about how typically developing children go through periods of reorganization as they make growth leaps forward. The process of development can be very stressful during times of concentrated change such as when a child is going through potty training. It is an absolutely normal neurotypical tendency for children to seek calming in one physical area while growing physically or emotionally in another. Children with special needs are no different. To compensate for growth in one area, they seek calming in other areas, of which the oral and genitalia areas have the strongest calming effect.

Although it's quite a natural inclination for parents to want to extinguish the overt behavior, it is important for them to realize that their child's sensory need for calming is ultimately a sign that he is experiencing stress. Initially, alternatives such as chewy tubes are used to validate the need while the child is actively engaged in a therapy program specifically targeting the areas causing the stress. Over time and with intervention the need for this overt calming will begin to decrease.

Prolonged Ear Infections May Have Lasting Impact

Another consideration that can impact audition and language is the residual effect of repeated early ear infections. When taking an extensive look at children's developmental profiles, we frequently encounter long periods of ear infections during times of crucial motor and language development. For some children, this does not affect their overall development; their central nervous system adapts and moves on. But for other children, the prolonged periods of having fluid in the ears does have strong implications on their development.

Sound is transported through the middle ear, which is supposed to be an air cavity. When the middle ear is filled with fluid, what is heard is much like what you hear when trying to listen to someone speaking underwater. Sound needs to be transported through clear air until it reaches the inner ear where it is then propelled through fluid. Ear infections prevent this adequate transportation of sound. It has also been found that by the time an ear infection is diagnosed, the fluid could already have been present for a number of weeks or months.

Feeding Difficulties

Many children have been referred to my center for feeding difficulties with profiles ranging from picky eaters to problem feeders (not eating more than seven foods). Feeding is a tricky subject and never the first difficulty to tackle in designing an intervention program. In order to more fully understand feeding difficulties, we need to also consider smell. Smell is not processed through the brainstem as are the rest of our senses; it takes a different pathway that leads straight to the limbic system, which is the emotional center of the brain. A baby can smell what his mother is eating while he is in utero as smell is transported through the fluid environment to the baby. We cannot consciously recall what occurred during our first two years of life, but researchers concur that memory engrams are laid deep in the subconscious of the brain from the very earliest time in development. Smell is attributed to about 90 percent of what we eat, so who knows what experiences could be memorized in the subcortical parts of our brain in early years. There could be many memories related to smell and food in those first two years of life that would remain noxious to a child without us ever being able to pinpoint exactly what they are.

Eating difficulties attack parents at their core in making them feel inadequate in the care of their children. The power struggles some parents describe are simply heartbreaking. Parents should know that there are also many emotional aspects to feeding that have more to do with *control* than with food textures or preferences, and what often starts as a sensory difficulty could develop into a behavior difficulty based on the need for control.

In an effort to use sameness as a tool to control their environment, children may choose to limit their food repertoire to very specific preferences. Sameness provides a sense of security and helps thwart the constant daily threat of having to deal with different sensory inputs at least three times a day. Knowing what is appropriate to each child's profile is important, but it is also true that certain children can also develop internal nutrient cycles, which are highly dependent on the child's intake of only certain foods. It is also quite possible that children could become dependent on short-acting, short-lasting energy bursts (carbohydrates) to maintain their energy level and sustain their attention to task during activities. It surprises most parents to learn that feeding issues can be so complex from a sensory, physiological, and emotional perspective. It is always in the best interest of the child to consider all of these aspects and involve a nutritionist when dealing with a picky eater or problem feeder.

Oral Motor Therapy... More Research Needed

Oral motor therapy, like other interventions, needs more research to substantiate its validity. Professionals are asking for rigorous control studies, but parents are simply asking for what works. What makes research difficult is that it becomes very specific to one function and one part of the brain, yet it's the relationship between functions that influences each child in different and multiple ways. More case studies need to be documented to prove the many oral motor therapy methods currently in use in order for rigorous, double-blind research funding to be approved.

Clinically speaking, I have seen much improvement using oral motor techniques for oral modulation, oral discrimination, and oral motor control when used with frequency and intensity, and not only once a week in a therapy session.

Praxis

Global childhood development depends as much on the ability to take in and process sensory information as it does on the ability to extend that information into a functional response. **Praxis** is the ability by which we physically and mentally *figure out how* to interact with and respond to our environment. Praxis is comprised of several components, which combine to form any physical response. It is an obscure yet essential element of all activity that drives childhood development and how we subsequently interact with the environment as adults. It is also frequently the hidden dimension that co-exists within other sensori-motor system difficulties. More often than not, a difficulty in the processing of the somatosensory system (the tactile system) leads to difficulties perceiving body awareness, which then leads to difficulties with praxis. Therefore, it is important not to lose focus on the body awareness element for children who exhibit motor planning deficits. I have also worked with children who do not have any sensory discrimination difficulties, but strong modulation difficulties, and have seen how this also impacts the ability to exercise praxis.

Playfully Obstructing the Structured Routine

The ideal classroom for a child with praxis difficulties is one with a set routine, yet one that carefully scaffolds the child's need for new and novel activities through playful obstructions that the child can securely negotiate. **Playful obstruction** simply means we throw an obstacle in the path of a familiar routine that the child has to work around to conquer.

For example, say a kindergarten teacher transitions to the expected time for a craft learning activity. There are usually six chairs around one table, but today one chair has been removed unbeknownst to the child. As he goes to his table he realizes that his chair is not in its regular place. If the environment has been structured and safe, he may feel some anxiety, but would feel safe enough to make a motion or point or say something to indicate he has a problem. The teacher could then use this teachable moment to carefully help him sequence through the steps to solve the problem. Another example is to specifically ask the children to use yellow crayon, yet there are no yellow crayons set out on the table.

The idea is to set up situations where something in the predictable order of the routine is changed so the child has to negotiate a problem and figure out how to solve it. The safest place to test the waters of new and novel is within the structure of a comfortable routine, and it most certainly can be done. The greatest potential for learning is in seizing bite-sized opportunities that open the door to new and novel experiences, while stretching the comfort zone only slightly.

1. The body must be in a regulated state
and ready to take in information.

2. Child has "idea" to take a
sip of drink.

3. Motor plan must be initiated
to reach for cup.

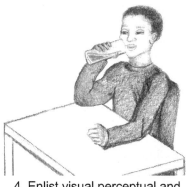

4. Enlist visual perceptual and
motor abilities to sequence
actions to bring cup to mouth.

5. Process the feedback of
positioning the cup back on
the table.

Praxis

Praxis is the ability to conceive an idea, initiate the idea, organize a plan, and sequence the steps to carry out a motor activity. For all children, this *idea to task* sequence should be completed with the same timing and rhythmicity as peers regardless of whether an activity is novel or routine.

A child's ability to feel in control of motor actions no matter what new situation he finds himself in is one of the most important concepts of praxis. Sometimes a child is able to build extraordinary skill in one area such as penmanship or riding a bicycle, but is not able to translate that same skill to other activities. You can train your central nervous system to adjust to any activity you've had much exposure to and are intrinsically motivated to do, and the more familiar the activity becomes the more adept you become at doing it. But the ultimate test of praxis is to present the child with an unfamiliar activity; not one that has been practiced.

The typically developing brain does not shy away from activities it has never seen before. It should be inquisitive and new activities should hold exciting new possibilities. A child with no motor planning difficulty is able to apply himself to a new gross motor activity, a constructive building activity, a fine motor activity or an imitation activity with the same speed and dexterity of average peers. Yet this is frequently not the case with children who experience difficulties in the area of praxis. Praxis difficulties are often the reason why children like steady routine and prefer to have activities be exactly the same every time they participate in them. It's also a reason why children don't handle transitions easily and don't like surprises. Typically developing children seek out new and novel, but children with difficulties in the area of praxis prefer things to remain the same. The problem is, the central nervous system is ignited by *new stimuli* and that's what is needed for effective learning to take place.

The Catch 22 of Praxis Difficulties

Many school reports recommend a structured teaching environment as the best approach for a child with praxis difficulties. It is true, once the environment is more predictable and the initial adaptation is over, the child is able to follow the sequences of the day with less stress to his compromised system. However, the Catch 22 is that the child needs structure to *support* his praxis difficulties, while also needing exposure to new and novel activities to *improve* his praxis difficulties.

Teachers have much to do to satisfy the needs of the curriculum, and they need to maximize group focus to achieve these goals. They work so hard during the first few months of a school year to find each child's comfort zone and create an environment of order within the classroom. For teachers to then think about how to introduce new and novel for each child becomes a daunting task. Though difficult, it is simply what we have to figure out how to do, collectively as a team, in order to keep igniting the central nervous system with new stimuli and raising the bar to achieve the best possible long range outcome for each child.

Adaptive Responses and Feedback

When a child's brain is unable to receive accurate or reliable sensory input, or receives the information at too fast or too slow of a rate, his ability to process information, organize it, and create an appropriate **adaptive response** is disrupted. An adaptive response basically occurs threefold: (1) experiencing a wish or want which is transported through your central nervous system in a timely manner, while (2) negotiating the environment in which the expectation should occur. Both these processes occur simultaneously, and then, (3) result in an efficient adaptation to which a response can be elicited to match your original intent.

To understand adaptability you must also understand feedback. Every time our bodies move, the brain receives **feedback** through our central nervous system regarding how it *felt* to execute that movement so that when an activity is tried again and again, each time it will be executed with stronger efficiency. Our bodies then rely on sensory processing and motor memory to initiate and complete the same movement again.

Many children with praxis difficulties under-register this feedback system, which is one reason why we feel we need to teach the same movement over and over. But we also must consider the value of **intrinsic motivation** and how it ignites the central nervous system and fires up the motor feedback system. If the child is motivated in an activity and understands the reason for participating, the feedback process becomes more efficient and will be far more automatic in his learning. If I were required to study law rather than study children, my motivation would be very poor even though I might have the cognitive ability for it. I would spend countless hours just getting myself geared up to try. But when I study something new about children, I am interested because I simply love the subject. Not only that, it is easier for me because I am building on knowledge I already have, which improves my feedback potential. I have an *intrinsic motivation* to learn about children, and therefore my *feedback* systems process this type of information more efficiently and with more meaning for me.

Avoidance

Avoidance is a classic flight instinct. Children who want their structure to remain the same are certainly in a fighting mode to secure a place of comfort. A child simply may not comprehend what *change* will ask of his body or mind, and will automatically resort to the safe harbor of avoidance and sameness. But when they are interested and meaningfully engaged in a subject or task, they will have more inclination to reach beyond their need for safety and security to apply themselves more readily to learning. Another component is the anxiety of newness, but by carefully exposing a child to new and novel stimuli through his intrinsic motivations, he will gain experience in processing *what it feels like* to enter new territory. The more quality feedback experiences he gets, the more he will be able to adapt and this will open a whole new world of possibilities for his learning.

Attention Difficulties Rooted in Development and Sensory Processing

Much has been researched and written about the area of attention. In addition to investigating all of the potential issues that could be at the root of attention difficulties, I am hopeful many more doctors and parents begin to consider the developmental reasons for attention difficulties before jumping directly into the chemical processes of the brain through medication. This is especially true in the early years of development when the central nervous system is still maturing.

Attention difficulties with the children I see are a common co-occurrence with sensory processing difficulties. If a child cannot rely on the processing of his incoming sensory systems, and if his processing time is slowed, then attention can certainly be affected. This does not mean that no children need chemical substances such as medication to assist them to pay effective attention; there truly are children who may need this kind of assistance. My hope is simply that intervention teams negotiate the early developmental profile to work away at possible origins of the difficulty first, before attempting to treat it chemically.

The Quality Process

In today's times, with legislature and insurance governing the rules for outcome, we have become quite an overly goal-oriented society. The problem is, most educational teams are so focused on the quantitative goal achievement that the quality of what we are asking children to accomplish is literally forgotten. This negatively affects the feedback system of the body and impacts development of the central nervous system in ways we rarely consider. When it's more about how many repetitions are achieved, how much more, and what percentage is reached, the *quality* of each repetition may not be considered and the body may not be receiving the right feedback in order for the motor pattern to repeat itself again successfully. A maladjusted pattern is then established, which then affects the motor plan of further activities.

Let's say we ask a child to sit on a platform swing to prepare for a suspended activity. A platform swing is a thirty-inch-square platform with four ropes, one fastened to each corner and joined together above the center of the swing. The multidimensional tilting characteristic of the platform swing make it a terrific tool for balance and postural control improvements. Suppose we need a child to sit in the center of the swing for proper execution of our activity. He climbs on and sits like a pretzel, but his bottom is not centered. Because the child has difficulty with body awareness and body position in space, he might not know exactly where he is sitting on the platform. He cognitively understands what was expected, and we might ask him to sit "in the middle" or "sit in the center" a couple of times. Since he is not processing the feedback of the feeling of his body tilting to the left or the gravitational imbalance pulling his left leg slightly lower than his right, he does not have the awareness that his bottom is positioned left of center. He might attempt to make an adjustment, shifting slightly or even overcorrecting because he knows what we are requesting and wants to make us happy, but he is simply unable to gain the needed feedback from his body position to know how to move his body to successfully achieve what we are asking.

How many times do we go over to the swing and assist the child to get centered? Unfortunately, this occurs all too often. We do this partly because we are good hands-on therapists or caregivers and we want to *help* the child be successful in the task. Admittedly, we also help in the interest of time as our goal is the activity to be performed after the child is centered, not the centering activity itself. The problem is this is a penny wise-pound foolish approach. When we assist the child, he is not getting feedback from his own movement pattern, and the next time he is required to do it, he will be doing it from the same exact place he is doing it from today. He will not have moved forward at all in making his own adjustment happen.

We need to spend much more time on the *quality* of all movements that feed a child's nervous system. Doing so, we ultimately spend less time repeating the same activity while scaffolding him to higher motor potential. In this example, the feedback of attempts at positioning and maintaining position are what the central nervous system needs to internalize what it feels like for the body to find its place of center given the subtle movement of the swing. The reality is we are so focused on achieving *our* goals in a session (because we have to report back on the progress we made to the family and team), that we forget what the goals of the child are in that moment in time. The central nervous system needs to experience the *process of adjusting* to learn what it feels like to achieve the desired outcome of an activity. **Process** is a child's greatest tool. If you give a child process, the product will always be there.

Flexibility is Critical to Theory of Mind

Rigidity of behavior is a key discussion regarding children with developmental delays and children diagnosed as being on the spectrum. Flexibility is critical for children with praxis difficulties and is one of the factors underlying the concept of theory of mind. If we can help a child flex himself out of thinking that the world and everyone else exists only around his thinking, he will be so much more open to the riches of individuality and the exciting awareness of being different. But being able to behave flexibly is very dependent on the early stages of a child's motor and praxis development. A child with motor deficits avoids involvement in attacking new situations and activities, robbing himself of the very experiences that target the development of flexibility and theory of mind.

Praxis Impacts Higher Order Thinking Processes

Difficulty with praxis skills can also lead to difficulty with imaginative play, creative use of objects, turn-taking, following directions, initiating age-appropriate play with peers, flexibility, and negotiating rules. Another important consideration is how the underlying skill of praxis feeds into higher order thinking processes of the brain in terms of sequencing language, active working memory, organizational skills, and the ability to pay effective attention. Motor procedural development supporting step-sequential activities acts as a building block for higher order functions of the brain where sequencing is especially needed.

Consider sequencing skills in the realm of **active working memory**. Active working memory is different from long- and short-term memory in that you do not need to store this memory for future use; you only need to temporarily hold ideas or steps in your mind while you quickly contemplate another aspect of a task. A simple example in a typical busy classroom can be seen in the multi-tasking needed to write down an assignment while the teacher is giving reminders, while a friend asks if you are going to the ice cream social, while twenty other students are noisily preparing to leave for the day.

The executive functioning skill of active working memory is very dependent on our ability to *sequence* and *multi-task*, both of which are very difficult for children with praxis difficulties. The same holds true for sequencing a sentence for language. A child must be able to hold and manipulate words, meanings, and grammar rules in his holding tank, and arrange them in the right order to produce the correct sentence structure. Sequencing has a role in all of these processes, and in early development it all starts with motor sequences.

Active working memory is also an important skill used during reading comprehension. A child must hold information as a story unfolds and keep it in the right order for full comprehension. Sequencing impacts a child's ability to organize thoughts for writing assignments as well as his overall ability to organize his desk to easily find what is needed for the next activity. The roots of reading, writing, and organizational difficulties skills can extend into multiple developmental areas, and we have an obligation to each child to find the origin in their developmental profile and start working from there to solve the resulting difficulties to the greatest possible extent.

Fine and Visual-motor Skills

Fine motor skills are the small muscle movements occurring in the fingers and hand. Development of these skills allows us to complete tasks such as writing, drawing, cutting, and buttoning. There are many little muscles in our hands called intrinsic hand muscles that are mostly responsible for in-hand dexterity skills. Following the developmental framework, hand muscles for fine motor work develop their intricate dexterity after adequate gross motor development, after having developed sufficient postural control. Parents are frequently referred to occupational therapists for tasks such as handwriting and scissor skills, and are often surprised when we complete an evaluation and talk about so much more than simply the hand or the upper extremity.

Postural control, praxis, and vision skills are foundational for efficient execution of any fine motor skill. If a child has difficulty maintaining seated posture and does not have synchrony between his flexion and extension postural control systems, he will not have a solid foundation for developing integrative fine motor control to apply in tasks such as writing. It is possible to only focus on handwriting, and through repetition and cognitive control, develop sufficient writing skill to get by. But if not supported by the underlying developmental building blocks, the handwriting may be *sufficient* but not *efficient*, and will require more effort to accomplish rather than developing the automaticity in writing that we as adults take for granted. This is why we see children who can produce letters and words beautifully when simply applying handwriting in a therapy session, but as soon as the child is back in the classroom and has to apply the handwriting skill to a sentence or essay, he cannot produce the same work with the same speed or legibility.

Writing is crucial to learning, but good writing skills are dependent upon more than the hand alone. Research shows that if the shoulder joint is stabilized, one would still able to achieve fine motor skills and would still be able to write—if writing alone is all that is needed. But a child must write, think, move, listen, and look, all with good timing, speed, and rhythmicity. Many children on the spectrum have quite good penmanship, but they often need to forfeit quality for speed. Or they have great penmanship, but when asked to write their own ideas down in a sentence structure that makes sense with respect to language and grammar rules, these added layers cause frustration, distress, and a noticeable loss in quality and legibility.

The importance of cursive writing is also understated in the general curriculum of educational systems today. Since the advent of computers, this important building block is being treated as being "not as necessary." The act of cursive writing is an important skill in moving fluidly from left to right with connectivity, exercising the intricacies of fluid movement of the hand, while improving the timing between thought and the physical writing process.

I certainly do not advocate for children not to be exposed to fine motor and writing skills, but in order to achieve the finest integrative outcome, therapy should first focus on the core muscles, postural control, and efficient laterality skill (the sense of both sides of the body, left and right). When we focus on these foundations, and because children are still practicing fine motor work in school, these skills improve naturally, even though they are not the direct focus of therapy. As with praxis, we must remain careful not to focus only on the product (can the child cut or write), rather than the process it takes to get there (the flexibility of applying different sensory and motor systems in different sequences). If you focus on process, the child will always gain the product, as he will have developed motor memory through adequate feedback to make the activity automatic.

Maladaptive Pencil Grasps

Parents are often concerned about maladaptive grasps when it comes to holding a writing utensil. Most maladaptive grasps occur because the child is not receiving adequate sensory feedback in his hands. He may not be registering the feedback of the actual positioning, which causes him to want to press down very hard on the utensil in an attempt to register more feedback. Inadequate pencil grips can also be caused by exposing a child to a writing utensil before his thumb abductor has developed fully enough to ease him into an adequate web space (circle formed between thumb and side of hand), which is essential for a good tripod grasp.

Fine motor abilities develop over time starting with primitive gestures, such as grabbing at objects, to more intricate activities including precise hand-eye coordination. Fine motor skills also depend on visual perception, visual-motor integration, and ocular motor control. If there are deficiencies in any of these visual capacities, we must consider that we simply do not know what the child is seeing, and we must remember that the child has no idea that he might be seeing any differently than we are. He could be visually hypersensitive to the glare of the white paper or experience double vision, seeing two fingers at the starting place where your finger is pointing. Or when you ask him to cut on a line, an astigmatism might cause him to cut alongside of it. Our eyes can create havoc in a fine motor skill activity and this has to be assessed appropriately to find out what the aversion to the activity is all about. You do not have to wait until a child is at a *writing age* to see signs of potential issues. If a child avoids touching objects in his early development, which are experiences needed to develop eye-hand coordination and visual-motor skill, he might not only be touch defensive, but he could be having difficulty visually perceiving the item.

We must also understand that the issue is not simply writing or fine motor skill; it is generally rooted in the child's praxis (motor planning) capabilities. The brain must be able to perceive the demand adequately, organize it in good timing and rhythmicity, and then produce it—all of which has very little to do with whether the child has actual fine motor skill or not. This is why parents are often perplexed as to why their child can detect the minutest detail on a rug and pick it up with the finest pincer grasp, yet he finds it difficult to write. The answer lies in the simplicity of the motor plan and that the child probably has adequate fine motor *skill*, but not sufficient motor *plan* for more complex and novel actions.

During classroom consultations, I often see considerable anxiety when it comes to any form of fine motor work. Any child will participate in activities he feels successful in, and writing is a very complex process even though we do it so automatically as adults. It's so difficult to see a child who is obviously compromised in his sensori-motor system carry the burden of a negative consequence when he does not want to engage in a writing task. Such solutions are imposed without regard for the tremendous effort it takes for the child to participate in the activity in the first place. If the influence of vision and visual perception is overlooked, you could be causing the child's resistance to the very act you are trying to teach. In a child's life, things are very simple. It's easy to lose site of the fact that children do not consider what is good for them or that we mean well, they shouldn't be expected to. They simply react to the situation at hand. If something bothers them, they avoid it. If we insist, they enlist their fight and flight responses and we are quickly heading toward a power struggle. All we are really achieving by this type of behavior plan is for the child to really not like any task that even remotely smells of writing.

Righty or Lefty?

Another question that frequently arises is the question of handedness. Typically developing children show a strong preference between the ages of two and six years, and teachers often choose to wait on therapeutic intervention until children have reached the six-year mark. Handedness is built on the building blocks of crossing the midline, bilateral integration (coordinated movement by both sides of the body), muscle strength, and endurance. If a child shows a cluster of these difficulties and if the teacher knows to look for these issues, it is recommended that a referral be made sooner rather than later. If we wait until the child is six, it will be much more obvious that the skill has not been achieved, but some crucial development time has also passed.

Parents should also be aware that true ambidexterity is a very infrequent occurrence. If a child appears to be ambidextrous, it would be advisable to have this checked out. However, we know that reversals (i.e. confusing "b" and "d") are acceptable in typically developing children's writing until mid-second grade. But if other indications suggest we are working with a child with learning differences and slower processing speed, it is highly recommended that you do not wait until then to intervene. The time to develop the maturation of these skills is best done in the earlier years before extensive compensatory strategies have had the time to become habit.

Reflexes

As infants first leaving the womb, we are equipped with **primitive reflexes** to aid in our survival in the world. Goddard claims, "Primitive reflexes are automatic, stereotyped movements, directed from the brain stem and executed without cortical involvement."

Primitive reflexes emerge in utero and should remain active until the age of six-to-twelve months. If these reflexes are not fully integrated by twelve months of age, there is an indication of immature central nervous system development. In typically developing children, as one skill is gained another skill becomes inhibited. This is the case with primitive reflexes where each reflex lays the foundation for higher level skills. If these reflexes are still present at an older age, it is an indication that the child has not gained sufficient control over that reflex. Non-integrated reflexes subsequently impact the fluidity and smoothness with which an individual moves.

It is from these primitive reflexes that postural reflexes emerge. Primitive reflexes emerge from the brainstem, but postural reflexes arise from the midbrain and are indicative of central nervous system maturity. Postural responses are automatic reactions for the maintenance of balance, stability, and flexibility throughout the body. As postural movement sequences are practiced, more mature patterns of response supersede primitive reflex responses. When absent or underdeveloped, postural reflexes negatively contribute to a [child's] adaptation, problem-solving, linking, multi-processing, sequencing, and coping with large volumes of information, coordination, as well as associated disorders such as dyspraxia, "clumsy child" syndrome, apraxia, etc. (Goddard, 2005).

There are many different reflexes, too many to detail within the scope of this writing, but it is worthwhile to describe one common reflex that is greatly discussed by therapists strongly interested in the developmental influence. The **Asymmetrical Tonic Neck Reflex** (ATNR) is elicited when a baby's head is turned to one side and the arm of that side extends forward while the opposite arm moves to a flexed position. The ATNR develops in utero and is a key player in the birthing process as the baby passes through the birth canal. It helps to increase extensor muscle tone, training one side of the body at a time, and lays the foundation for future reaching. It also supports eye-hand coordination in its earliest form and the development crossing the midline of the body. **Crossing the midline** is when one side of the body, arms or legs, crosses over the vertical center of the body (imagine a line from the nose to the navel). Being able to fluidly cross the midline without the body stopping or twisting indicates that signals from one side of the brain are efficiently being sent to the other side of the brain.

We could look at the following scenarios as a possible influence of an ATNR that has not been fully integrated by development. A child sitting at his desk could be laying his head on one extended arm while writing with his opposite hand in a flexed elbow position; or a child jumping on a trampoline, and each time he is in the air, one side of his body flexes while the other side extends. According to Dr. Masgutova, this reflex supports the development of the auditory-vision connection, auditory memory, and crossing the midline in terms of the activation of auditory and visual midfield. It further supports the development of binocular vision and binaural hearing. I see so many children with reading difficulties who also exhibit non-integration of this ATNR reflex. This is but one example of one reflex, but sufficient to say, there are many hidden treasures in looking at reflexes when considering the developmental profile of any child.

Social Skills

It is inevitable that having difficulty with sensory processing skills contributes to difficulties with social skills. If a child has spent his early developmental years in a state of fight, fright, or flight due to strong avoidance of environmental stimuli, his largest concern is going to be keeping himself safe. Not only will he avoid the unpredictability of peers, but he will also avoid the very activities that typical peers play with and not gain experience from them. Children who appear extremely passive and who are under-registering sensory information are simply not paying attention to the social cues needed for social interaction. They are more focused on their physical and sensory neural needs than on paying attention to the social cues around them. In a child with a spectrum disorder, you have this experiential difficulty, but you also have the inherent difficulty of not having sufficient theory of mind, where the child is not able to project that another person may be thinking or feeling something different than him.

Mirroring Mommy

There is interesting research regarding *mirror neurons*. These neurons are available to every child at birth and are responsible for the baby being able to mimic mommy from the earliest stage of newborn life. When mommy coos over baby, you see the reflection of the same pleasure in the baby's facial expression. There is an innate social-emotional response to mommy's overtures that sets the stage for bonding, attachment, and social-emotional connection with caregivers. This forms an important base for social-emotional connection and the instinctive understanding of non-verbal communication.

Because social skills are so affected in children with developmental delays, parents rush in very early to have their child participate in social skill groups. As important as early intervention is, very frequently this type of intervention might be too early for the child's developmental age—even though his chronological age says differently. If a child has acute sensory processing needs, a group situation with multiple stimuli may become too overwhelming and end up causing the very behaviors we are trying to avoid. In many cases, to argue that the child is only going through a transition and will get over it would be misdirected and cause much unnecessary stress. If a child's sensory needs are not being met, he will simply not be able to take in the learning from the social situation anyway.

There are two keys to timing the introduction of social interaction: 1) an individualized profile and 2) a team approach. With a complete picture of each child's sensory and developmental profile, the team of parents and professionals will more easily see the right timing and approach for social exposure. A better approach is to work with a child individually first (with the parent), then introduce one peer to a session. A child could stay in this stage of development for quite a while, and that's more than okay. Only after the child is really comfortable and able to play with great connection to a single peer should he be introduced to group social skills training. This does not mean the child is not exposed to groups at all, since in many cases the child is still being exposed to social groups in preschool or school. It is important for a child to be exposed to group activities that allow him to become more aware of social situations. But the goal is *awareness* and *observation* initially, until the child is ready for social skill.

Developing social skill relies on many of the same fundamental building blocks as complex writing tasks. Adequate social skill requires the integration of all of our senses at rapid timing and processing speed. Many social skills programs today rely on the child's cognitive skills such as memory to *learn* certain skills. It is almost an oversimplification to regard the *observable behavior* as the most important aspect of the social interaction required. The truth is typical peer engagement is rapid fire. Almost all of the sensory and developmental capacities described above are needed for a child to take in a social situation, plan an organized response, and participate with meaning in a timely manner before the smallest moment has passed. The seemingly simple action of waiting until someone else has completed a sentence relies on understanding the reciprocal nature of conversation and a certain sense of timing that is lacking in so many profiles I encounter.

With a global approach to sensory intervention, I frequently see that as we start working on the sensory processing difficulties, more social ability comes to the fore without directly targeting this area in the intervention plan. Foundation comes first. With a strong foundation, higher order skills such as social thinking will have more support and the child can then develop the ability to use them more effectively.

Your Sensory Jumping-Off Point

This discussion was not meant to be an educational tour of theory and should not be considered as the total conversation on the topic of sensory processing. My goal is to provide you with an overview of what to consider in terms of your own child's development as a jumping off point to learn more. The many examples described were to highlight some of the pitfalls I frequently see in my work.

Though we continue to evolve in our knowledge of sensory processing and how it impacts a child's learning and behavior, there is one clear fact that transcends science today and will continue to do so for many tomorrows to come—the basic development that was true for you still holds true for your child. We should remember this truth thoughtfully when planning and considering any intervention for our children.

"...our teaching was only part of the equation that was going to make Matty whole... his learning was a distinctly individual factor that only he could control.

What I learned in those five short minutes and five simple letters was that I simply had to entrust part of this journey—to him."

Chapter 5

Floortime and Schooltime…a Whole New Ballgame

"Hello?" Karen answered the phone with a gentle, unassuming voice. The mom who recommended her was so excited about how well her son was responding to his Floortime sessions that I anxiously called her the night I came home from the support group meeting. I remember being immediately struck by her calm manner and genuine care and understanding.

We talked for over an hour as I explained my initial Floortime experience with the EI speech therapist, and how it had somewhat soured me on the concept. We talked a lot about play and how important it is as a foundation for so many social expectations as kids get older. I realized I had jumped to the conclusion that *following the child's lead* was the end goal of Floortime. I assumed the sole purpose of Floortime was to boost a child's esteem by *appearing* to be interested in what he's interested in. Karen explained that following the child's lead was not the goal, but a strategy to allow a child to reach his own goals. *His* individual goals based on *his* individual development.

"Floortime," she explained, "is a strategy under a larger framework called DIR, which is like a roadmap for a child's social and emotional development. It puts a child in the driver's seat, and Floortime is one of the tools we use to help him get where he needs to go."

She told me what the DIR acronym stood for, but I readily forgot. What did stick with me about our DIR discussion was that it was all based on the child's unique course of development, allowing the child himself to sure up developmental areas that may have stalled or gone off course.

"It allows children to do it in their own time and in their own way," explained Karen, "but with DIR, the child is in control of the pace of his own development."

It sounded like it was connected to a more organic approach. It had a sense of naturalness that appealed to the child's individuality, and appealed to my sense of finding roots and making connections. Giving a child the opportunity to make himself whole is a much more gracious intervention than assuming he is irreparably mis-wired or disconnected, and forcing an approach upon him that just tries to make the best of the hand he appeared to be dealt.

Opening a New Door

A couple of weeks later I answered the door for Karen's first visit, welcoming a tiny smiling frame largely outweighed by the bags of toys she brought for Matty's first session. I showed her the classroom with all of our new sensory options. "This is great because the first level of DIR is regulation," she said.

She was thrilled to hear about what we were doing from a sensory perspective. I explained the sensory path we'd taken over the prior year and the differences in Matty when he was regulated vs. being driven by sensory seeking or avoidance needs. I told her about how Matty craved deep-pressure, jumping, crashing, and the tactile input from the rice bath. Not surprisingly, her first session and many more to come would be spent in that rice bath.

Matty was always very cooperative and really liked the ABA sessions, but he loved his sessions with Karen from the get-go. After her first visit, she left me with a list of toys that would help get their sessions off and running. The list included all kinds of toys for fantasy play, nurturing and empathy. I liked where this was headed. We touched on some play schemes during Matty's ABA sessions, but the play approach in ABA seemed more scripted and contrived with drills that were more about training him to go through the motions and less about a purpose for engaging in the play to begin with. If Matty wanted a lion to drive a train, he obviously had a purpose for wanting a lion to drive a train. We may not have understood his purpose and he may not have been able to articulate his purpose, but he did have a reason for wanting to play that way that day. I immediately felt good about Karen and the way this approach seemed more in tune to a child's natural inclinations.

Lagniappe and White Gloves

Lagniappe (lan yep) is a Cajun word meaning *an extra gift* or *unexpected bonus*. It often describes that extra something a merchant may give to customers as a gift of gratitude for their business. It's that baker's dozen or the few extra green beans thrown in after the scale has been read. Lagniappe is all about is appealing to your emotions rather than your intellect, and the delight factor is a powerful thing. Lagniappe goes a step further than simple appreciation—it's the connection of your experience to your enjoyment of it.

Everyone has experienced lagniappe, and it can be experienced in many different ways. A friend of mine once completed a computer course and took her completion certificate to a craft store to be framed. It wasn't a sentimental photograph or expensive work of art, it was a simple certificate. When she presented it to the employee for framing, he promptly reached under the counter to put on white gloves before touching it.

"Really, it's not anything expensive, it's okay for you to handle it," she told him.

"Oh no, ma'am, but it's important... it's important to you and that makes it a work of art."

Showing her that respect, letting her know that what made it valuable was her emotional connection to it was what made the experience of getting a simple certificate framed more pleasant and memorable for her. That, to me, is the essence of lagniappe. It's the emotional connection that defines how a person experiences a moment.

I'm the last person to comment on how the human mind works, but I visualize lagniappe in the brain as one experience being mapped in two areas, the emotional area and the intellectual area, with a line connecting them to each other. The line is what gives more meaning to an experience. I may be stretching the definition of lagniappe in my mind, but it has suited me well as a single word to describe those experiences that are more powerful because they're mapped with both intellectual and emotional meaning in the brain. Children learn more and more easily when a learning moment is meaningful to them. That's what childhood should be all about... lots of lagniappe and respectful white glove moments. Maybe most children are just born with more natural capacity to connect to the meaning of their experiences and to map those lines in their brains, and perhaps some children like Matty seem to have less of that capacity. But that didn't mean he had no capacity at all.

I once attended a lecture by a sensory integration therapist who explained sensory regulation in terms of a sliding window. She illustrated how regulatory activities can ease the window open, but how sensory defensiveness and avoidance reactions can slam it shut in a heartbeat. That comparison made sense to me as I saw more and more how Matty responded to SI intervention. Like the balls of Newton's cradle, Matty's sensory window would open and shut at any given moment depending on his state of regulation. I imagine that when you live life through a swing door of sensory regulation, you would tend to map life experiences as though you're on the periphery of them. It's like your life is played on the field, but the experience mapped in your brain is from the perspective of the bench. You're there, but you don't adequately feel the grass under your feet or the ball in your hands. You may feel somewhat connected to the loss but never the full exuberance of the win. And unfortunately, for some children, too often all they experience is a metal bench and a cold butt.

Most kids go through childhood with windows wide open and a natural capacity live life on the field. Maybe Matty wasn't a child with those natural inclinations, but I now felt closer to understanding where his gaps were. I saw that in order for him to step onto the field of life, he needed help in keeping his regulation window open as wide and as long as possible to allow his experiences to be mapped with more meaning… more delight… more lagniappe.

The Five Letters that Spell "I Can Learn"

Like the image of Matty with his head tilted in his bouncy seat as an infant and the way he communicated in our Christmas portrait less than a year later, Matty again helped shape my perspective of our journey. Only this time, it wasn't something I saw in him—it was something I heard. Matty was almost two and a half when I took him to see our third and final developmental pediatrician. I remember sitting at a traffic light waiting to make a left turn to find the hospital campus. Matty was in his car seat behind the passenger seat. He had been silent for the entire drive. I was unsure whether I was making the correct turn and I was looking around for a street sign. I don't know whether everyone does this, but whenever I'm driving and begin to feel lost, I turn off the radio so I can hear myself think. Matty was looking out the window to our right and the car was now quiet. I was the first one at the light, so we were sitting there for a minute or two. Without warning, I heard Matty speak: "F," "E," "D," "E," "X."

At first, I didn't make any connection to the letters he uttered; I just thought he was babbling. Then I glanced out the passenger side window and saw that a FedEx truck had pulled up next to us. My first reaction was, "Wow, how did he know that? He even recognized the uppercase and lowercase E." He hadn't been working on the alphabet in therapy and I was puzzled by how he would have learned the letters. My girls had an alphabet video on during the prior week, but I didn't remember Matty ever sitting down long enough to watch it. We went to the appointment and he recognized most if not all of his uppercase and lowercase letters for the doctor. While Matty slept on the way home, I remember thinking about it for much of the ride. I remember thinking that by him uttering those five letters, he was telling me so much.

He was telling me that he could learn and that he was acutely aware and listening even when he didn't *look like* he was taking anything in. He was telling me that although he was in therapy three of his twelve waking hours each day, the other nine hours were not void of learning. He was growing and learning 24/7, whether he looked like it or not. He was telling me that what my eyes saw wasn't always the whole picture, and that I couldn't sculpt my entire perception of him based solely on what I see. I realized that just because I didn't see him sitting in front of an alphabet video attentively absorbing every letter like the typical sponge kids are supposed to be, that he wasn't learning. He learned it somehow and in his own way. He wasn't like my four other sponges; he was like a little chamois, always taking more and more in with never an indication of how much he was absorbing or how saturated he was.

The value of the appointment with the developmental pediatrician had less to do with the thirty minutes I spent in the doctor's office than the five minutes before we arrived. Before then I thought all of Matty's learning would be at the hands of our teaching, but I now know the type of learner he is and I can guess how his learning likely happened that week.

I now know that he doesn't always integrate visual and auditory information in real-time when he learns. He's a snapshot kind of kid. He often takes a quick snapshot of a visual image then diverts his eyes away from the target image so he can listen better. He probably didn't look like he was tuned into the alphabet video because he never had his eyes glued to the TV. Rather, he could take a quick visual snapshot of a letter, then look away, or even have his back to the TV while he acutely listened. He didn't look like he was paying any attention to the TV at all, but he could still visually see the letter in his mind while processing what he heard. Although much improved, even now he sometimes switches back and forth between visual and auditory input in the initial capture of information, then replays it in his mind to integrate and process it.

What I learned that day was that *our teaching* was only part of the equation that was going to make Matty whole. *His learning* was a distinctly individual factor that only he could control. I now knew he could learn, but it was going to be in his way and on his terms. It may seem obvious now, but it made me realize the real value of Matty's contribution to his own learning and development. What I learned in those five short minutes and five simple letters was that I simply had to entrust part of this journey—to him.

Play is Demanding

Over fall and winter I watched how Karen's style cultivated more of Matty's natural inclinations during play. With each session she would help him ease his window open, then calmly reach in with her satin white gloves to respectfully share in his experiences. During those sessions I also realized a lot more about play. Play is demanding. I never thought about all the skills you really need to play. You need fine and gross motor skills, imitation skills, social skills, attention, and imagination— just to name a few. All the things you need for learning in school. I can admit that I never was and probably never will be a *good player*. I never really did the doll thing, yet I didn't play with typical boy things either. To be honest, I don't know what I did as a child when it came to play.

I do have one play memory at Christmastime when I was in first grade. We had a Pollyana gift exchange in our classroom and a boy in my class gave me a Barbie doll. I clearly remember taking the doll home, removing it from the box and thinking, "Okay, so what am I supposed to do with this now?" I had absolutely no idea how I was supposed to play with that doll. Pretty sad, I know. I guess it's not too hard to see how the lack of imagination and play skills apple didn't fall far from my tree. But I'm glad I knew this about myself. As we shifted to using more of a Floortime approach, I knew without a doubt that I would not be much help in trying to do serious Floortime with Matty. As I saw in Karen, it took equal parts of experience, art, and skill to do what she did. When it came to creative and imaginative play, I had none of these and I knew it.

Maybe it was a blessing that my play skills are so bad. Knowing this, I was well aware from the beginning that I would not be capable of stepping into the role of a therapist. I knew some parents who were supporting intensive ABA home programs, and were trying to curb costs by learning how to do therapy themselves. I was very fortunate this was never a realistic option for me. I knew I was no Super Mom, but even if I did have some inclination toward imaginative play, turning myself into Clark Kent the therapist would have been a disaster on all levels. For Matty, a child who lives a perpetual journey to be grounded in his own body, confusing the most foundational and grounding relationship in his life would certainly have been detrimental to him. For my family, I was already living dual role of a mother working outside the home; splitting my identity again would simply be unfair to them. For me, knowing there was not much expectation by anyone that I could assume the role of the therapist was definitely a relief. I knew I couldn't do it, and more importantly, I knew I would be setting everyone up for failure if I pretended I could. The role of the therapist would have to be the work of others... sisters, peers, and therapists, but not me. And that was okay. I'm the Mom, not the therapist.

The Speech is Back

We had a break in speech after converting Matty's speech therapy to ABA, but during a summer meeting with St. John's, we were granted a full speech evaluation and two hours of speech therapy were added back into his EI program. Fortunately, a different speech therapist was assigned and she was not at all like the first. She was very agile and had lots of spunk. She knew a little about Floortime strategies, was eager to learn more, and was very open to embracing SI within what was now becoming a very eclectic program of interventions.

Sensory work was becoming an elemental part of all therapies and Floortime strategies would soon follow. Throughout the winter all therapies focused on three strategies: 1) follow Matty's lead; 2) provide plenty of validation; and 3) introduce playful obstruction to foster problem-solving.

Happy Birthday...Now Blow Out the Candles and Off to School

Matty would soon be turning three; he was on a good course, and I was starting to recover from the stress of the prior year. But even before the ground began to thaw I found myself gearing up for what would likely be an instant replay of that same intensity, as it was soon time to plan Matty's transition to preschool. Transitioning from the EI system to the education system was somewhat of a hard pill to swallow, but I had to put the pieces in perspective. Moving to a purely educational focus would be a whole different game and I needed new insight on the forces at play. Until then, Matty's intervention plan really had only two players—Matty's needs and the medical community's interventions. Even though I knew Matty's needs better than anyone else, it would now be a new challenge to develop a program to continue to meet his needs within the constraints of the education system.

By law, the last day a child is eligible for Early Intervention services is the eve of his third birthday, but the process to begin the transition begins a full three months prior to that. You begin with an identification meeting to determine whether further evaluation is warranted. In Matty's case, since he was already being serviced by the Early Intervention system and we had a diagnosis, there was no question whether he qualified to be evaluated.

Over the following two months the school district conducted a series of evaluations including social, psychological, speech, and OT. Throughout the evaluations, I began to realize just how much I really knew about Matty. I was able to provide a sensory history, a summary of the gross and fine motor progress he'd made over the prior fourteen months, and a helpful account of his communication challenges. I went into the evaluations expecting that I would provide some information, but that the bulk of the knowledge transfer would be in the other direction. I expected to learn more from the evaluator than the evaluator would learn from me. I soon realized that wasn't the case; but in retrospect, I now know this was a good thing. In the end, all of Matty's evaluation reports contained accurate characterizations of his needs as I knew them, and this helped tremendously in the development of his IEP.

Looking back, I now believe this was the biggest contribution I made to help establish the most appropriate suite of interventions when he entered school. I didn't realize it at the time, but I understood him in ways the IEP team needed to know in order to create a program to meet his real needs. I was so glad I had spent more than a year really watching him and making connections between what he needed and what he did to satisfy his needs. I understood him from a sensory perspective and was beginning to understand him developmentally. I was able to answer not just their initial questions but also their follow-up questions, and I could explain some roots and connections not typically discerned through the typical school evaluation process. I discussed how much of what he does is rooted in his physiology and how the need for him to focus, be still or pay attention will always take a back seat to his need to respond to his body's demand for regulation. I explained that for Matty, movement, structure, and control were ways he satisfied his physical needs. They were not behaviors in the socially undesirable context of the word.

After completing all the evaluations and requirements, our first IEP meeting was held. I say first because we probably held five or more meetings before I felt comfortable enough to actually sign it. The evaluation process was one thing, but the process of developing the IEP was, I would soon learn, a whole new animal. Going into it, I didn't know much about writing an IEP, but I did know one thing—Matty's program had to reflect his true needs. I soon found this would be easier said than done.

The Big Eye-Opener... Not all Aspects of Development are Educationally Relevant

Moving from an all-encompassing medical intervention approach to a purely educational perspective was a real eye-opener, and it didn't take long to realize Matty's weren't the only needs on the table. First, the educational system is required by law to consider equal opportunities for every student on a level *commensurate with peers*. This vision differs from school system to school system, and it certainly may not always reflect the child's best potential. When the goal is to be *on par* with peers rather than to reach the child's individual potential, many possibilities for intervention remain out of reach. Beyond that, certain aspects of development are considered *educationally relevant* while others are not. It's rare to find a school system well-versed in early development as they don't consider it to be a focus or their responsibility. But the connection I can now make is that what is educationally relevant at a given point in a child's chronological age may not always be where the child is developmentally. And when the level of expectation mismatches the level of competence, a child will most often comply with rote memory and little meaning, or go into a shutdown or avoidance mode to escape the situation and self-protect. I am only hopeful more parents begin to understand this and educators begin to allow this understanding to influence the focus of goals, expectations, and interventions.

Besides the expectations of the school system, I also struggled with keeping my own expectations in check. I think all parents do. Parent expectations run the gamut of academic, social, and emotional goals. Some parents might like to see their child act exactly as appropriate to fit into his peer age social circle, yet not know what it really takes for the child to develop and maintain that level of interaction. Other parents may focus on making sure their child learns the alphabet or reading and writing skills to prove his level of intellect, not knowing the strain this can cause on the system of a child still in need of foundational skills learned through play.

Going into the process, I thought I was sufficiently prepared in knowing what Matty's needs were, not asking for miracles, and being grounded in keeping his program tied to those needs. But for me, the broader challenge throughout the IEP process was learning to accept the education system's goals and developing a program to accommodate both. Much of the time spent in our IEP meetings focused on writing and rewriting goals to meet educational objectives in ways that met Matty's real needs.

Eventually, after more than a few exhausting meetings, we did it. We finally settled on a core set of measurable academic and functional goals, supports, and services to meet his needs through educational objectives. And like tens of thousands of parents like me do each year, I woke my child up on his third birthday, put him on a bus, and sent him off for his first day of school.

The mind embraces "early intervention"… but the heart says "too soon."

Matty's Seat at the IEP Table

I always kept a seat for Matty at the IEP table, as he was also a member of the team, with me as his surrogate. To me, Matty's role was to constantly project his needs and mine was to simply be the ambassador of those needs. Within the pages of the IEP, the goals were always written to meet Matty's needs within the framework of educationally relevant objectives, but in the many IEP meetings I've attended over the years I've learned to keep my own set of goals in sight as well. After every IEP meeting, I now try to debrief myself with some simple questions:

1. Did I really know Matty's true needs?
2. Was I the best ambassador of those needs by injecting them in every nook and cranny of the IEP?
3. Did I keep expectations in perspective?
4. Did I trust my gut and have the courage to ask for everything he needed?
5. Are we doing things at the right time (developmentally)?
6. Do the goals reflect the patience and time Matty deserves? That is, are we rushing anything because of the education system's goals and external pressures?

I find that keeping these questions in the front of my mind keeps me as closely tethered to Matty's true developmental journey as possible.

School Days

As stressful as the process leading up to the transition to preschool was, the first days and weeks were very positive for all. Matty was content, his teachers and therapists welcomed him warmly, and I was relaxed and relieved everyone was feeling the groove. Matty gravitated to movement and away from the fray of classroom activity because he needed to, and it was my role to make sure everyone involved in his program knew that. He avoided transitions because he could not easily regulate to new environments or demands, and loved letters and numbers simply because they never change. He liked to talk about the rainbow color order because he needed order and predictability. He craved this stability because his body could not regulate and adapt to a quickly changing environment. Teachers and therapists soon saw these connections too, as well as the difference in Matty when he was regulated.

The first month was focused on meeting his physical and sensory needs. His sensory diet became an important tool to help him maintain regulation throughout the day, with swinging and movement activities prior to transitions and times when he needed to focus. Two of my other children attended his preschool as typically developing peers in inclusion classes. Within a month or so, Matty began visiting my five-year-old daughter's inclusion classroom for a short time each day, and by the end of the year he was spending the entire morning session there. Academic requirements were not a stressful concern; we were simply testing the waters to see how well he could handle an inclusive educational environment. He neither embraced nor rejected the larger social setting by way of meltdowns or other stressful reactions. In fact, he was then given placement in both the morning and afternoon sessions of an inclusion class for the following school year to provide the most complete experience possible, given his therapy schedule.

In June, two months after starting in preschool, it was already time to develop Matty's IEP for the next school year. After spending a year having monthly team meetings with Matty's Early Intervention team, it was kind of a shock to be thrown into a process where progress and direction is only evaluated once a year. It seemed crazy to me that we would have IEP meetings in June to develop goals and objectives covering the entire following school year. It was beyond me how in one meeting, we were expected to predict what a three-year-old child would need over the next full year of his development. It was always noted that we could convene an IEP meeting at any time, but going by what it took to get the first meetings scheduled, I had my doubts that it would be easily accomplished. In fact, that year it was written into Matty's IEP that it was to be automatically reopened after November conferences, and for the two years Matty spent in preschool, I made sure his IEP included ample consult and meeting time with everyone on the team.

We had monthly team meetings for me to meet with teachers and therapists to share and compare what we'd seen in him. I did have journals going back and forth with individual team members, but that system was limited to communicating daily notes, not fostering the group's collective knowledge. It was only at the face-to-face team meetings where I felt we were all able to share an understanding of Matty in a whole sense. Through the school's summer program, Matty was able to continue working with Karen and this helped to keep him moving in a good direction.

During the summer, Karen told me about an OT she had been working with on another child's program; her name was Maude Le Roux and she had a practice about forty-five minutes away. Karen explained that Maude had been working in other school districts in a consultation role for children with needs similar to Matty's. I thought about calling her, but my insurance had stopped covering Matty's OT visits for SI work and I knew it would not likely cover an appointment with a new OT for a similar consult. With the craziness of summer and getting everyone back to school, I just never ended up making the call.

Back to School

September came quickly and Matty was back at school in his double session of inclusion. At home he seemed happy and it appeared as though he was handling the new environment well. However, at our first school team meeting in October, his teacher noted areas where Matty was struggling. He was unable to focus and sit still during circle time, was having difficulty processing multi-step instructions, and was perseverating more than ever on numbers and letters. I was a bit taken back. He seemed to be doing well at home; he wasn't unhappy and never showed a negative reaction to school. I guess I was a little dismayed to find he wasn't making the brilliant adjustment I'd hoped for.

The OT tweaked his sensory diet and made more recommendations for regulatory activities, but I left that meeting feeling less confident than I had in any other school meeting thus far. I wondered whether, even with the sensory accommodations, Matty was going to be able to function in a typical classroom environment. We left the meeting with a plan to try some additional sensory strategies, but I couldn't help thinking, "What if they don't work... what do we do next?" I left that first meeting feeling not disappointed, but more unsettled about what this new school year would bring.

Can Matty Cut it in Inclusion?

For weeks after our first team meeting, I spent more than a few loads of laundry thinking and worrying about whether Matty was going to cut it in a typical school environment. He was my fourth child to go through preschool, yet I was experiencing his journey on a whole different level. Up until then, I never had to really think about the expectations of preschool. At three years old, we expect children to be able to listen to a story, work together, share toys and tools, and express their needs. If they lack physical capacity to cut, color, jump, skip or climb, it's an OT to the rescue. If they have less than optimal ability to communicate, it's a speech therapist to the rescue. Even if they have difficulty regulating to the environment, it's a sensory diet to the rescue. But we had all these interventions in place and it still seemed like a challenge. I began to wonder whether it would ever be enough to get Matty to a place where he could not only succeed, but thrive. I really started to wonder... .

I thought about the many challenges Matty faced each day and the differences between how he navigated through the same preschool day as his four-year-old sister. Where she could sit fully engaged at circle time or watch a teacher model instructions—Matty looked away and lost his bearings after the first step. Where she had no problem regulating to fluctuating classroom noise levels—Matty withdrew. How she could easily jump right into the fray of free play time while he had to escape to the security of the classroom walls. Why?

Insights into SI had taught me that Matty's behavior was sensory behavior rooted in "I need to do this," not social behavior rooted in "I want to do this." I felt comfortable that his sensory needs were being addressed, but it seemed that even with all the accommodations for his sensory needs, he wasn't taking the steps and making the strides I envisioned. I feared we were reaching a point of accepting that Matty's struggles were not within my or anyone else's power to change. Maybe this was the point where I just count my blessings and adjust my expectations. Maybe it just wasn't in the cards for him.

By the next team meeting not much had changed. Teachers offered more observations and therapists recommended more sensory tweaks. It was beginning to feel uncomfortably familiar. No big changes, no big breakthroughs. After the meeting I strolled down the hall to peek into his classroom. He was sitting at a table with a few other children who were building with blocks. He didn't look unhappy to be there, yet he didn't look happy either. "Maybe he was intended to be more of an observer of life than a spirited participant," I thought. I'm that way in a lot of ways. I prefer the role of silent observer in many social and professional areas of my life. I'm just not inclined to go out and mingle, stand up and volunteer, or get up and dance. These are things I'm just not comfortable doing. So why isn't it okay for Matty not to want to either?

I Just Don't Want To

For Matty, it wasn't that he *wouldn't* build. It just seemed that he just *didn't want to build*... or play... or participate. It was hard to say he couldn't, because at the time there was every reason to think he could. It could be the stimulation, but every effort was being made to mitigate the environment through sensory interventions. It seemed he had most every capacity to engage in many of the classroom activities he was avoiding—except the desire to do so.

When Matty started working with Karen over a year before, it was, for me, the beginning of a new perspective on respecting Matty's experience. I had learned that the way he experiences a moment defines how much meaning he will derive from it. I had seen how the more he experienced regulated, validated, and boundary-less play, the more he seemed to tap into the delight factor and process experiences with more meaning. But when he was at school he wore a protective armor against the new and novel, shielding him from challenges and denying him the lagniappe-filled experiences he deserved. I thought about it up and down, through and through, but I still felt the heaviness of one daunting question—how on earth can you inspire a child to *want* to jump up off the bench, run onto the field, and participate in life?

Reaching out to Maude

I finally decided to give Maude a call. From what Karen told me, she seemed to be an ideal fit for all areas of Matty's program. She was a sensory OT, she encouraged a strong developmental perspective and she was soon to be certified in DIR. I was initially reluctant to call because her office seemed so far away, but after we talked, I ended up feeling fortunate she was so close. I don't remember what day I put the call in to her, but I do remember what day she called me back. It was on a Saturday morning. No medical professional had ever returned my call on a Saturday morning. We talked for quite a while that day. Well, actually I talked for quite a while, Maude mostly listened.

I was encouraged by Maude's broad background and experience and I had a good feeling that her perspective could help shape Matty's program in many ways. Our conversation happened shortly before a school meeting regarding Matty's current difficulties and other IEP concerns, and the timing worked out perfectly for me to request a more in-depth sensory evaluation by a professional outside the school district. The district agreed, and Maude was scheduled to conduct an in-school observation of Matty followed by a full sensory evaluation at her center. The school observation was conducted in December, and Matty's sensory evaluation took place at Maude's center soon after the winter break.

Matty seemed to be tolerant of his new inclusion environment, but was far from being an active and enthusiastic player in it. I had high hopes that this evaluation would bring a deeper understanding of his sensory systems; but beyond sensory, I hoped for any new nugget of direction in cracking the nut of "participation" he so avoided.

Always an Uphill Climb

We headed to Maude's office, Matty perched behind the driver's seat of our van. As we reached the highpoint of the bridge over the Brandywine River, Matty sat up as though he saw something interesting in the water below. I wondered what he could possibly see beyond all the gray. The gray bridge, gray water, gray skies didn't offer much to interest me, but something obviously piqued his curiosity. A few miles later, I found myself waiting to make a left turn onto the road leading to Maude's office. I remembered how a single left turn spoke volumes to me more than a year earlier as we arrived at the Developmental Pediatrician's office. Sometimes even when I see a FedEx truck today, I still think of the moment when those five letters spelled out so much for me that day. He can learn and he will learn… in his own way and in his own time.

No signs or premonitions this time. I turned left, only to find a steep hill and winding road to challenge my transmission. "Boy, I hope this isn't an omen," I thought. A steeper climb for Matty was not what I hoped this evaluation will bring. Matty had been living an uphill climb every day of his short little life. But I was very hopeful to learn even more about him from a sensory perspective, and possibly find more insight into how to help turn his daily uphill battle into, at the very least, a journey on flat open road. If I couldn't make his journey as easy as most kids, I just wanted to find a way to not make it so damn hard for him. And, with a little luck, maybe even find a way for him to get a glimpse of the downside of the mountains he scales every day of his little life.

"With the first page of his chart filled with many notes about the essence of who he was...

We were now ready to build our repository of clinical evaluations to define Matt's sensory and developmental profile."

Chapter 6

A Deep Dive into Matt's Sensory Processing Systems

Matt looked around, bewildered, suspicious, cautiously inquisitive. He held himself quite erect, almost rigid in a way. He glanced at his mother before slowly steering away to circle the room, reluctantly exploring. Steely eyes, timid reach. He carefully touched different objects and then let go. He wandered around the room, seemingly aimless, yet with his senses on high alert to anything that might cause a defensive response.

I could tell he was curious about what he saw, but didn't know how to plan a response to be able to do something with what he found interesting. His face was one of intense concentration with no hint of a smile, his big blue eyes intently roving. He came back to his mother and held her hand. She was his place of comfort, the place of the known. This new room was the unknown.

My thoughts raced as I tried to feel what he was feeling... to step inside his mind... to know what he was thinking. "Trapped" burst into my mind and stayed there as we silently watched him move.

What does it feel like to have thoughts but to have nowhere to put them? To have ideas that are never validated because no one knows about them but you. To not understand that your thoughts cannot be read or interpreted by your family and those around you. To listen to people talk but only take in half of what they say—only to understand one word, maybe two. To look at people's faces without being able to listen to them at the same time, and to watch emotion ripple over faces yet derive no meaning from it.

And what lingering memory might he be pondering at this moment? Might he still be thinking of the discomfort of getting ready to come here? The prickle of the bristles in his mouth causing him to clench the toothbrush in his teeth so hard that pain shot through his jaw. The fear of last night's bath as Mom rinsed the shampoo, screaming as she tilted his head back under the running faucet, not able to tell her it felt like he was falling backward with no one there to catch him.

There was so much we did not know about what Matt was thinking, and would not know for quite some time. At this point, we simply could not assume anything. To do so would be disrespectful, even arrogant. We must give him the ownership of himself, and allow him to teach us about who he is.

Matt was three years nine months old when he came to my center for an evaluation. Lauren explained the journey of his first three years with much insight into who he was and what made him tick. Her eyes filled with tears as she described his sweet nature in always wanting to please, yet somewhere deep down she felt he knew he couldn't. I didn't yet know Matt in a clinical sense, but I did know I wanted to change that feeling for both of them.

With the first page of his chart filled with many notes about the essence of who he was, we were now ready to start building our repository of clinical evaluations to define Matt's sensory and developmental profile. Our approach would leverage the following tools: 1) background information collected from Lauren detailing Matt's sensory and developmental history; 2) an observation of Matt in his preschool classroom; 3) a *Sensory Profile* (created by Winnie Dunn), also completed by Lauren; and 4) evaluation at my center using our clinical assessment tools.

Step 1. Parent Input

Background information was collected specific to Matt's sensory development and sensory preferences through a sensori-motor history questionnaire. Lauren also noted the following in detailing her concerns:

- **Focus:** Matt would tune in and out, he focused on unimportant details, was easily distracted by visual things, missed important information, could not follow through on instructions, concentrated too deeply, and had difficulty remaining alert.
- **Flexibility:** He had trouble shifting attention from one activity to another and was fearful of new situations.
- **Control:** Predictability was highly important for him; he avoided challenging situations, and he over-reacted to stress and frustration.
- **Social:** He did not initiate play with peers, he gravitated to adults, and withdrew when a lot of people were around, such as at a party. He was also described to be affectionate, appealing to adults, accepting of rules, likable, and generally happy.

Step 2. School Observation

We also had the opportunity to visit Matt's school environment to view him in his preschool classroom to see how he functioned in his community of children. I am always pleased when we are able to do this because in a one-on-one situation a child can look very different than in a multi-sensory environment such as the classroom. Following are highlights of the feedback from the educational staff.

- **Strengths:** Matt was cooperative, followed classroom routines, responded well to intervention, and seemed to have the ability to generalize new skills when given practice.

- **Speech/Language/Communication:** Matt exhibited variable performance in his willingness to speak. He did not always speak in full sentences or use words in the right order, and sometimes said things that seemed irrelevant. He had decreased willingness to ask questions and had difficulty understanding instructions and following verbal directions. He also had difficulty using time words (*before, after, now, later*) and prepositions such as *in* and *on*.

- **Focus:** He lost interest easily, concentrated too deeply at times, and focused too long on the "wrong" thing. He was easily distracted but easily redirected, seemed to be in a daze at times, and became tired when not moving around.

- **Play:** Matt exhibited difficulty using imagination/ creativity and had little to no interest in games.

- **Social:** He was slow to make friends, tended to play alone, was timid or passive with other children, and sometimes isolated himself from other children. He depended on his teacher or adults for help in engaging socially.

Our classroom observation revealed all of this and more.

- **Focus:** Matt was unable to remain seated in a chair in circle time, but thrived on music and movement activities. He needed maximal assistance during tabletop activities to complete the expected tasks. As the morning wore on, Matt became more distracted and less focused. The incessant noise of the classroom caused him to want to hyperfocus in an effort to shut everyone out, but this took its toll in terms of endurance.

- **Regulation**: Matt became distressed and started to put his hands in his mouth in an effort to provide sensory input to calm himself. He was taken to wash his hands, but did not want to resume any table top activities afterward.

- **Motor Activities:** He was noted to exhibit fine motor and bilateral integration difficulties (both sides of the body working together) during the fine motor activities.

- **Social:** At no time did Matt make any social contact with anyone after the music and movement portion of the morning routine.

Our hearts went out to this little boy who knew enough to hold himself together, but at great cost to his sensory, emotional and learning profile.

Step 3. Sensory Profile (created by Winnie Dunn)

The *Sensory Profile* is a caregiver-based questionnaire that I use at my center. This questionnaire measures sensory processing abilities and profiles the effect of sensory processing on a child's functional performance. It was designed to contribute to a comprehensive assessment of a child's sensory performance when combined with other evaluations and clinical observations. It is considered to be a standardized tool that has been used in several research studies as a pre- and post-measurement.

The Sensory Profile relies on caregivers to provide their best estimate on a series of questions across the different sensory systems. The caregiver who has daily contact with the child completes the questionnaire by reporting the frequency with which certain behaviors occur. Lauren completed Matt's profile. His scores were derived in each sensory area and are reported in one of three categories: *definite difference*, which showed that Matt demonstrated difficulty in the area; *probable difference* showed he had trouble in the area, but to a lesser extent; and *no difference* meant his scores were within typical range.

In the findings, all of his systems (auditory, visual, somatosensory, vestibular, and oral) noted a *definite difference*, though multisensory indicated a *probable difference*. Regarding the multisensory score of probable difference, his classroom observation clearly indicated a *definite difference* when compared with his typical peers. This modulation finding is quite common when the questionnaire is completed by the parent. The caregiver at home simply cannot simulate the multisensory environment of an actual classroom situation and usually sees the child in his safe and comfortable home zone where the same stress is not detected. This is why it is important that information is obtained from all areas of the child's life in order to develop an accurate profile.

Matt's modulation difficulties were also found to affect all of the following quite strongly:

- Sensory Processing related to muscle tone
- Modulation related to body position and movement
- Modulation of movement affecting activity level
- Modulation of sensory input affecting emotional responses
- Modulation of visual input affecting emotional responses and activity level

Overall, Matt experienced a **definite difference** when compared to his typical peers in six of the factors scored:

- Sensory seeking
- Emotional reactivity
- Low endurance/tone
- Oral sensitivity
- Inattention/Distractibility
- Poor registration—ability of the body to become aware that sensory information is coming in

The Sensory Profile is a tool commonly used in educational systems today. It is frequently described as *the total sum of a child's evaluation of his sensory experiences*. Although it provides a comprehensive view of the sensory systems, it should be made very clear that this alone is simply not sufficient in gaining the total picture of any child's development. The assessor still needs to use other assessment tools and clinical observations to gain sufficient understanding of the individual profile. Since some children are unable to comply with the rigorous measures of standardized tests, we use many peer referenced clinical observations and rely on the clinical judgment and experience of the therapist.

Step 4. Clinical Evaluation

Lauren brought Matt to my center where we conducted a battery of tests. Along with Sensory Profile, Lauren's input, and the school observations, the following describes the findings from Matt's initial overall sensory processing evaluation.

Sensory Processing Profile – Matt O'Malley

Somatosensory System—Tactile-Proprioceptive System
Observations & Evaluation Results • Mixed reactivity to touch input in terms of modulation. • Matt needed to direct his touch experiences in an effort to remain secure and feel safe. • Matt expressed distress during tooth brushing, was irritated by shoes, and withdrew from splashing water. He had difficulty standing in line, a decreased awareness of pain, and preferred to touch rather than be touched; however, he enjoyed exploring finger paint, and did not mind touching any object or texture. **Profile Notes** • With mixed reactivity, a sensory system can be both over-reactive and under-reactive to stimuli. The mixed messages he was receiving from tactile input were very confusing for his system to interpret; hence, he tended to want to control his environment. • His difficulty with tactile discrimination leads to difficulty with body awareness and experiencing his position in the space surrounding him.

Vestibular-Proprioceptive Processing

Observations & Evaluation Results
- Hyposensitive/under-reactive to vestibular input.
- Sustained balance for one to two seconds but unable to perform with eyes closed.

Profile Notes
- Vestibular Input—Clinical judgment is very important here. The reason Matt sought more vestibular-proprioceptive input could have been due to an actual delay in his vestibular system. But it was more likely that he had to overcompensate for his weaknesses in his *visual* and *auditory systems* through the support of more movement and deep-pressure.
- Balance—Balance is another tricky area for clinical judgment, along with the consideration of gravitational insecurity. Both are highly impacted by the function of the visual system, depth perception in particular.

Postural Control

Observations & Evaluation Results
- Maintained prone extension position for one to two seconds with encouragement.
- Unable to assume or maintain supine flexion position.
- Exhibited adequate protective extension.
- Low average muscle tone.
- Used momentum rather than efficient grading of postural control mechanisms.

Profile Notes
- Prone extension (Superman pose) is associated with vestibular function and should be considered in conjunction with other vestibular-proprioceptive measures. Matt was barely able to maintain this position for one to two seconds, whereas typical peers would be able to maintain it for up to ten seconds.
- Matt was unable to assume the supine flexion position. Supine flexion is associated with somatosensory (tactile-proprioceptive) processing. Typical peers would be able to maintain this position for up to ten seconds. Matt was able to come into a sitting position with support on a therapy ball and demonstrated no difficulty transitioning from supine to sitting position. He was, therefore, able to use his flexor muscles for short bursts but was unable to assume and sustain for an age-appropriate period of time.
- Protective extension reactions are the ability to use body limbs to protect oneself from falling. While supported on the therapy ball, Matt had adequate protective reactions, but demonstrated some difficulty sustaining his balance when the ball was moved back and forth and his center of gravity was altered from side to side.
- Matt tended to use *momentum* rather than efficient *grading* of postural control mechanisms when climbing. Grading is the ability to use controlled movement over varying degrees of an activity, such as slowly picking up something heavy vs. picking it up quickly while maintaining body position against the pull of gravity on the muscles. Momentum is used to compensate when grading is inefficient.

Praxis

Observations & Results
- Matt demonstrated difficulty with grading the control of his movements for climbing on/off sensory equipment.
- He experienced difficulty with the sequential tasks required to play with toys.
- Matt indicated decreased body awareness, poor bilateral hand skills, difficulty crossing the midline, and inadequate balance skills.
- He had noted difficulty with imitating movements and diminished adaptive responses to adjust his plan in relation to environmental demands.
- Matt exhibited a limited play repertoire and preferred to stay within play activities that he was already familiar with.

Profile Notes
- Matt's praxis difficulties were negatively impacting his ability to use his body effectively to explore his environment.
- He experienced difficulty knowing *how* to play with toys in a variety of ways and had difficulty completing what he started.
- He tended to want to take control of the play schemes, remained in familiar play patterns, and was not observed to readily accept or expand his play with new ideas.

Auditory Processing

Observations & Evaluation Results
- Matt experienced a delay in speech and language development.
- He had difficulty functioning if two to three steps of instructions were given at once.
- He occasionally responded negatively to unexpected noises, and he did not readily respond to his name.

Profile Notes
- Matt required visual cues combined with auditory requests to maximize his responses.
- During our classroom observation he was noted to be easily distracted when the noise level in the room increased. This appeared to negatively impact his ability to sustain attention to task.

Visual Processing

Observations & Evaluation Results

- Visually hypersensitive, visually distracted, and avoided eye contact.
- Difficulty performing visual pursuits (following an object with his eyes) and crossing midline with his eyes. He lost visual focus on the object though he would regain visual focus when verbally cued to do so.
- Disliked having vision occluded (obstructed) and appeared to have more difficulty following objects with his left eye.
- *Test of Visual-Motor Skills (Revised)* showed a visual-motor age equivalence of three years, two months (23rd percentile rank).
- Demonstrated difficulty having adequate adaptive responses to ball catching and throwing.
- *Peabody Developmental Motor Scale—2: Fine Motor Section,* he received a standard score of seven for Visual-motor Integration, which is considered to be below average.

Profile Notes

- Eye Contact—Matt was noted to avoid eye contact; however, eye contact should be considered very carefully. In order to make eye contact while listening to another person simultaneously requires the integration of at least visual and auditory information. Many children are unable to interpret both systems at the same time. Forcing eye contact through cognitive strategies is not the answer. We have to lay the foundations of sensory integration to enable the child to make this connection with automaticity within their sensory systems.
- Visual-motor—Matt showed difficulty with several visual assessments, but what also needs to be considered is that his deficient postural control is not forming a sufficient base of support to enable him to independently move his eyes while keeping his head still.

Fine and Visual-Motor Skills

Observations & Results

- Matt placed in the poor range for his overall fine motor skills.
- He demonstrated difficulty with fine motor control and strength, pencil grip, and inefficient bilateral hand skills.
- He was able to build a block tower of nine blocks, draw a cross, remove a twist on cap, string beads, insert basic shapes into a form board, use scissors to cut paper in two, and trace on a straight line.
- He was unable to build a block tower of ten, reproduce age-appropriate block designs (bridge, train, wall, steps), fold paper to produce a crease, use scissors to cut on a straight line, and unfasten buttons.
- Emerging fine motor skills included drawing a circle with closed ends and drawing a square.

Profile Notes

- Matt's bilateral hand skill (ability to coordinate two hands together) was considered to be fair; however, he had difficulty controlling his writing utensil and the directionality of his movement to produce smooth and accurate strokes.
- Matt used an inefficient digital type pencil grip for paper and pencil tasks.
- He used his whole arm to draw on paper instead of dissociating movement at his wrist.

Taste and Smell Processing/Oral Motor

Observations & Evaluation Results

- Matt demonstrated a definite difference in modulating oral sensory input.
- Oral sensory profile appeared to be that of mixed reactivity.
- Difficulty with planning and coordinating the movements of his tongue and oral muscles.

Profile Notes

- Matt avoided certain tastes and limited himself to particular food textures/temperatures. He had difficulty wrapping his lips around a spoon, did not like to use a fork and rotated his wrist externally when using a feeding utensil.
- The oral area is frequently used by children in an effort to calm themselves. Matt was under-reactive to some oral input yet over-reactive to other input.
- He had difficulty imitating tongue movements and it was noted that he required additional time and practice to figure out how to imitate and plan the movements. He also had some difficulty isolating his tongue from his head movement when asked to move his tongue in a side-to-side pattern.

Social Skills

Observations & Results

- Matt could become easily verbally or socially frustrated.
- He had regular sleep patterns, was an early riser, and immediately on the go.
- He loved predictability and was set in his ways.
- He was easily distracted and preferred the company of adults or older children.
- He had poor frustration tolerance, could be overly serious, had difficulty making friends, and did not display a sense of humor.
- He did not readily initiate and sustain interaction with his peers.
- When excited or stressed, Matt reverted to perseverative type behaviors (i.e., over-focused on letters and numbers, liked spinning things such as water going down a toilet).

Profile Notes

- Matt needed to control his environment and his activities in order to feel safe and protect himself from unwanted stimuli. He was motivated to maintain harmony in his environment and avoided opportunities that would increase challenge and learning.

The Whole Child... A Whole Team

A sensory processing evaluation is not a process that should be considered by a single score or result. The whole child must be considered with respect to the effects of each system on its own, as well as how the systems relate to and impact each other. It requires a true view of the child in different environments. It would be misleading to draw the extension that what is seen in one environment will always be the same as in another, and this would lead to an inaccurate profile. Very frequently a child can hold himself together at school only to really let loose on family members once he gets home. The opposite can also be found. A child can have an extremely difficult time in his school environment, but be at complete peace at home once he is in his comfort zone. It is very important to consider each environment and not to make the assumption of "we do not see it, therefore, it must not exist."

More assessment tools have been added to our toolset since Matt's initial sensory evaluation, but this assessment gave us a fairly comprehensive picture of how his different systems were playing out functionally in all areas of his life. Now that we had our starting line, much work needed to be done in planning and executing an intervention program. A good intervention program considers all functional areas, including the effect of these systems on all activities of daily living as well as social and emotional implications. A responsible intervention is one that is not fragmented in execution, but is always a team approach consistent across environments to eliminate further confusion for an already confused little person. With this baseline, we now knew where the bricks in Matt's developmental foundation were weak or misaligned, and we could now begin a program targeting intervention at those specific sensory, developmental, and emotional areas to strengthen his foothold in all future learning and development.

"It's a mouthful, but I encapsulated it like this...

DIR is like the blueprint for building the connection to the guidance system that imparts purpose and meaning to a child's developmental experiences."

Chapter 7

The Student Body... the Anatomy of Classroom Performance

When the evaluation report arrived in the mail a couple of weeks after visiting Maude's center, I couldn't believe the detail. It was a comprehensive eighteen-page sensory profile built from an assessment of each of Matty's individual sensory systems and core developmental capacities described within the framework of the DIR model. It not only discussed his sensory makeup, but also how this profile impacts his ability to function in a learning environment. It took me a few days to dissect the report, sentence by sentence, and sometimes word by word, to really absorb a deeper understanding of the connections. It detailed a host of findings, some minor and some not so minor, but taken as a whole, it gave me an entirely new perspective on the body-mind connection and physiological roots of a child's ability to function in a classroom. I have no educational or professional expertise in any of these areas—I'm just a Mom; but I venture to offer how this information changed how I look at any child's ability to perform in today's learning environments.

Regulation

Everyone needs regulation, and as adults, we generally know what we need to do every day in order to get it. For me, it's a combination of morning exercise and my carefully concocted cup of Joe, a precise brew of regular and decaf coffee. Too much caffeine... I can't think straight. Not enough caffeine...

I can't think straight. If I stick to my routine, I feel pretty good. When I don't, I have a much harder time getting things done and dealing with the day. Children are no different. Their learning environment demands physical regulation no less readily than my work demands of me. As an adult, I am cognitively aware and able to meet my own needs for regulation, but children are not. Most kids have a pretty finely tuned inherent ability to keep their bodies regulated, but there are many children whose physical makeup can't keep pace with the level of regulation today's learning environments demand.

The report discussed how the tactile deep-pressure and movement systems work together for regulation, noting that Matty was under-reactive to this type of input, and therefore needed movement to satisfy his brain in its attempt to regulate him to the environment. This was certainly no surprise. In sensory terms, this is part of sensory modulation. Understandably, in a classroom environment, kids can't just stand up and jump or walk around on an as-needed basis, so it's a constant struggle for some children to remain focused simply because their bodies can't calibrate to the regulatory state it needs in order to function.

An invaluable connection for me was to understand that when a child seeks movement, regulation may not be achieved by the movement input alone, but by the combination of the movement input plus the *response* to the movement input. The regulatory effect is a result of the combination of the brain soliciting movement input to calm, *followed by the actual calming response of the proprioceptive system.* In sensory terms, this handshake is part of sensory integration. For some, the vestibular and proprioceptive systems may not work together as well as they should, and if the system seeking input to satisfy the need doesn't work efficiently with the system that should respond to the input, the need may never really get totally satisfied. That is, the vestibular input is the water being drunk, but the proprioceptive response is the actual quenching of the thirst. Hence, some children may constantly seek out movement, yet never get the calming response they're seeking. The sensory recommendation for Matty was to follow movement input with deep-pressure, which makes sense to ensure the proprioceptive side of the equation was satisfied.

The Foundation

As I immersed myself in the report, more roots of classroom performance surfaced. One very enlightening area for me was learning more about postural control and praxis, the body's infrastructure for sitting and executing learning activities. Postural control, which is less of a root and more of a trunk, is our physical foundation for stability. Although not part of the sensory set, the connections between postural control and sensory processing were very enlightening for me. The role of postural control began to make perfect sense as I started to see its structural contribution to the vestibular system, visual processing, and fine and gross motor skills. When you think about it, most daily activities in school, particularly preschool, involve sitting in a chair or on the floor. A child with a weak trunk may simply not be able to stabilize the demands of the learning environment, particularly for fine motor skills such as handwriting. This was an "aha" moment for me, as it had never dawned on me just how many learning and developmental demands depend on the foundation of good postural control.

Matty's teachers noted that he lost focus easily during circle time and table top activities. He would fidget and slouch while at circle, and he would lean and almost lay on the desk or table during focused activities. While other attention issues could also be in play, I hadn't really considered the fact that part of the difficulty could be his actual core strength to keep his body in the sitting position for an extended period of time. Part of what looked like lack of focus could actually be rooted in a lack of core strength to maintain body position. The role of postural control in providing a stable base for visual processing was also an interesting revelation. When preschoolers sit in circle time on the floor, they're often there to focus on a teacher reading a book or for some other demand for visual focus. But these visual attention capabilities must be supported by a stable base. It seemed like such an obvious relationship, but I just never made the connection between postural control and the sensory systems that depend on it so literally for their foundation.

Praxis in Action

You only have to look as far as any school playground to find motor planning and praxis in constant action. Say a child has the idea to go down a slide. To make that happen, he must be able to arrange the set of motor actions in the right steps to carry out the idea. He needs to sequence the body movements to climb to the top of the ladder and the motor execution to sit down, lean forward, and push his body off with his arms. As he slides down he must have the postural control and core strength to remain sitting while his body moves against gravity, he must time the placement of his feet on the ground as he nears the bottom, and he must instantaneously process the feedback of feeling his feet touch the ground to push his body up to a standing position.

Excited by the thrill, he may want to immediately re-execute the same motor plan that just brought him so much joy, but just as he turns to run back for another trip up the ladder, another child bumps into him and asks him to go climb on the jungle gym. He sees the line for the slide has grown, so with this unexpected change in plans he must adapt with a new plan and a sequence for motor actions must be instantly derived.

This is what childhood is and what it should be. Children in perpetual motion, getting ideas, sequencing, planning, and gaining feedback from their execution, all with the ability to adapt to changes in the environment or when other children's ideas get in the way of their own.

Execution

To my collection of roots I could now connect the trunk, the physical core of stability for so many school demands. But beyond the structural stability, I also learned about the role of praxis as the foundation of *execution*. Praxis is the coordination of mental and physical information (your brain telling your body what to do) to interact with the environment. Of the four elements of praxis (ideation, motor sequencing, motor execution, and adaptability), I was most enlightened by the first step, **ideation**. To me, you *had an idea*. An idea was an end product of some magical synapse in the brain. I had never thought of it in the broader terms of ideation, the *process of having ideas*. But when you think about it, an idea has to be the product of some process. I just never had reason to consider the actual process that creates an idea and how that process is a feeder system for much of the cognitive and motor actions we take for granted. When it comes to imagination, most kids thrive on a rich process of ideation to allow them to tap into a deep well of imagination and creativity. While for others like Matty, difficulties with ideation can reduce their flow of ideas to a trickle, pervasively impacting all areas of learning and development.

The next steps were fairly straightforward. **Motor sequencing**, the ability to sequence the movements to carry out a plan, and **motor execution** which describes how well one is able to execute those movements. These were areas where I knew Matty had difficulties. But the last element of praxis, **adaptability**, was another area I hadn't really considered, though I now realize how very critical it is to thriving in school, home, and any environment. The capacity of one's body and mind to accept new stimuli, respond to change, and refocus in new directions is such an essential life skill. Learning about adaptability in the perspective of a physical process gave me much more patience in understanding why Matty craved sameness and why it was just so difficult for him to be more flexible.

Anyone who's ever built a home or been involved in a construction project would agree—a good general contractor is about as important as the foundation you build your house on. Praxis is like the general contractor in building developmental capabilities. Imagine hiring a contractor who looks at a blueprint, but cannot formulate the ideas or sequence and execute the steps to build the house. Imagine a contractor who can't adapt his plan due to weather, materials not arriving on time, or when you change your mind on the dimensions of a room. This is a general contractor who won't be a contractor very long. Praxis is like the body's general contractor for executing motor tasks to achieve learning and development. And like a good contractor, it's taken for granted when it works well; but when there are problems, the results are very similar... inefficiencies, delays, and poor work quality.

Attention

Beyond the ability to regulate to the environment and having a solid foundation for learning comes the larger expectation for maintaining focus and paying attention. Walk down any elementary school hallway and you'll hear a familiar plea. "Listen up...;" "Eyes on me...;" and other requests for focus billow out from every open door. As the bar of learning expectations rises with each passing year, so too does the appeal for on-demand attention. Every need for focus generally depends on the integration of at least the visual and auditory systems along with the relative strength of the foundations they rely upon (postural control and praxis). The report described the nature of what stood in the way of Matty's ability to sustain focus, including the need for regulation, difficulty discriminating auditory and visual information, and inefficient postural control. To top it all off, praxis and motor planning difficulties were further cause for the lack of focus and responsiveness in his overall execution of activities.

In classroom observations and in the report, visual elements were also noted as a cause for Matty's distractibility. Of all sensory areas, visual processing was one area I had given the least thought to before Matty's evaluation. There are so many areas of visual processing that impact how children see and experience the environment, particularly at school. Of no surprise, the report noted that Matty was easily distracted by visual stimuli, he sometimes had difficulty zeroing-in on what to focus on in competing backgrounds, and he tended to focus on details and lose spatial relationships. The connection that struck me most regarding attention and focus was how Matty was stuck in the dilemma of needing postural stability for visual focus while needing movement for regulation and cognitive focus.

From the perspective of auditory attention, it was also not surprising to learn that Matty had difficulty processing auditory information in a busy environment due in part to difficulties in distinguishing foreground and background noise. Many children, including Matty, come to the table of learning with visual and auditory systems that don't work together in a balanced and integrated way, causing further inherent difficulty for sustained focus.

Participation

Matty's evaluation gave me a new view of the real anatomy of classroom performance. I now had a deeper understanding of the physiological starting point for learning. But before you can begin to learn you have to *want* to engage in the learning process, and unfortunately for some kids, this motivation to participate seems to be a missing link. Lacking competent sensory processing skills and a solid foundation of execution, for Matty, many environments soon shaped themselves into a ball of confusion he spent too much energy dodging.

But as I understood more about how much we rely on praxis and processing skills to participate in new and novel activities, the opposite side of the adaptability equation also began to make more sense to me—this being the inclination to *control* the environment. The easiest way to control the environment is to simply not participate in it. The brain thinks, "If I can't effectively regulate or process input from the environment, I'll block the input from coming in; therefore, I won't have as much of a need to respond to it." A child soon learns that his most efficient coping strategy for controlling an environment to which he can't adapt is to simply shut the door to it and not participate in activities that may require a response to the unknown.

The evaluation helped me realize how the complexities of sensory and praxis difficulties can form a deep taproot of avoidance; but understanding the physiological connections gave me more patience in cultivating the intrinsic motivation that would ultimately empower Matty to *want* to participate.

Maude Joins the School Team

Two weeks after receiving the report, a meeting was held with Matty's school team to discuss the findings. The team fully agreed that the evaluation was extremely comprehensive and on the mark with most observations. In fact, more than one team member commented that they wished they had this type of information for more children sitting in their classrooms. We went through the detail of each sensory system and discussed how Matty's program could be modified to foster improvements from the ground up. There was significant discussion about the praxis/motor planning component described in the report. The OT was completely supportive, noting that we needed to start from the beginning and give sufficient respect to the *ideation* component of motor planning.

"Hopefully," she said in a note to me, "a more intense and focused DIR approach will help with Matt's ability to come up with new ideas during play, and he will then want to practice motor planning skills through play."

In addition to an increased focus on motor planning during OT sessions, the team would look for opportunities to incorporate sequencing and motor planning activities and encourage him to express new ideas throughout his day.

More Sensory and a T-Stool

Sensory regulation had been a priority in Matty's program and his teacher and the school OT were always supportive of his sensory diet, but the sensory report seemed to gel the team and give everyone new momentum in viewing sensory regulation from a proactive perspective. More proactive sensory intervention and subtle sensory breaks were included throughout his day to help him stay regulated, and per the report's recommendations, we would start a daily oral motor program to help with keeping his system calm.

We also implemented a postural control program that included daily core strength activities and using a T-stool at circle time. I had never seen a T-stool before, but apparently it's not an uncommon sight in many preschools. It's basically a chair with a one leg in the center of a round seat about the size of a Frisbee®. The child sits on the seat but has to maintain his balance on a single pole. It's not as easy as it sounds. You really have to use your abdominal and back muscles to keep your balance. It makes you sit up straight because that's the easiest way to keep your balance, and strengthens your core while doing so. A hidden benefit for children with under-reactive vestibular systems is that it provides constant subtle movement as the child makes adjustments to keep his balance. Matty immediately started using the T-stool during circle time, adjusted quite quickly, and actually ended up preferring it over sitting pretzel style on the floor.

Given this new level of the understanding of the interrelationships between postural control, sensory integration, praxis, and where Matty was developmentally with respect to the

DIR model, we understood that the pieces were not independent of each other and should not be approached that way. Matty's program needed to be more integrated to build his capacities from the ground up, and to do this it needed to be refined to target three foundational areas: sensory regulation, postural control, and praxis/motor planning. I also expressed that there was a need for oversight of the DIR area, and since the school district did not have the resources to fill the void, a DIR consultation was written into the program. In other words, Maude would now be brought in to provide training, consultations, and guidance on the DIR portion of Matty's program. For me, Maude's contribution would soon bring the leadership I'd been hoping for, and for Matty, there could have been no greater gift.

DIR at School

Maude immediately began working closely with Karen on Matty's DIR goals. His first goal beyond regulation was *ideation* to facilitate his ability to develop new and novel ideas through play. Karen started with a renewed focus on regulatory activities using back-and-forth rhythm and shared timing games using musical instruments. She would continue to use playful obstruction strategies to try to foster new ideas when Matty started to move toward his comfort zones, such as talking about letters, numbers, and the rainbow color order. One day, Matty really needed to *talk colors* for comfort, so Karen pulled out a Twister® mat, hoping to bridge him from his need to stay in a safe color zone to a place where he could build new ideas based on colors. That Twister mat, we would soon learn, would be the door to a new beginning for Matty, one that would teach us all more about him than we could ever expect.

It was sometime in February when Matty and Karen stepped onto the Twister mat. They stayed there until June. Every day, Matty would pull out the mat to talk about colors, and Karen would follow his lead with enthusiasm each day as though they were doing it for the first time. Day after day, Karen played with Matty on that Twister mat, trying to follow any glimmer of a lead to allow her to scaffold him to initiating new ideas. Things started out slow. When Matty did offer ideas, they were pulled from the same daily list. Each day he would start with yesterday's play schemes followed by reenactments of scripted dialogue from the same set of TV shows.

In our first DIR consultation with Maude, Karen described the Twister challenge.

> *"I really think Matt uses Twister as a regulatory tool. It calms him. He spends the first fifteen minutes detoxing from the classroom stimulation, and the Twister mat seems to help him get in and stay in a more regulated zone," she said. "He is communicating and engaging with me, but he seems stuck. I feel like I've probably spent twenty-four straight sessions on those twenty-four dots without Matt initiating a single new unscripted idea."*

We were all frustrated. There we sat in a hot, tiny preschool library as Karen explained all the strategies and play schemes she had tried to help Matty ignite his idea engine. Using high energy, she brought in new toys, pretend play props, and puppets, hoping each day that this would be the day Matty might take a huge leap. But so far he wasn't jumping. Every DIR session sheet that came home began with, "We played on the Twister mat today," which I soon learned was code for "No new ideas yet."

This being our first DIR-focused consultation with Maude, I didn't know what to expect. It was a long meeting, during most of which Maude and Karen talked in detail about DIR level three and strategies to scaffold Matty into initiating new ideas. Although I thought I understood the overall philosophy of DIR, when the discussion started getting into the weeds of DIR levels and strategies I kind of zoned out, too consumed with the lists in my head and the clock on the wall. But as I slowly began to emerge back into the moment I heard Maude say, "Stay on the Twister mat, Matt is a smart cookie. He has proven to Mom, teachers, and therapists that he's aware of everything going on around him. He's processing it all. It will come."

Maude went on to explain why it was so important to follow Matty's lead, and at the time, his lead was to remain on the Twister mat. "He's there because he needs to be there—he has a reason."

Although I still felt unsure of Matty's future, I left that meeting feeling absolutely sure of two things. First, I realized how very fortunate Matty was to have a person like Maude caring for him. She has proven time and again that every child's journey must begin with an unshakable foundation of respect for the child's potential. Her intuition and genuine belief in Matty's ability to move beyond the Twister mat on his own terms were unwavering. She thoughtfully encouraged us to continue to lie in wait on that mat, and the reassurance of her leadership gave us the patience to do so. Second, I knew I had to put all excuses aside and really sit myself down to do the DIR research I had been planning to do since I received the evaluation report. Maude was scheduled to conduct a full-day training session on DIR a few weeks later, and I was inspired to learn more so I could make the most of that session for the entire team.

So, What is DIR... Really

My research began with a quick scan of a borrowed copy of Stanley Greenspan and Serena Wieder's book *The Child With Special Needs*. It didn't take long to find the following explanation of sensory processing that would put Matty's sensory evaluation in perfect perspective for me.

According to Greenspan and Wieder, *"Sensory reactivity is the way we take information in through the senses, and sensory processing is how we make sense of the information we take in. Muscle tone, motor planning and sequencing are the ways we use our bodies and, later, our thoughts to plan and execute responses to the information we take in. When these systems work together smoothly, they create a continuous feedback loop where we take in sensations such as sights and sounds, react to them with emotions, and then organize thoughts and behaviors as well as feelings to interact smoothly with the world. But when one or more parts of these systems go awry, we are less able to function well.[1]"*

Matty definitely had some parts gone a little awry, but now knowing what parts they were, and gaining the understanding of why he was less able to function efficiently filled a deep well of patience for me.

Next, from a few click-throughs on a Google® search on *DIR developmental model*, I landed on references to Greenspan's *Affect Diathesis Hypothesis*, the foundation upon which the DIR model was built.

More than forty pages long, the hypothesis summarizes well as follows: *A child uses his affect to provide intent (i.e., direction) for his actions and meaning for his words. Typically, during the second year of life, a child begins to use his affect to guide intentional problem-solving behavior and, later on, meaningful use of symbols and language. Through many affective problem-solving interactions, the child develops complex social skills and higher-level emotional and intellectual capacities.[2]*

As with Matty's sensory evaluation, I had to read the whole document a few times to absorb it all, but soon many more connections would emerge. The crux of the Affect Diathesis Hypothesis is that there is a deficit in the ability *to connect affect or intent to motor planning and sequencing capacities as well as symbol formation.[3]* Admittedly, it took me more than a couple of reads to absorb what this meant. The first step in my understanding was to define what "affect (or intent)" referred to. There are many definitions of the word *affect,* but I initially assumed this reference, since it was used in the context of engaging with children, was simply the tone, volume, and spirit in one's voice and body language. To use a lot of affect meant to exaggerate the emotion in your voice, facial expressions, and body movements. But I was thrown by the pairing of *affect* with *intent* throughout the hypothesis.

After reading, re-reading, and again looking the word *affect* up in the dictionary, I finally realized it was referring not just to the exaggerated expressions I might use when telling a story, but to a person's affect in a broader sense. It was referring to one's intuitive sense of their own and another person's emotions and emotional intent. It was not only referring to my affect when speaking to Matty, it was referring to Matty's affect when engaging with others. It was describing Matty's sense of his own intent and desires, as well as his sense of the emotional intent of others. The hypothesis presented how affect and emotional intent act as the developmental guidance system that imparts meaning and purpose during development. It offers the following example:

Consider a 14-month-old child who takes his father by the hand and pulls him to the toy area, points to the shelf, and motions for a toy. As Dad picks him up, and he reaches for and gets the toy, he nods, smiles, and bubbles with pleasure. For this complex, problem-solving social interaction to occur, the infant needs to have an emotional desire or wish (i.e., intent or affective interest) that indicates what he wants. The infant then needs to connect his desire or affective interest to an action plan (i.e., a plan to get his toy). The direction-giving affects and the action plan together enable the child to create a pattern of meaningful, social, problem-solving interactions.[4]

This example couldn't have hit me more squarely between the eyes. Thinking back to my first conversation with my neighbor, I now realized why she inquired about how Matty would communicate his needs to me. If he did want a cookie on the counter, was he able to recognize his own desire and come up with the motor plan (pointing or gesturing) to convey his desire to me? No, he wasn't. Maybe it was because he didn't recognize his desires, or, if he did, maybe he couldn't connect his desire to a motor plan to communicate it.

It really made me think about how much we rely on sensing others' intentions. We do it every day in reading facial expressions and body language, and if we're unsure of our read, we can use verbal language to confirm or clarify our interpretations. But what if you're incapable of reading others' intentions or have difficulty processing language? You don't have much to rely on to help you discern their intent, do you? Everyone has been in a driving situation when you and another driver are signaling each other to go, but you're both reluctant to move because neither knows quite what the other plans to do. So you both sit there with hands waving, but neither goes because you don't want to hit each other. "C'mon... what are you doing?" you think, or say, or shout as the frustration builds. Imagine living every day with most interactions being this bewildering. Imagine constantly having this kind of distance between you and the intent of others.

The hypothesis explained that processing emotional intent is further connected to fundamental developmental capacities including motor planning and sequencing, symbolic formation, sensory processing and modulation, and other processing capacities. Here again, I needed to put some thought into breaking down each element. Motor planning and sequencing I now understood along with sensory processing, modulation, and other processing capacities which included just about everything covered in Matty's sensory evaluation.

I needed to do a little further digging to get a grasp on symbolic formation, which is a child's development of understanding the *representational* aspects of the world. This is his ability to use objects, words and concepts symbolically. When a child uses an object or toy to represent something else, such as using stick to represent a magic wand, he is developing emerging symbolic understanding. As described in the hypothesis, symbolic capacities are a prerequisite for a host of developmental capacities such as pretend play, imagination, problem-solving, connecting ideas, abstract thinking, and more functional use of language. *(Affect Diathesis Hypothesis)*

Another element I thought long and hard about was *purpose.* In trying to understand the essence of purpose in guiding development, I thought about my own experience and my own lost moments. We've all been there. You walk into a room only to ask yourself, "Now why did I come in here?" We've all felt that void when we're temporarily disconnected from our purpose for doing something. It's a bewildering moment. My body executed the sequence and motor plan to walk into the room, but the feeling of not knowing why I did so is nagging.

I draw from this feeling in trying to understand the role of purpose in development. In a similar way, a child's potential for development could be standing at the ready, but his developmental capacities may remain suspended in execution because they're not adequately connected to their purpose. As presented in the hypothesis, the connection between affect or emotional intent and a child's developmental capacities is the conduit to deliver purpose. If the mechanism to impart purpose is deficient, developmental capabilities may exist, but they remain disconnected from what should guide them.

You Can't Get in Gear without the "Prindle"

With four girls, we have a lot of ponytails and are always looking for hair bands. Whenever I'm desperate to find a hair band, I know I can always find one on the *prindle.* What's a prindle, you ask? The prindle is what my kids call the gear shift in our car. I think they heard it on a Disney show. The PRNDL (Park, Reverse, Neutral, Drive, etc.) is where I slip all the hair bands I find on the floor of the car. One day while making my umpteenth trip to drop someone off somewhere, I got to thinking about how the foundational elements of a child's development are much like the basic functions of a car. As a child relies on motor planning, sequencing, sensory processing, etc. for his developmental journey, we rely on a car's basic park, reverse, and drive functionality for our journey. And the prindle is our connection to directing those functions. If our desire is to go forward, the prindle is the mechanism connecting our intent to the functionality we need.

After days of thought, my lasting interpretation of the Affect Diathesis Hypothesis went like this. A child's ability to process affect or emotional intent is what imparts meaning and purpose to developmental actions. Some children may have a deficiency in the connection between affect or emotional intent (which imparts purpose) and the foundational elements of development. It's like a child is sitting in the driver's seat of development, but his prindle doesn't work efficiently or at all. He may have an adequately operational vehicle to take him on his journey, but he's missing the capability to connect his intent and purpose to the mechanisms to get his journey in gear.

With this slight grasp on what was at the root of DIR, more connections surfaced. If I dropped Matty into the blend of the hypothesis, it would assert that he had a diminished ability to sense his own desires and emotional intent as well as the intent of others, and this is what imparts meaning and purpose to his development. That is, there was kink in the fuel line that delivers the *purpose* to his motor planning, sequencing, symbolic formation, sensory processing, and other developmental capacities. It may have appeared that he didn't want to participate in school and play, but I better understood that it might be because his sense of desire and purpose were not adequately connected to the developmental capacities needed for execution in those activities.

Finally, the Connection to DIR

After spending much time absorbing the tenets of the Affect Diathesis Hypothesis, I began to see how it drove the DIR model. It was all finally starting to make sense to me. Apart from focusing on the foundations of sensory processing, DIR is rooted in harnessing a child's affect, emotional intent, and desires to cultivate purposeful connections to his developmental capacities.

As I had done with the elements for the Affect Diathesis Hypothesis, my next step was to explore for myself what the "D," the "I" and the "R" of DIR actually meant.

- The "D" (**Developmental**) is looking at a child's capacities from the perspective of where a child is in his development, not where he should be if compared to external factors such as his chronological age, the ability of peers, or the desires of parents, society, or an education system. It considers the child's individual developmental profile and is the level-setting, baselining component that filters out external expectations and sets the pace for the journey.

- The "I" (**Individual Differences**) is all about understanding the child's sensory connections and other unique qualities. It's having a deep understanding of a child's sensory, regulatory, and emotional makeup to discern the *why* of his actions and the choices he makes in relating to his environment. With much appreciation for Matty's sensory evaluation, we now had a pretty broad understanding of the "I" part of Matty's DIR equation.

- The "R" (**Relationship**) acknowledges a child's developmental capacities by leveraging the security of trusting relationships. A child who exists in a world dominated by a defensive posture to the environment will certainly not let down his guard without feeling secure that he can trust the relationships he has formed with family, teachers, and the therapists who encourage him to take risks.

With a cursory read of the six levels that comprise DIR, I was starting to grasp that they are the set of developmental interdependencies which are the foundation of a child's social and emotional development. They are the framework to harness a child's purposeful interactions and to empower him to make meaningful connections to his own developmental capacities. The DIR levels are the general milestones to ensure a child has a fully stocked developmental toolbox.

It's a mouthful, but I encapsulated it like this: DIR is like the blueprint for building the prindle, the connection to that intangible guidance system that imparts purpose and meaning to a child's developmental experiences.

By George, I think I had it. It had taken more time than I care to admit, but the painstaking parsing of Matty's complete sensory profile and the understanding of the DIR model shaped my perspective invaluably. As I gathered with Matty's school team in the school administration building one sunny day in April, all eyes were glued on Maude as she kicked off a full day training session on DIR.

"With the DIR model I have seen so many children flourish and grow in ways that have, on occasion, taken my breath away..."

Chapter 8

Developing the Child through Relating and Understanding

To describe a child from a sensory perspective is simply not enough. Though necessary and enlightening, we cannot focus through this single pane of glass. What about relationships and communication? What about problem-solving, ideation, and creativity? What about emotional range and abstract thinking and theory of mind?

Every child is a beautiful work of stained-glass art. Each child's totality is projected through many individually shaped pieces held together by a strong lead frame. And like those colorful fragments, the many pieces of sensory and developmental capacities depend upon a stable framework to shape them into what ultimately reflects his or her brilliance back to the world.

DIR is that framework. It is the sturdy yet pliable lead of a stained-glass masterpiece. It is the place to fit the pieces, the shape to define a child's uniqueness, and the strength to hold it all together.

The Developmental, Individual Differences, Relationship (DIR) model was originated by Dr. Stanley Greenspan and we owe much to him for this important work of understanding with regard to children with developmental delays. The principles of DIR are instilled in every aspect of my clinical practice and in my view of all children. With an understanding of a child's sensory capacities, DIR allows us to then begin to build the broader landscape to determine where they fit and how they drive the child's overall development. With this model I have seen so many children flourish and grow in ways that have, on occasion, taken my breath away.

The Concepts of DIR

The DIR model embraces the following concepts: **Developmental** capacities that integrate the most essential cognitive and affective processes; **Individual** differences in sensory processing capacities; and **Relationships** that are a part of the child/caregiver and family interaction patterns. DIR is the umbrella term for the model, and Floortime is the actual work of play and interaction with children using a variety of techniques. The fact that DIR considers a child's sensory profile as an important building block for higher levels of thinking and communication is great validation for what sensory integration occupational therapists have long believed. The very first level of the DIR model is regulation—the level of work occupational therapists embrace as the stronghold of early development.

The DIR model creates thinking because it involves the child in the cognitive processes of problem-solving, and depends on the child to become the initiator. The whole idea of the DIR model is to link to thinking by using affect to tap into intrinsic learning. This results in the integrative learning that creates connections of permanency. By working with a child's differences and steadily scaffolding him into higher levels of functioning in a safe environment within trusting relationships, the DIR model has proven what many have believed for the longest time. Children become active thinkers by working on their preferences and within their comfort zones. Before they know it they are scaffolded into a new risk or activity, but rather than *us* creating the learning and prompting the first step, DIR inspires *the child* to initiate that first step himself. From these first feelings of accomplishment, the child intrinsically wants to try more and learn more.

You may ask why I focus so much on *play*. The reason is simple. A child's occupation is play. That's it. Play, play, and more play. During developmental years, play is where the child learns to problem-solve, negotiate, and see someone else's point of view. Play also sets the stage for future academic work. There are many reasons why this is true, but a quick example is when the child stages or acts out a story in his play, he is integrating a play sequence of beginning, middle, and end. This is important for following, comprehending, and later writing a story.

While a child is physically growing with gross and fine motor skills, he is registering feedback, while at the same time developing how he feels about it. As with motor activity, where feedback regarding the quality of the movement is crucial to gaining automaticity, children need to parse social and emotional feedback with the same kind of intensity. They need to likewise build quality into their subconscious range of feelings. It's not unusual to see that after some time in regular therapy, some children do very well clinically and even test in the average range for their age, but parents are often frustrated because their child is not changing functionally. What should be understood is that the child's emotional readiness is at stake in these instances. It is often a *lack of emotional development* that creates this hurdle as the child is not able to fully accept the changes. We simply must consider the child's emotional process to fully harness the entire child.

Self-Concept

Self-concept is another often overlooked driver of learning. Self-esteem is not built through endless, trivial "good job" exclamations for every move a child makes, especially when the adult does all the prompting and the activity has no meaning for the child. Self-esteem is built when a child knows he is the initiator, when he sees the meaning, when he is the one driving it through his internal motivation, and when he is emotionally invested in the learning. So often I hear parents and teachers voice frustration about teaching something to a child repeatedly, wondering if the child simply does not possess the ability to retain the information. This assumption is too easily made, especially if we are teaching something in a conventional way that only makes sense to the child's chronological age and expected curriculum, but does not make any sense to the child.

Self-concept is built on genuine self-esteem experiences. When a child learns that his ideas are meaningful to himself and others, that he has conquered a problem situation in his own way, and that he drove the learning, he is building on his own idea of how he fits in this world. He learns who he is, how capable he is, and how powerful he is.

Colwyn Trevarthon writes much about **intersubjectivity**, which means that in early development a child learns his view of himself through how he perceives the world is perceiving him. This is such an important aspect for any family or therapist to consider. Through every command we give, what does the child think of how he is viewed? When a child's entire day is so scheduled with one therapy after another, one set of expectations above another, how much power does he experience with regard to his effect on the world? During stages of early learning in a typical sphere, parents are very supportive of the independence of each new step a baby or toddler takes, and they delight in how a child achieves in almost *taking over* their world. This should be the case for our child with special needs as well. We have to assist in helping him in finding out who he is and how powerful he can be, as this, in turn, will contribute to his own self-concept and intrinsic learning.

Another important facet that led me to embrace the DIR model was because it truly encompasses and validates what the child brings to the table. With DIR, the child is the focus and it is our task as adults to be led by his motivations. This is done by understanding his language the best way we can, whether through speech or gestures or whatever he has to give, and to validate and follow up every step, one step at a time. It doesn't mean we work in the absence of goals, but it does mean more work and a deeper understanding of the child's needs so he will become intrinsically motivated to engage in what we will be asking him to reach for. It does take training to really know how to apply the DIR model in a way that enhances each child's unique profile. But teachers soon realize it's more of an art of facilitation rather than traditional instruction, and that every child in a classroom can benefit from it.

Harnessing Individuality Starts with the "Individual"

I have attended many IEP meetings and I frequently ask the IEP team to really look at whose goals are written down on the forms in front of us. After much reflection, they inevitably answer that much of what they see are the team's goals, not the child's. Though the professionals on the team should certainly have goals in mind, I ask what the child's goals are, what his preferences are, where does he fit into everything we are trying so hard to teach him.

I realize this is not an easy concept to grasp in a traditional school setting with traditional expectations, but development for each individual child is not predictable and it never will be. To truly harness individuality, you must start with the individual and weave your goals and expectations into his. The child will ultimately develop a more cognitive understanding of what it means to be a school student, what it means to be a part of a group, and what it means to have unwritten social and educational rules. But the bridge to that place must be built on his individual needs.

So frequently, curriculum is applied with no understanding of core deficits, especially in our children with autism, and yet we expect them to start learning simply because we've created a plan for them to do so.

DIR Embraces School and Parent Partnering

When parents learn to apply the basic Floortime ideas at home, it accelerates the learning process tremendously. Over time, parents see that what seemed like a difficult task at first quickly becomes fun engagement time with their child, and that DIR techniques apply to all of their children, not just the child with special needs. DIR embraces development for all children and the whole family structure; and through its flexibility, there is more time for the family structure to remain intact. Coaching with Mom and Dad considers their individual styles and empowers them to feel the difference they are making with their child. It is not about a therapist getting more out of their child. It is about the parent being able to be with the child and playing in a way that fosters the developmental processes that support the academic and social learning that needs to occur. Parents can really become parents again and be free of homework tasks from multiple therapists, as these goals are worked into play.

Many parents tell me they think they don't know how to play, that they didn't play much as children themselves, and that they have fears and anxieties about their own children rejecting their overtures. Lauren described similar feelings, and although she may never have sat down with Matt in an actual Floortime session using play, she embraced the concept so wholeheartedly that she infused *applied Floortime* in everything she did. She attended every meeting and DIR training and incorporated that way of thinking and style of interacting with all of her children. Whether in play or during everyday engagement, there is nothing that can replace the joy on parents' faces when they realize the power of genuinely connecting with their child for the first time using some of the techniques. It is thrilling to see and definitely an experience parents are intrinsically motivated to repeat.

Play is natural to a child. It is through play that experiences are internalized and feelings are externalized so the child can understand and bring meaning to the events and learning occurring. DIR is a model that truly embraces school and parent partnering, once we can get over the hump of hundreds of IEP goals we as adults would like to see achieved. Remember, once the child feels safe, once he knows he has been validated, once he is taken through the process, the product of true development will inevitably be there.

The Foundation of DIR

This discussion cannot do justice to the entirety of the DIR model, and as with our examination of sensory processing, I will only highlight the aspects important to foundational understanding of DIR. This model is based on the Affect Diathesis Hypothesis, which states that children may have a neuro-biologically based processing deficit that involves the way *affect* connects to motor planning, sequencing, and sensory processing capacities, as well as the child's ability to use symbols and abstract thought processing. Affect provides the intent, internal drive, and internal motivation to participate and be a part of communication, learning, and play.

At first read, the Affect Diathesis Hypothesis may strike you as a highly complex model of intangible concepts—but it's not. It's not some labyrinthine theory requiring an intensive intervention model that's too hard to understand and even harder to execute. What it says is this: If cognitive, emotional, and motor skills are built on *meaningful* use of ideas, and if a child is less able to *impart meaning*, then many actions and ideas in his world have the potential to be rote memory or execution. Affect imparts meaning and provides internal drive. Some children may have a deficit in linking affect to their sensory processing and developmental capacities, and are therefore less able to see the meaning of their own and others' actions and ideas. This hypothesis is what shapes the goals and strategies of the DIR model.

Affect and Intentionality

The first place to begin to digest DIR is to start with an understanding of *affect* and *intentionality*. A child's intentionality drives his acquisition of language. A baby spends the early months of life using the affect gestural system as his predominant mode of communication. Babies, say researchers, "enter language 'hands first.'" [5]

A baby points. His ability to express intention lies, literally, at his fingertip. He reads the affect we emit from facial expressions and the tone of our voice, and must use his affect to connect with us because at that time in his development that's really the only tool he has for that purpose.

And let's think about intrinsic motivation. Learning occurs when experiences are internalized, and it is affect based gestural cues and facial expressions that fuel the connection to the internalization of learning. In the early relationship between mother and child, the mother's voice and face are an important beginning for the child to start to internalize non-verbal communication, and a first connection to the motivation to later turn to the mode of verbal speech. This is one of the reasons why using an affect-based model is so effective when applied to children's learning and communication needs. Because the model imparts learning through a child's instinctual learning capacities, the child is intrinsically motivated to embrace it. It's the most predictable construct of all my work with children.

In a regular sense, the use of affect is a strong therapy tool for any therapist. On countless occasions, I've gone to a playground with a child during recess with nothing more than a few play tools, lots of energy, and a boatload of affect. High affect and excitement draw typically developing peers to our play like a super magnet, and keep a child with developmental differences engaged that much longer. Affect is the natural conduit for connecting to any child and it is no different for children with developmental delays. We do not need to beg another child to play or make it another typical peer's job to look out for our child with special needs. The sheer act of having fun and being excited is the natural draw and invitation to participate. And in one-on-one sessions with a child, it is through the use of affect that we can extend engagement and hold a child's joint attention to an activity for longer periods of time.

The idea of *intentionality* is built upon through affect gesturing by using limited language and communicating with gestural exclamations. Intentionality can be conveyed by simple things, such as a thumbs-up sign or a facial exclamation of pleasure. This makes engagement much easier for children with auditory processing challenges, allowing them to more easily maintain speed with us as their play partner.

In working with parents, I often baseline them with their first step in learning the model and understanding the meaning of intent by asking them to try to use no words with their child, no matter how verbal the child may be, and to only communicate through affect and gesturing for thirty minutes a day for two weeks. The first reaction is always a predictable raise or squint of the eyebrows. If the primary goal is to gain speech and verbal expression, why suppress it? But parents always return amazed by what they learned, surprised by how much their child actually was communicating without them realizing it. This exercise is an invaluable tool for connecting parents to the foundational aspects of DIR, and it also sets the stage for them to embrace what it means to read their child's intent and truly following the child's lead.

Though I describe the journey of Matt and his mother at a certain point of his development beginning at age three, there really is no age limit for using the principles of DIR, and the fact that it is a play based model should not deter parents of an older child from learning to use this model.

Developmental Subtleties Set the Stage for Learning

The DIR model underscores that all the development you really needed *to enable you to learn*, you developed *before* kindergarten. That is, your potential for all future learning is fostered by the developmental capacities you acquired even before the age of five. Your mother and doctor may have documented your obvious milestones such as crawling, walking, and talking. But beneath all that, you journeyed through the more subtle developmental milestones without mention or notice.

If you had never walked or talked, obvious intervention would have occurred, but what if you missed some of these subtle milestones? They're not nearly as obvious to see. A child who doesn't develop the capacity to regulate himself by three months of age may not look or act all that differently than one who does. He may look like a quiet baby when he's really shutting down or he may look like a high-strung baby when he's really over-stimulated. A baby who doesn't mutually engage or respond to affective overtures by seven months of age might be thought of as a *Mr. Serious* because he doesn't respond with facial expressions or gestures to demonstrate his connection to your emotional intent. And so it goes.

A child can miss all or parts of these crucial developmental milestones without obvious red flags at all—that is, until it comes time to actually put these abilities into action in learning environments and social experiences. And even then, a void or gap in these capacities could eventually also be present symptomatically within shyness, speech or communication issues, severe learning deficits, or other diagnosed difficulties.

The Six Levels of DIR

My goal is to introduce you to the general concepts and philosophies of DIR and provide you a springboard explanation of each area. Though I describe my own experiences with DIR, all honor of the original development of this model goes to Dr. Stanley Greenspan.

DIR is generally described through a framework of levels, but don't think of it as a ladder or staircase where each step is taken independently in a linear upward progression. Think of it more as one of those vertical climbing walls where your overall goal is to reach the top, but the exact path you choose to take on any given day can vary. In scaling a rock wall, your body moves as a package upward; however, your feet and hands grip and step independently to map the path that suits your size and strengths. DIR is similarly agile. And just as climbing depends on the strength of the grip, DIR is anchored in the stamina of regulation and co-regulation with a play partner. Regulation is a child's grip strength to keep him connected to the climb through the levels of DIR.

The six levels of DIR are:

1) Attention and regulation
2) Forming relationships and sustaining mutual engagement
3) Communicating back and forth with intent
4) Purposeful interactions, complex gestures, and problem-solving
5) Elaborating on ideas, imaginative play, and creating symbols
6) Emotional thinking, problem-solving of complex ideas

To explain the levels and some key concepts of each level, they will be put in the context of Matt's core capacities during our initial clinical and school evaluations.

Matt: In the Context of DIR

Throughout all of Matt's evaluations, he was pleasant and verbal; he expressed warmth to Mom, and dabbled in some play schemes. At a chronological age of almost four years old, had he been progressing through the typical developmental milestones of the DIR model, he would have been deeply embedded in levels five and six. He would have demonstrated his own unique ideas and would be connecting them and building upon them in pretend play. But the DIR evaluation and classroom observation revealed a different process for our Matt. In combination with sensory difficulties, Matt was developmentally teetering between levels one, two, and three.

Level One – Attention and Regulation

From zero to three months, a child develops the ability to attend to multisensory, affective experiences while being able to maintain a calm, regulated state. That is, by the time Matt was three months old, he would have had the internal capacity to normalize himself physiologically within the sensory experiences of the environment. He would have had a sleep-wake cycle, an eating cycle, and an internal rhythm that set the foundation for having the ability to inhibit a rising arousal level or stimulate a lower arousal level to get to an optimum place of being for the physical and emotional aspects of early development.

Matt appeared to have the ability to maintain regulation for a period of ten to fifteen minutes with an affective play partner such as his mother, though this same regulation ability did not appear to be sustained during a peer play situation in his classroom setting. His ability to co-regulate (sustain a rhythm of back and forth engagement with a play partner) depended greatly on the effort of his play partner. Matt craved and sought opportunities for deep-pressure and crashing types of activities. He showed interest in playing with some toys, gravitated to sensori-motor and comfort toys, and demonstrated only islands of focused play. When his preferences were challenged by introducing a new activity or toy, he lost regulation and withdrew from the engagement.

This is a powerful level that affects all other functioning in all spheres of development. Since this development occurs

Calm and content

Dysregulated   Shut down

States of Regulation

fairly early in the baby's life when fight and flight reactions are closely available, it makes sense to look closely at this level of functioning when a child repeatedly avoids certain activities. Children are wonderful in their ability to adapt, and if adaptation is not occurring, there is a reason for it and we must view the avoidance for the flight reaction it is—not as bad behavior. If we really want to help a child attend to an activity that will progress him further, we must give him the regulation grip strength he needs to climb through the developmental levels by ensuring his body is in the calm and organized state that will allow him to learn.

When you know what you're looking at, sometimes it only takes a little additional effort to meet a child's regulation needs to help him attend to a play engagement or school task. Children want to play with their parents, but I've seen children literally turn their backs on their mothers to escape from the auditory stimuli while Mom unknowingly increases her volume and pitch in an effort to keep the child engaged. As the child becomes increasingly detached, Mom becomes anxious and feels rejected, not realizing it is simply the child's sensory systems that are disallowing him to continue. With just a little bit of coaching, Mom can soon learn how to recognize the child's pace, adjust to his modulation needs, and use her therapeutic self to scaffold her child forward.

We learn much about the child's individual differences by using the key concept of *following the child's lead*. By watching a child intently and getting to know his interests and cues, we build a bank of secure ideas and regulatory preferences we can go to when working through difficult periods. The idea of following a child's lead does not mean we follow him around the room ad infinitum. Rather, we use his preferences to achieve his next goal in a way that maintains his idea of safety, comfort, and control. The strategy of following the child's lead is used throughout the six levels of DIR, but it is especially important in level one, so we can work on maintaining the child's regulatory level through preferred activities in preparation for the higher levels to follow.

___

Sensory Diet... Not a Carrot or Stick

Consider a teacher expecting a class to be seated at their desk and to ready themselves for a teaching activity. Our child may not be able to settle down in the morning and might need a five-minute period of deep-pressure activities. One important thought in the school environment is that it is not sufficient to simply accommodate for the child's sensory needs with a sensory diet. It really is necessary to have a sensory processing trained occupational therapist on your child's team to actively work on rehabilitating his sensory profile while the sensory diet at school or at home assists him with staying organized in the meantime.

It is for this reason that a sensory diet should never be put in place in an IEP for a period of a whole year. The sensory diet must be monitored constantly for change as the child's sensory profile changes. A sensory diet is also not a carrot or a stick and it is never *as needed*. It has to occur before focused activity needs to take place. When a sensory diet is used correctly and prescriptively, it prevents the pitfall of being used as an escape from the very schoolwork we're trying to engage the child in.

___

Pace and Space

Pacing is another important regulation strategy. If a child is inclined to move slowly and processes information at a slower pace, it really does intrude in his thinking process if he is bombarded by language, questions, and the interruption of an adult's ideas. In most cases he will simply resort to shutting down because we are overusing the very areas he has difficulty with. On the other hand, if a child's pace is fast action with lots of crashes and booms and other exclamations, he is not going to pay attention to a very calm adult with low facial expression. Finding his exact pace and matching him in that pace becomes an art of joining him where he can enjoy you and you can enjoy him. If he becomes disorganized in his play, you have to bring calmness to him and tone him down by lowering your voice and steadying the pace, though not losing your affect and excitement for his play.

Children also need space. Just as adults have a need for personal space, so do children. It is amazing to see how many times a day a child's personal space is invaded by well-meaning adults. If we want to be allowed into his inner space circle, we must be invited. We're going to have to simply stop being so demanding of our goals and leading him away from where he wants to go. If someone threatens your security, your home, or your family, you do exactly what children with these difficulties do. You immediately go into a self-protect mode and other quality of life issues become quite unimportant. And where did we learn this? In our early childhood. Don't expect children to be different than you. Think about entering their space respectfully and attempt to achieve learning goals by enticing them to be interested in your creation or idea–not by demanding it.

Level Two – Forming Relationships and Shared Mutual Engagement

Between two and seven months, Matt would have had to develop the ability to engage with and show affective preference and pleasure for those who cared for him. His first smiles, the way his face would have lit up at the mere sight of his mother, and the way he would have flapped his arms when she smiled and cooed at him would have been his first steps in connecting to and imparting meaning to her affect.

During his evaluation, Matt showed contentment and neutral affect, was comfortable being touched by his mother, and was able to indicate emotional interest with her by vocalizing and

Mother and Child Engaging with Mutual Affect
Mutual Affect

smiling. He made social reference to her, visually referenced her across space, and verbally connected with her when needed. He could be engaged in preferred activities (his comfort zone), but it was more difficult for him to be engaged in unfamiliar play activities and it required effort on the play partner to gain his interest. The classroom observation revealed that a high level of affect and interest was needed to maintain his engagement.

We must remind ourselves that children with developmental delays and spectrum disorders have a core deficit in relating to other people. During this level of development, the focus is on the child's ability to remain in an activity while acknowledging and enjoying being with a play partner. Dr. Greenspan talked much of being able to *woo a child* into engagement with us. He discussed the need for children to decide for themselves whether they would like to join us or not. To woo a child is to use high affect, for example, to bridge him into his own motivations. This creates a much different thinking response in a child than a direct instruction prompt. When a child is intrinsically motivated to participate, he has to tap into his own resources for motivation and intent.

When a non-preferred task does come along, typical children will suffer through it to please a caregiver. But our child will not have a vested interest in the learning activity simply because it has no meaning for him; and further, he has not developed a foundation for intrinsic relationship values to make him want to do it just to please the teacher. If a child is making more visual contact with the task at hand or the toy he is playing with, he is deriving his internal drive from the object rather than the person trying to engage him. For teachers, this might be sufficient temporarily, as he will perhaps complete a task; but it runs short of learning when and how to apply the social rules of pleasing a teacher or adult.

This does not mean we must *enforce* relational eye contact, but it is a red flag for us to think of using some technique such as drama and high affect to draw the child into wanting to make a connection with us rather than the object he is focused on. It is very important during this early level of development that the child gains the momentum from wanting to be with people and wanting them to be in his play, as this starts the process of working on his theory of mind and fuels his excitement for having other people around him.

WooHoo!

When Dr. Greenspan talked of wooing the child, it was not about asking or requesting the child to come to us or to do what we expect him to do. It is about following the child's lead. One example would be to parallel play with the child, build the exact scheme he is building, and then sound so excited about it that he turns his head to see what excited you. Rather than relying on our prompting, he will become internally motivated to initiate the next idea. If a child is intent on spinning his toy or pushing the button of an electronic toy repeatedly, it is not about redirecting him to an activity we find more appropriate. It is about taking the time to join him in his play, do what he is doing, and then add one more exciting thing to it such as crashing the toy with great excitement and high affect.

It is important at this stage to move only one step at a time. There are many reasons why some children indulge in these repetitive actions and this discussion is too short to cover them all. Consider his sensory profile, his difficulty sequencing to the next step, his difficulty organizing himself in his spatial surroundings, the stimulation, and his need to create an inner calmer world amidst turmoil and too many expectations. When we think of the child as a self-protector, as looking out for himself to remain safe and in control, we begin to think very differently than someone trying to *extinguish a behavior*.

Questions Do Not Make for Mutual Engagement

I also leave you with a thought on the issue of asking questions during a playful time together, and I encourage you to think twice about doing so. So often we hear parents and teachers ask children the same question multiple times, seeking a response. Our typical human nature tells us to expect responses from the people around us. We want to have an effect on people, we want them to respond to our overtures and recognize us as a part of the play or learning or interaction. But how many times does the child actually respond?

I see it over and over again. It almost becomes a desperate plea from the adult for the child to respond, raising the anxiety in both the adult and the child. Think back to the time you spent in a classroom yourself, hoping the teacher did not glance in your direction because you didn't know the answer or didn't understand the question. Remember that feeling. It was a distressing experience, even though you may have had typically developing capacities. A child may not know the answer, may not hear you correctly because of auditory processing difficulties, may be afraid you will be taking him off his tried and true path of play, may not be able to retrieve a word or formulate the language to respond adequately, or he may simply fear the new and novel of the direction you are leading him into and therefore will choose not to respond. Yet, we insist upon his affirmation as if his very act of a verbal response will bring the outcome we seek.

Many professionals spout the use of questions to build language, but I find they raise unnecessary anxiety and cause the opposite reaction as the child withdraws from the learning situation or play, especially during these earlier levels of work. I coach parents to use *comments*. I encourage them to simply repeat or rephrase what the child says, or say one-word comments about something the child is touching or doing. Be careful not to say anything that would lead him away from his own thought formation, giving him the time to formulate his own next idea. This is another way of joining him in a way where he feels safe with us entering his comfort zone, and allows him to begin to recognize us as being non-threatening, validating, and most importantly—fun to be with.

Level Three – Intentional Two-way Communication

It is difficult to put exact ages to this type of development, but during the prior level's time span to about ten months, the child begins to initiate purposeful interactions with gestures and circles of communication. One circle of communication is defined as a child initiating, the play partner responding, and the child responding again in the same vein of the initial topic. It is not a circle of communication if a child asks for a cookie and he gets one. There needs to be a give and take, not simply having a need met.

During the clinical evaluation, Matt was initially able to open circles but did not readily close the circles he opened. He was not always receptive to a new idea presented by his mother and he liked to remain in control of play. His communication consisted primarily of directing his mother on how the play should go. He was also observed to initiate eye contact when speaking but had great difficulty sustaining eye contact.

At school, Matt's educational speech therapist and teacher reported that he did well with structured activities but needed prompting to interact. He demonstrated emerging initiation with peers but was not able to sustain it due to his inability to close communication circles. This would be like Matt saying, "Hey, wanna play?" and a peer responding, "Sure, what should we do?" but Matt having no follow-up response. He was unable to close what he had opened. Some peers might take the ball and suggest an idea, but most would simply walk away, confused by the sudden halt to the overture.

Circles of Communication

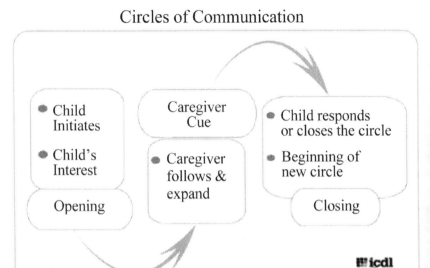

IMH 401, FEAS Reliability Training, Cecilia Breinbauer, MD, MPH

Circle of Communication

As you can see, a circle of communication has three points—open, acknowledge, and close. With two people involved, it's obvious that one person owns two-thirds of the engagement and the other owns one-third. The goal of a circle of communication is to foster two-thirds of the ownership to the child. We want the child to open and close the circle, leaving us the job of acknowledgment. Too often the opposite is the norm where the adult initiates the interaction, the child is expected to respond, and then we reward the response the child has provided. The child is the one who needs to develop interaction, yet this latter pattern works against the child initiating the interaction himself.

The first and obvious question regarding circles of communication is: How do you get the circle started if you're not supposed to be the one to start it? The answer lies in *purpose*. Again, the goal of DIR is to impart meaning. We often use a technique that simply makes every action a child does purposeful. To encourage a child to begin initiating we have to help him connect to *when he is initiating*. When he touches something, we can simply touch it ourselves. The very action of our repeating his behavior starts to instill a thought in him that he caused something to occur. He might not have intended it, but we are putting a sense of purpose to his action. If he repeats it again, we know we have succeeded in creating a bridge to him feeling he's in the driver's seat, and we are letting him know that his actions matter.

Some children take to this quickly, almost as if they have been waiting for it to occur, while others need more practice in this communicative behavior before they start using it with meaning. If a strong level of comfort has been established you can also attempt to do one step with an object he's touching, almost guessing at what you thought he might possibly have been thinking of doing. If he repeats your action or does something else in the same vein, he has closed the first circle and also opened another circle as the start of further interaction. In a way you have expanded the interaction while following his lead in maintaining his interest level.

This level is all about reciprocation and give and take. This is the same thing we do when we converse as adults. We listen and respond with the assumption that the same idea will be followed through with a deepening of the idea. Children with developmental delays often feel ineffectual in their environment as their initiations are frequently missed. It is so wonderful to see their empowerment when they first realize that they have the ability to make us do something, and this in itself becomes the motivator to try it again.

Internal motivation is built on a sense of empowerment and it is very difficult for a child to feel this empowerment if we continue to make decisions for him all day, every day. There must be time built into his day when he can feel someone listening to his language and finding his overtures valuable.

Additionally, because so many children with developmental delays struggle with auditory processing difficulties, using very limited language is always a good idea in play. It's best to use one word at a time, and for children with vestibular and motor planning difficulties, the use of verbs is encouraged to bring action into the play, inviting more circles to occur.

Stringing Circles

Dr. Greenspan also discussed the value of *stringing circles;* here is where playing dumb really works. A typical scenario: Use a familiar activity such as putting on your child's socks in the morning, a daily routine that he has a certain comfort level with, but instead of putting the sock on his foot, you quickly pull it over his hand. He looks at you puzzled and responds by pulling it off. You respond with fun and laughter, and perhaps say, "Mommy is silly!" as he takes the sock off his hand and tries to put it on his foot himself. But you do it again, keeping it at the pace where he can enjoy the moment and not become overly anxious. Acting dumb with huge amounts of affect and enjoyment has allowed many parents to string reams of circles while encouraging problem-solving and having extreme fun. This kind of problem-solving attitude with familiar routine activities acts as a scaffold to start building new and novel problems for the child to solve.

Remember that it is very important to always start where there is a familiar base. Use this technique while setting his place at the table with no spoon to eat his cereal or give him milk instead of the juice he asked for. Look for opportunities like this throughout the day to facilitate his mind into a thinking process of problem-solving. This builds a base upon which to work out problems, think of solutions, express concern, and build flexibility. You are now developing a thinker and not someone who simply responds to a prompt given in a certain circumstance.

Frustration and Meltdowns

The role of frustration should be considered here. Many caregivers, parents, and teachers express a reluctance to upset the applecart, tending to walk on eggshells around their child. Not wanting to cause him to reach a tantrum level or become emotionally upset, they do everything just the way he expects so he can maintain his comfort zone. The child might appear to be doing *fine*, but it takes a tremendous amount of work to make him *fine*, and the thought of causing yourself or others to work your way back to an even keel is a big driver for avoiding anything unexpected. The problem is that his comfort zone is not allowing him to take the necessary risks for new learning, and now we too have become imprisoned by it.

Nobody wants to see a child upset and disorganized, and it is heartbreaking when it happens. But we have to risk it from time to time, otherwise the bar will never be raised and we further constrict his learning opportunities. We have to get him to dance. We must watch his cues very closely, extend our hand at just the right time, and guide him onto the dance floor. Then we take it step by step, always allowing him to lead with his preferences and through his differences. And if we engage him in a problem-solving opportunity and sense we are reaching his threshold of frustration, it's okay to back down, come up with the solution ourselves, and help the child feel the sense of relief over the challenge.

Much value is gained in the process of such seeming failures. First and foremost, he stepped onto the dance floor, he felt what it feels like to approach frustration, and then, through the security of your relationship with him, he experienced your calming influence on his arousal level. It doesn't matter that you didn't achieve the end product—the solution or the dance. What matters more is the feedback he gained from the process of trying. Please don't avoid raising the bar in fear of facing a meltdown. You can build quality into the entire process including the meltdown and his recovery from it. Many adults feel more angst than the child over a meltdown, and they unknowingly carry this anxiety over to the child in the way they deal with it. It is very important that the child is not left alone in moments of distress and feeling out of control, and that he knows there is a boundary and a stable person who also believes in his ability to calm himself. The first few times this process might take longer, but as he learns that he has the ability to exercise control for himself, it will take less and less time.

Level Four – Two-Way Purposeful Interactions with Complex Gestures and Problem-solving

Pretend Play and Ideation

Between the age of nine and eighteen months, Matt needed to start putting words, gestures, and actions together in communication. When we met him, Matt demonstrated the ability to open circles, though he often tended to require someone else to elicit and open the circle first during play, and he needed prompting to close a circle or respond to a request or comment made to him. Reciprocal communication (continuous back and forth circles) was difficult for him and he appeared to be highly dependent on the person playing with him. He was not observed to readily incorporate a new idea in his play pattern and he tended to stay with rote and familiar types of play by committing previous play schemes to memory and initiating those play schemes at another time. Matt's ability to initiate his own ideas spontaneously was quite limited at the time.

This level is where some of the pieces of earlier social-emotional development begin to come together. It consists of the child's ability to organize chains of two-way social problem-solving communications by stringing together a series of gestures, actions, and words to maintain communication (whether the child is in close proximity to the caregiver or on the other side of the room). At this level we continue working on opening and closing many circles of communication on a sequential theme, and expanding the ideas of the previous level into more elaborate sequences of pretend play themes. A very important goal during this phase is to facilitate the play situation in such a way that he has his own ideas. The child may put together pretend play scenes of everyday life situations, such as taking a bath, going to the store, giving a baby a bottle, or going to the doctor. In setting up the scenes, he starts to work on his own role and the roles of others in the family. He will also start to identify basic emotions, such as happy and sad, and acknowledge them as a part of his life in dealing with situations.

One core deficit in children who struggle with a spectrum disorder is being able to express what they are thinking, and it is therefore quite important to find ways to validate their ideas in order to set the course for the development of abstract thinking. Many children find it easier to start working with their cuddly animals or TV characters at first. I always encourage parents to purchase the characters of favorite TV shows so their child can exercise the power of making the characters come to life. At first, the child may want to play out scenes exactly as they are in the show and not allow anyone to introduce a new direction; but as the comfort level grows and we use more playful obstruction, he will begin to allow changes bit by bit. Care should be taken at first, as we do want to maintain the dance of just enough frustration accompanied by loads of playfulness and fun. It is important to only go one step at a time so that especially the child who may have a sequencing difficulty can follow. When we reach the point where playful obstruction becomes exactly that—*playful*—we know that flexibility of thinking is right around the corner and an achievable goal.

If a child only wants to line up objects and not do anything differently, we need to remind ourselves that this is what he learned to do to organize himself while working through earlier levels. Even though he might not need order in his life as much anymore, this type of activity connects him to the memory of calming and safety. Simply requiring him to change is not an option. This must be approached carefully. Parallel play is usually a good idea. Sit next to him and line up your own objects, and then woo him in by making a change to your line up. Turn one object upside down or hide a block or car you know would be next in sequence so there has to be a search for it. Again, be reminded of using high affect whenever you are initiating a challenge.

Hats On!

Parents can take on the roles of different characters to help the child become securely involved in play and to be motivated to work on playing different roles himself. This again works on theory of mind, empathy, and flexibility of thinking.

I encourage parents to wear different hats at home... literally. Hats are an inexpensive and easy way to assume different roles such as a policeman, fireman, or doctor to assist in this pretend role play. As always, parents are urged to follow the child's lead. If the child does not want to explore pretend sequences through soft toys and characters and prefers playing with blocks or cars, different objects can be coaxed into the play scheme by having names or attributes of favorite characters. The objects can become representational of other life or story sequences. Remember, you're pretending—anything goes.

Level Five – Elaborating Ideas, Pretend Play, and Creating Symbols

Deepening the Plot

In entering the twenty-four to thirty months stage, Matt would have had to start to have his own ideas and been using them in play. He would have needed to begin to understand symbols such as power, independence, nurture and love, as well as other emotions such as anger and jealousy, and evolve these emotional ideas in pretend play. Typical two-year-olds are very skilled at communicating emotional intent. They make it very clear exactly what they do and do not want to do, and they are not shy about showing their anger and frustration when they don't get their way.

At four months shy of four years old, Matt was not observed to engage in any symbolic play, although he was demonstrating emerging pretend-play skills with nurturing themes (i.e., feeding a tiger some juice). The pretend play that was observed was gained from ideas that were modeled or memorized from some idea he had seen or done before. He was not observed to expand on any ideas presented to him.

It is during this level that we frequently talk about *deepening the plot*. It is where we foster the child's ability to create and evolve ideas in pretend play, give meaning to symbols, and begin to communicate some emotional intention. It is the acknowledgement and validation of the emotional themes expressed by the child that truly advance this level. Children are very honest in their play and easily reveal areas they are stuck in along with what they are focusing on next. This level is an important step in understanding and forming the abstract thinking processes, which ultimately affect academic skills such as reading comprehension, organizing ideas, writing essays, and social skills. It helps work against becoming a literal thinker and not making connections to hidden meanings or innuendos, and is a building block for understanding humor and making appropriate jokes. This is also the level where children can act out their fantasy world and work toward testing fantasy against reality. This level contains the richness of imagination and reveals the struggles of emotional development that are so necessary for every child to experience.

At three years of age a child is deeply engaged in imaginative play:

- Using imaginative thinking
- Expanding on any ideas
- Beginning to understand symbols
- Forming the abstract thinking processes that work against becoming a literal thinker
- Setting the foundation for facing struggles of emotional development

Imaginative Play

Emotional Themes

I have listened to Dr. Serena Wieder, who co-authored two books with Dr. Greenspan, speak many times over the years, and I especially enjoy her insights with regard to a hierarchy of emotional themes that are important for strong emotional development. The first themes played out in this level are *dependency, nurturance,* and *attachment.* This can be seen when a child re-enacts little scenes that depict his mother's care such as feeding a baby and putting it to sleep.

Another theme is working through *separation anxiety* and having the ability to *lose* someone, albeit temporarily. So many parents find themselves in a position where they have become the extension of their child and the child feels totally inadequate when the parent is not around. When working on this theme children test the waters of independence and internalize their feelings of their own competence in the world. Another frequent theme is the scenario of *being hurt* and having to go to the doctor. The idea of being broken in some place could become a symbol of the child himself being broken. It is very important that these themes are worked through in a commenting and facilitating way, allowing the child to process through emotions in his own way. It is not up to the adults to *save* the child from being exposed to these emotions or to solve the emotional play schemes for him. In order to really internalize change, a child must come to emotional conclusions himself.

Children attempt to deal with *fear* in magical ways first before turning to a symbolic route to face their fears. It is a stage of development for all children and could be a fear of large animals, large spaces, or a fear of growing up and facing the world with more independence than they feel they have within themselves. They also work though *sadness, anger, joy,* and *surprise*—experiencing the differences in how each emotion makes them feel. In a world where communication is often so difficult for our children, it must be frightening to be so aware of your own body's needs and not know the meaning of any of it. It helps to give a feeling a place by learning that the tight feeling you get when you are mad has a name called anger, and the teariness you feel is called sad. We did not learn these meanings as adults; we learned them during childhood play and in experiences with our own parents.

Less Play... More Anxiety

Today, with more and more advanced technology and entertainment, children are playing less and less. As a result, I am not at all surprised to see increased anxiety and an inability to handle difficult emotions as they become teens and young adults. Children often fear the feeling of anxiety so much that they do not even attempt a task they possibly could achieve simply to avoid the experience of anxiety in their own bodies.

I cannot stress enough how important it is that these symbols and emotions are worked out in play and are normalized for our children. This is frequently a major stumbling block of development. And if we are not aware of it, we often think the child is stubborn, has a behavior problem, or simply is unable to develop a certain skill. We must remember that it is early play that draws the blueprint of a child's ability to later process through different emotional states during teenage years and adulthood.

It is natural for children to encounter feelings related to *jealousy, competition,* and *sibling rivalry.* It is also healthy to see these emotions addressed in play. Once a child is really doing well exercising many circles of communication with one adult play partner, siblings are frequently brought in to Floortime sessions. This is where these themes play themselves out even more. Children would lead play schemes such as where it's only Mommy and the child going to the zoo and everyone else has to stay at home.

Competition in the sense of winning and losing is tough for our children since they frequently are too afraid to take risks that could stir their inner feelings of inadequacy. As adults we take so much for granted, but each of these emotions is very risky for children with special needs to face. Just as we attempt to hide from stress or potentially difficult situation, children are no different. We're all inclined to defend ourselves against negative emotions, but in adulthood we have the cognitive ability and a history of maturational experiences that help us cope. Children don't.

Power is another large emotion that holds much fear, but also much reward in children. As adults, it's difficult for us to imagine what it feels like to be powerless, to literally have every decision made for us every day. Some might say this is an exaggeration, but it frequently is the case for many children I see. They get up, get dressed, eat breakfast, go to school, come home, have dinner, do homework, and go to bed. The feeling of powerlessness is pervasive. It robs the child of the opportunity to work with his own strengths and weaknesses and form his own identity. In play, we see power begin to develop first through magical thinking such as waving a magic wand or electing to use power figures in play. This can then develop into reenactments of fighting, aggression, war, death, and dying. Older themes of loss and separation anxiety may also very likely resurface again temporarily.

Parents are often anxious about witnessing aggression in their children. We must remember that children do not have the abilities we have to inhibit emotions and guard against showing them. It took us a lifetime to gain this ability. It's okay to let the child play out his aggression in the safety of a play session, and it is also okay to take a time out to re-establish safety rules (but not to inhibit the play of emotion). It is important to remain calm, as it's often our anxiety that causes the child to act out their aggression even more.

We also know that a child will frequently choose the person he feels safest with to show these underlying emotions. Many children turn around and bite or push their mothers when they become frustrated. This is always an unfortunate situation as the parent has no warning and feels anxious and rejected by these actions. But most mental health professionals will tell you this is very normal and actually means the child is feeling safe with you and is wanting to communicate the full extent of his feelings with you. The child wants the parent to share in his feeling of frustration, have empathy for him, and show understanding of what he is going through. At a time like this, it's best to tell the child that it hurts, that it must be so hard to feel so frustrated, and if you know the source of the frustration, add this to the recognition of the emotion.

Once a child has established power in his life (to a child-appropriate degree), themes of friendship and loyalty begin to appear in play and we see him become more ready to face peers. This is a great time in play, usually one that parents have been waiting for. Just be reminded that friendship is not automatic, and developing empathy for a peer's preferred play is not easy for a child who is intent on maintaining his comfort zone. It is also during this point in development when the child becomes more cognitively aware of love and the meaning of the word. These *friendship* and *love* themes set the stage for the next theme of *justice* and *morality*. Some competition themes might resurface in terms of what is fair and not fair and what it means to *get even* as a sense of good and bad choices are developed and played out. When we see this process come to life in play, we see the child then start to build themes of the future into play. During this process we often see the child's uncertainty in play as he vacillates between themes of power and nurturing, only to suddenly switch over to a baby role and curl in Mommy's lap. Some even start talking baby talk. This also occurs commonly when a new sibling arrives on the scene. Children might also express these feelings of ambivalence by insisting to do things themselves, only to turn to Mommy in the next moment for help with something they have conquered before.

The Good and the Bad

Many children with developmental delays really struggle to accept both the good and bad in their own persona. They may play themselves out as good or bad guys, but have difficulty accepting that their one little body could be good and bad at the same time. It is especially difficult for children who are constantly reprimanded for bad behavior. They learn that adults are not pleased with them during these times and, therefore, they do not want to accept it in themselves. Self-identity then suffers under the strain of their own self-acceptance.

Once this theme has played itself out, it assists in the concept first talked about by Dr. Margaret Mahler in that the child is able to individuate and separate from the umbilical cord of his mother. This is an extremely important process as it provides a sense of self-reliance and taking responsibility for one's actions.

Level Six – Building Bridges Between Ideas (Emotional Thinking)

Finally, between three and four years of age, all these seeds of development would have had to come together for Matt in order for him to form his ability to connect ideas within a framework of logic, reality, thinking, and judgment. His ability to make connections between different emotional ideas would have been forming during this period. One example of development at this level is seen in a child's ability to negotiate his own needs and wants around parents' rules, while also being able to apply causal thinking within the ambiguity of emotional context. Matt was unable to indicate the necessary skills this level of development requires, and he would have had to work on solidifying all other levels to fully harness the complexity of level six.

Working at level six, I have had many *be careful what you ask for* conversations with parents. This is where negotiation skills appear more frequently and when asking and answering *why* questions starts to be the rule of the day. This is also the time of development where the child is able to effectively formulate a story with a beginning, middle, and end including emotional nuances with causal influences. The child is able to relate what happened yesterday, today, and tomorrow in ways that have logical sequence. He is able to put meaning to the relationship between his thoughts, feelings, and actions, and to more readily define subtler feeling states such as feeling pleased, secure, and lonely. He is also able to adapt more flexibly to the needs of others, seeing a larger picture than the one created by his own needs.

Role identification becomes more established and his ability to move in and out of familiar routines becomes easier. Events and transitions have more meaning for him now, and feelings of extreme insecurity and vagueness start to dissipate, leaving a lesser need to hold on to a comfort zone. You will still see a child with childlike needs, but a more flexible, less routine-bound, less anxious child. Once we have spent quite some time solidifying level four (purposeful interactions with problem-solving), we frequently see children wanting to tackle levels five and six at once. They tend to want to skip the deepening the plot work and go straight into causal thinking styles. Be careful of this trap as solid work on level five is needed to expand the literal thinker, the child who does not get the hidden innuendo of conversation. Literal thinkers become inhibited in their social growth because they have not fully harnessed the meaning of different emotional states in their own lives.

DIR/ Floortime -- Play, Concept Development, and Academic Achievement

Many teachers ask questions related to the educational relevance of this method. Whether you agree or disagree with the pace of curriculum today, it is what it is. There are many underlying skills we expect a kindergartner to have because that is the time they are expected to have readiness to learn in an academic environment. Teachers expect a child to be able to achieve one-on-one correspondence in order to start the process of counting objects effectively to do math. If a child does not understand sequence and order, which are skills worked on in levels three and four, he will have an insufficient base of support to attack math. Every teacher likes to read stories to children in circle time, but if a child does not understand sequence and does not have an abstract thinking process happening at the same timing and speed as his peers, he will have difficulty fully comprehending the story in its entirety with regard to the message and the details that underscore the story. For example, for a child who has not developed the theory of mind to differentiate Cinderella's wicked step-mother and step-sisters as being different from his own mother and sisters, the meaning of the story is impacted quite extensively. All of these skills are formed and fine-tuned through the richness of play.

The underlying concepts of understanding *change* and *cause and effect* are also expected skills in school-age children, but quite often these are the very skills our children fight against or lack experience in. During play a child learns she can cause a baby to cry if she lets it fall, learning that she is the cause of the action and the baby crying is the effect of the action. These are the same principles you need to understand math. If I put one and one together, the effect is going to be two. Many children on the spectrum struggle with self-identity and do not feel any power over their environment and daily lives, let alone feel that they could cause something to happen and have an effect on something. These are crucial developments in concept formation that only experience through play can provide.

Many high functioning children on the spectrum really do appear to function well in kindergarten. This is when material is introduced at a slower pace with many visual reminders and models of what is expected. By the end of first grade, however, they start showing signs of struggle with reading comprehension or understanding multi-step instructions, which call for faster speed of sequencing and content acknowledgement. Active working memory also creeps in more strongly at this point. The child has to remember the facts of a story in sequence to be able to answer comprehension questions, or must hold a math question or definition in his mind while working on each step of a math problem.

We must also consider the concept of time, the comprehension of past, present, and future, and a child's understanding of how long it will take to complete a task. Considering a child on the spectrum, much apprehension comes from not knowing how long he is going to be out of his comfort zone. A new task raises anxiety in and of itself, only to be compounded by the fact that the child does not have the ability to understand when it will end. These executive functioning skills will strongly impact the child later in his academic career, as he has to plan projects, remember to take things home, and be organized in his attempts to do homework.

Typically developing children who have vast play experiences have exercised all of these components in their play with other children. Children on the spectrum usually have limited experiences of play, yet we continue to expect them to somehow have these skills when they enter school. Most adults believe that if children are exposed to specific learning frequently enough at high repetition, they will get it; yet we continue to hear frustrated teachers speak of constant repetition holding limited success. The real answer is that we are exposing children to academics without the necessary foundations to hold onto the information or have the information gain any meaning for them.

Support for Relationship-Based Approaches
The National Academy of Sciences (NAS), in its report "Educating Children with Autism," stated research support

for a number of approaches, including the DIR model, though also stated, "There are no proven relationships between any particular intervention and children's progress (p. 5), and no adequate comparisons of different comprehensive treatments (p. 8)." The report supported the development of relationship-based approaches and cited ten programs with some evidence as being effective, one of which was DIR/ Floortime.

I salute Dr. Greenspan for developing a method that is so child sensitive, so emotionally validating, and so socially rewarding for both parents and the child. I also applaud the Interdisciplinary Council of Development and Learning Disorders (ICDL) and faculty for their continued rigor in training more professionals and parents every day to further this work.

Lower Levels—No Less Important

A child may be working on all six levels during the same period of development, but it is important to make sure the child solidifies each level to the extent necessary to fully harness and take charge of his development. Many parents make the mistake of seeing levels one through three as lower levels, making them seem of lesser importance. This is not how these levels operate and you do not conquer each level before moving on to the next.

It is very important to understand that a child functions on multiple levels at one time, and can play on levels four, five, and six, yet still encounter regulatory difficulties of level one. Keep in mind, as mature adults, we are constantly using all six developmental levels at exactly the same time. As always, the goal is to follow a child's lead in play to reach the highest level of attainment for that child, which is the integration of all six levels of development.

"Through play, Matty opened a door and let us begin to see his emotional range—showing caring, nurturing, anger, and frustration."

Chapter 9

One Step off the Twister Mat... One Giant Leap for Development

The training Maude gave to Matty's school team crystallized my understanding of DIR even further. The discussion focused on the DIR model with much attention to level three—circles of communication, ideation, and specific classroom strategies to foster these important developmental goals. Maude explained where Matty currently stood and what he was moving toward. But as important as it was to understand how to help Matty achieve his goals, the larger value of the discussion was the focus on the physiological, emotional, and developmental *whys* that hampered his ability to move through these levels as easily as his peers. She explained his sensory needs, why he gravitated toward his comfort zones, and why engagement with peers eluded him. She explained why Matty avoided new ideas and new activities, and why he needed to control play situations and had difficulty sustaining them. By the end of the day, I felt a collective "aha" from the group, myself included, as many more dots were connected.

A Venue for Stealthy Progress

With new insight from the training, everyone went back to the classroom with a renewed sense of where Matty was headed and new ideas on how to scaffold his next steps. Karen headed right back to the Twister mat where she and Matty had spent the prior two months. Just days before the DIR training session

Matty had started to verbalize a little more, but over the next few weeks, he really started to show us that much more had been happening on the Twister mat than we ever imagined. I knew it was a comfort zone for him, and I always thought the role of his comfort zone was for self-preservation against the demands of the environment and self-protection against taking risks during play. In the beginning, these were likely his reasons for needing to be there. But Matty soon began to show us, and has proven to us time and again, that his comfort zones are as much a venue for stealthy progress as they are a place to take refuge.

Maude respected Matty's need to be on the mat and Karen turned it into a carnival of ideas. If Mattel® gave an award for the 1,001 most creative uses for a Twister mat that year, Karen would have been the hands-down winner. She continuously expanded the use of the mat using various Floortime strategies, sometimes through one-step modeling, other times through playful obstruction. And after having spent two months on the mat, my little chamois finally gave us a peek at what he'd been absorbing all along. Matty started coming up with original ideas and then began putting his ideas together with Karen's. By April's end, he was snuggling with puppets as he put them to bed, bringing our home environment into his play schemes, and showing first steps toward sequencing events. By mid-May, he was taking turns with puppets, he had tucked dinosaurs into bed after they had gotten stuck in the mud, and had even solved an argument between Karen and another therapist, spontaneously getting them tissues when they were sad.

As May came to a close, we began to see the first glimpses of what would be our main focus for the next year. Through play, Matty opened a door and let us begin to see his emotional range—showing caring, nurturing, anger, and frustration. I was not surprised to see his caring side emerge, as I never doubted he had deep feelings for me. I had seen him show sadness on only a few occasions, and when I saw anger, I attributed it mostly to sensory overload. I always thought he just went with the flow and didn't feel negative emotions strongly enough to project them. Deep feelings of anger, fear, sadness, frustration, failure, or disappointment seemed to not be a big part of his emotional repertoire. Or maybe, if viewed from the perspective of the Affect Diathesis Hypothesis, these emotional capacities were there, but he lacked the prindle connection to attach them to their purpose and the developmental capacities to express them. Whatever the reason, the reality was he had very little real-world experience in just about all negative emotions.

Following is an excerpt from Karen's session notes on what turned out to be a breakthrough session on anger.

Today, we played back and forth "I Spy" before heading to the Twister mat. When Twister finally came out, Matt enjoyed straightening out the mat. We did a few things that came together nicely. Matt had the idea to skate on the mat and I slipped on the ice. I challenged him by falling and scrunching up the mat when I slipped. Matt was very expressive of the mess I made of the Twister mat. I forget his exact words, but he said something like, "I fixed the mat and it's NOT okay." I validated that he was not happy with what I did, but he fixed it and seemed okay.

We used a broom to sweep the colors and I gave him one more challenge with the mat. When talking about astronauts and in bridging my ideas with his, I counted down for a blast off, and shook the Twister mat up again. Again, with a tone of anger, he verbally requested for me not to do that anymore. He was definitely a little more frustrated. When a classroom assistant came in and said it was time for lunch, Matt said to her, "Not right now, I want to play in the rice... come on, Miss Karen." The assistant said "No rice, Matt," and Matt said, "YES," in a sterner voice.

Matt did agree to go to lunch but he left with facial expression and body language that said he was clearly angry. Before he left I went up to him and said, "Are you mad, Matt?" With his head down and lips pursed, Matt said, "Yes, I'm mad." I validated his feelings and told him it's okay to be mad. He did not cry, but looked like he was on the verge. I asked the assistant to talk to him about it and don't dismiss his anger.

After lunch, I brought up the incident and validated again. I asked what he was mad about.

"The mat," he said, "...and the sand," he added, which meant he wanted to pretend he was at the beach and the rice was the sand.

Nice representational thinking, too! This is a very good occurrence. I talked to the teacher and she said Matt hadn't shown anger in class and she also felt this was good. It would be a good idea to bring this up at home as well. Identify when his sisters get angry and talk about it. This will help Matt experience negative emotion when seeing others in similar situations.

Matty was now starting to explore negative emotions and this moment of showing anger toward Karen when she messed up the Twister mat was what we'd been waiting for all along. It may not seem like much for a child to tell a playmate "I'm mad," but for Matty it spoke volumes. Karen had been working with him for almost half his life and his relationship with her was based on deep trust. Expressing negative feelings toward her was a huge personal risk for him. He could have abandoned the whole ship and just walked away after the first time Karen messed up the mat, but he didn't. He trusted her enough to know his anger wouldn't drive her away; and more importantly, he was telling her that what he wanted mattered.

By validating his anger, Karen let Matty know that it was okay for him to feel what he was feeling and she didn't try to avoid it. He was able to move on, stick with the play scheme, and forgive her. At the time, I would have been inclined to chill things out and try not to heighten his anxiety, but Karen knew to ask for even more. She was careful not to push him over the edge, but messing up the mat for a second time raised the emotional bar even higher. And Matty hung in there, proving he trusted her enough to risk expressing his feelings. Karen again validated his lingering feelings of anger toward the educational assistant and made sure the loop was closed after he had calmed down.

In the years since we first began doing emotional work, I've come to learn that a strong foundation for dealing with negative emotions is like a strong immune system. Your immune system is always there, doing a little work here and there, fighting off bacteria and viruses every day. But when that killer cold or terrible flu comes along, it's your immune system that steps up and takes you through it, strengthening itself along the way.

Dealing with negative emotions is no different. Too often, with our natural need to protect our children, we simply don't allow them to experience negative emotional feelings completely. We've become germ-o-phobes when it comes to allowing our children to be exposed to even the slightest negative feelings. But like immunities, they need to be exposed to some of the bad stuff to strengthen the underlying emotional systems they'll need to protect them throughout their lives. I'm as guilty of it as anybody. It's always easier to straighten the Twister mat, sweep the colors clean, and assume all is well because your child now seems happy. But I've come to learn that seizing opportunities to allow children to fully experience negative emotions is like the minor exposure to bacteria and viruses we all need to keep our immune systems strong. It's no picnic, but it's something we just have to do.

The Anecdotal Progress is all that Really Matters

It was already the end of Matty's first full year of preschool, and it was soon time to write Matty's IEP for the upcoming summer and his last year of preschool. Maude had been contributing to Matty's program for only six months and good things were happening all around. Whether Matty was making progress that could be analytically measured by some test or scale that IEPs and Child Study Teams know and love, I didn't know. I was beginning not to care.

What mattered to me was the anecdotal progress he was making. He seemed a little calmer and happier, more flexible and interactive, and was beginning to be more verbally and emotionally expressive. That's all I cared about. I understand IEPs must be written with certain rigor from an educational and legal perspective, but it's frustrating that so much time and money is spent parsing the words, when in some areas, it's the anecdotal progress that's all that really matters in the long run.

New High Watermarks

As school came to an end in June, Matty was immersed in levels three and four, using puppet play on the Twister mat to connect ideas and solve problems. One day Matty's class took a walk to a farmhouse and playground up the street from the school. After a full morning of sensory activity, Matty and Karen both arrived a few minutes late for his session. Karen told me she hadn't had time to set up any toys or puppets, so Matty walked around the room looking for something to play with. As he moseyed by the Twister mat, neatly folded in its box now broken on all four corners, he reached out with both hands as if to pick it up. Then he stopped. The room was quiet and Karen heard him whisper, "No Twister today." The Twister mat had done its job and was now retired.

Looking back, the *Twister period* as we've come to call it, was no different than the time two years earlier when Matty suddenly blurted out the letters on the FedEx truck. He didn't look like he was processing the alphabet he'd been seeing and hearing, but those wheels were spinning all along. The Twister mat has since grown into my little euphemism to describe the times when Matty retreats to a place of comfort, sometimes for weeks or months, to prepare himself for developmental change. I don't worry as much anymore when Matty's *on the mat* because I know he's there for his own reasons and that he's processing and preparing himself to move forward. I now know the best thing I can do is respect his need to be there while keeping him exposed and in tune to the business as usual realities of life. I've also learned that the mat creates tremendous developmental momentum. Although I give him distance, I always keep a close eye out for the signs that tell me when he's ready to move.

I may not be a pro at doing Floortime, but I do have a knack for following Matty's developmental lead. His "No Twister today" signs tell me he's opening the door. They're the sign of opportunity and it's during those times more than any other that Matty is ready to hit new developmental high watermarks. It seems he gives himself permission to move in all areas of development, giving me and others around him the nod to raise the bar. It's during these times that I look to his teachers and coaches to help bridge him to the next level. Maybe it's higher expectations when it comes to school responsibilities or participation in sports. Maybe it's wading through a new emotional experience or social situation. It's during these times when Matty adds new layers to his self-concept and inches himself closer to his peers. There is no formula for how much to raise the bar or in what ways to do it; but it has served me well to simply rely on my gut to see and seize the opportunities to help Matty make the most of his Twister mat momentum.

DIR has been a partner in Matty's developmental journey for over seven years now. Sometimes it takes a larger focus and at other times it's in the background giving support and perspective. It's always there helping to clarify where he is developmentally, what's in front of him, and how to scaffold him forward. It's had a calming effect in my life as well. It's a tangible framework to grasp when intangibles such as time and development seem to be in control. With this understanding, I just don't feel that unnerving, floundering feeling quite so much anymore.

The Expectation Dutch Boy

More often than I should, I find my role to be one of keeping expectations at bay. There are days when I am completely disillusioned by the unreasonable amount of time the education system demands of our evenings. Teachers are not to blame. They are just trying to do their job and meet the exceedingly high standards of the curriculum. The gods of reading, writing, and math curriculum are demanding way more than teachers, children, and families can give. With five children now in third through seventh grade, it's often simply impossible to accomplish what is expected for homework. I've heard that a reasonable expectation for homework is ten minutes multiplied by the child's grade. That's 250 minutes per night in my house before you tack on the required twenty minutes of reading per night per child. And please don't tell me how children should be *independent*. Nice thought, nice expectation. But it's just not reality. Sure, there are times when kids can tackle homework completely on their own, but what about helping to study for tests? What about the times when you have to teach or re-teach the material before the child can even get started on the homework?

Raising five children isn't hard. Educating five children is. I find myself playing the role of the expectation Dutch Boy more often than I should. I sometimes feel I'm the lone soul with my finger stuck in the hole, stemming back the sea of expectations. It's certainly not that I don't want my children to achieve, I just believe in timing. Learning occurs more easily and meaningfully when a child is developmentally ready for it and is intrinsically motivated to embrace it. We can teach something over and over until we're blue in the face, but if a child is just not ready to learn it, we're only wasting our time and theirs. And I often wonder what unintended damage we're doing along the way. How about what we're doing to their self-esteem as we come at them from every angle, trying to teach things they're just not ready to learn? With today's education system and high expectations, we seem to be constantly hovering over our children with collective "did you get it yet?" body language, and it's not hard to imagine we're not making many of them feel like failures in the end if they don't.

Expectations and curriculum demand more focused attention from our children than ever before. Downtime is being reduced and often eliminated. The pace of curriculum is so tightly structured that teachers have little flexibility to slow down when needed. Step into any elementary school class and you'll find twenty kids who are developmentally all over the map. For any given subject or concept, some children simply need more learning time than they're given. Curriculums are designed to throw more content and concepts at our children, seemingly to meet *our* need for children to prove their intellectual capacities in earlier grades. Sadly, we're expecting children to take off at younger and younger ages while giving them less and less runway to do so.

Process over Product

The IEP process can certainly become a mountainous one, but no matter how high my pile of IEP paperwork grows, I always I try to focus on keeping Matty's objectives tied to the developmental climb—not the summit. I understand his needs and I now have more patience and courage to work toward his developmental goals while the rest of the world works toward its goals. This is **process over product**. If I've heard Maude say it once, I've heard her say it a thousand times, "Give the child process and the product takes care of itself." Product is the end result; process is what gets you there.

In my mind, *process over product* is much like my notion of *need trumps guilt*. In letting go of the *product* I realized that all my children needed was the process anyway. I remember when my eldest daughter was in third grade, she brought home her first big project. It was what I came to affectionately refer to as our annual "dreaded diorama" of mountains, valleys, plains, and plateaus. In helping her get started, I asked whether the class had learned anything about how to do a project like this. "No?" she responded with question in her voice.

So I proceeded to help her write a project plan that included all the steps needed to complete the assignment. It started with a materials list and ended with a plan to get the project to school. One of the final steps was, "Ask Dad if he can drive me to school on Wednesday," just to show the importance of assumptions and contingency planning. I remember her list was more than twenty-five steps. I also remember that once we were done with the list, she never asked for any more help and finished the project completely on her own. What I don't remember was the grade she received for it.

IEPs Can Take You Back to the Basics

Every generation perseveres through its own unique adversities. For today's kids, true developmental needs are being silenced in the echo chamber of expectations and product. And when it comes to developing Matty's IEPs, it has always served me well to get back to the basics—process-based goals, realistic expectations, and respect for his real needs. Beyond these, I have also learned to always keep two more elemental needs at the top of the list—these are simply *time* and *self.*

Time is our ultimate natural resource. It can't be changed, bought, or sold—but it can be a gift. When we give children the gift of time, I think we'll find they can do amazing things with it. They'll use it to heal themselves and grow themselves in ways we can't see. One of the beauties of an IEP is that it can simply give a child more time. IEPs give more time for tests, assignments, classroom work, and overall educational progress. I take advantage of any opportunity that presents itself for Matty as *more time.* It seems crazy that as our increased demands and expectations steal time away from our kids, the number of IEPs needed to give the time back have steadily increased. Seems we've put a lot of money into raising the bar of expectations, and even more to fix the fact that maybe we've raised it too high.

Another more elusive yet elemental aspect I've found to be at the roots of much of Matty's growth has been his sense of self. I don't look to the IEP to necessarily build Matty's self-concept, but to protect him from the expectations that could tear it down. I always try to remember that Matty owns the goals; everyone else owns the expectations. The larger the gap between the two, the larger the hole for his self-concept to fall into. IEPs are never perfect, but in a nutshell, I always try to keep them tightly woven with the time and process Matty needs to meet his goals, while keeping expectations in check to allow him to develop a genuine sense of who he is along the way.

The Sounds of Summer

For the summer between his first and second year of preschool, Matty's IEP included OT and DIR services, and he attended a local day camp at a gymnastics academy. This was a great way for him to have access to daily jumping, tumbling, and typical peers. During the summer, Matty also began a series of three loops of auditory therapy at Maude's center. Although he was making progress, he was still delayed verbally. He was certainly talking more in recent months, but not to where he could easily interact on a conversational level. From an auditory perspective, we also knew he was always tuned in to the sounds around him, almost too tuned in. It was ironic how some auditory input was over-stimulating, yet other sound such as music kept him regulated. He just loved to listen to music all the time; I often wondered whether he heard more in music because he was so hyperfocused auditorily.

I remember one time, I don't know how old Matty was, but he was still in a crib. It was before I learned about sensory and regulation. For a week or two he had been having a hard time settling down to take a nap in the afternoon. He would hold onto the railing of his crib and jump up and down, never seeming to get enough. One day, I decided to lie down on the bed next to him, thinking it might calm him down. I pretended I was asleep while he continued to jump and jump. After a few minutes I did fall asleep, but I don't think he ever did.

A day or two later, I tried putting on a classical music CD. Matty wasn't as jumpy that day, but was still fidgeting a little as I lay still on the bed. After a few minutes, I realized Matty was quiet and I assumed he had fallen asleep. I remember opening my eyes and turning to see what time it was, but looking at the CD player rather than the clock. The CD player displayed something like 4:02, the amount of time the music had been playing, and I was confused because I thought that was the time of day. Then I realized Matty was not lying down. He was sitting up—still, silent. His face was pale and somber with a look of deep, profound sadness. Large tears rolled down his cheeks, but he was not breathing heavily and made no crying sounds. He was breathing very slowly and he didn't move. Even as I sat up, he didn't move or react. He sat still, hands in his lap, shoulders drooping forward. I didn't know what he was feeling, but I just knew I shouldn't pick him up. I sat still on the bed. All I could muster to say was, "It's okay." Maybe I should have said or done more, but for some reason I didn't. I had never seen him or any of my kids like that. After another minute or two, he lied down with his back to me. I crept out of the room. I don't know if he ever fell asleep

I didn't know what to make of what I'd seen, but the next day when I put him down for a nap he seemed a little jumpier. I lied on the bed again and turned on the CD player. He moved around for a minute or two but then seemed to be settling down. Before I knew it—dead silence. I looked over at Matty and it was déjà vu all over again. Confused and wondering if I had fallen asleep, I glanced at the CD player, again looking for the time, and saw that it was within seconds of the same point in the music when this happened the day before. He was eerily silent, still, and looked deeply sad. I didn't pick him up and just kept telling him "It's okay." I found myself feeling the depth of his emotion and I too felt tears well in my eyes. Again, he lied down and faced the wall. Something about that piece of classical music seemed to ignite a deeply emotional reaction in him. That night I changed the CD and never played it again.

Matty was quite young when this happened, and knowing what I know now about fostering emotional experiences, I probably should have handled things differently. I changed to a new CD because I was trying to protect him from the sadness that Mozart piece brought out in him. I just didn't realize the emotional opportunity I had in that moment, and I do wish I could have a Mulligan on that one. But it's okay. Although it was opportunity lost, it was perspective gained. I sometimes think of

Matty's *Mozart emotions* when a situation presents itself to walk my children through the feelings of negative emotions. It gives me the patience to give them the time to fully experience what they're feeling, no matter how sad, mad, or bad it makes them feel, and it encourages me to stay with them through the music, and hold their hand through the emotional crescendo.

"Through the occupational therapy intensive with Tomatis Sound training, we would be working to give Matt a stronger connection to his own development by establishing a stronger foundation of body awareness, adaptation, and feedback."

Chapter 10

Gaining Ground through Sound

Sound therapy is a method of using the auditory system as a conduit to stimulate change and enhance responses in the brain and nervous system to improve listening quality, communication potential, and body awareness. It uses music altered in specific ways to uniquely trigger the parts of the auditory system that affect auditory and motor functions. Though it is true that many professionals and parents remain skeptical of this additional form of sensory stimulation, for many families, sound therapy has proven itself to be much more than just music to their child's ears. I can understand the apprehension though, as I too was leery until I saw and documented its many successes.

I was first introduced to the world of sound therapy through the work of Sheila Frick, an occupational therapist who designed a sound therapy called *Therapeutic Listening*. Admittedly, when Sheila referred to one of her CDs as affectionately being called "the potty-training CD," many doubtful thoughts went through my head. My extensive clinical training had developed me into a hands-on therapist who needed to manually manipulate a body-mind system into progressing along the developmental continuum. What I could not see and touch did not have the capability of being manipulated. I questioned everything. How could listening to music enhance postural control? How could it increase motor response time? How could our work as hands-on therapists be assisted by a program in such a way that it could make a traditional therapeutic approach more productive?

Baby Steps

Trying to keep an open mind, I embarked down this road extremely tentatively, almost apologetically, with only two families in my practice. To my great surprise, one family experienced extremely remarkable changes in only a two-week period, while the other family started seeing changes four weeks after initiating the program. Changes included a faster rate of progress in the children's physical goals with regard to postural control, their ability to follow through on verbal requests, and their ability to verbally express themselves in play. My team had been so frustrated that our weekly treatment options never seemed to be enough to close the gap of developmental delay for the children we were treating. But this was different. There were plenty of physical changes that sparked my interest as a clinician. We started working with more families who saw similar results in varying degrees. For weeks and months we sat in our offices with jaw dropping disbelief. I was completely at odds with myself. With my heels dug deeply in my roots as a steadfast, analytical clinician, I couldn't easily subscribe to an intervention that was, at the time, largely intangible to me. How could listening to filtered music create change so quickly in areas that had previously taken many months to see the same progress?

My curiosity continued to build as I saw more and more functional results. Calming and inhibition of over-aroused central nervous systems, decreased tactile sensitivities, increased language, and much more. In comparing these changes to previous work we'd done with these children, I knew the changes were far more pronounced than using the traditional once-a-week approach, even when parents complemented therapy with home programs. The changes were different. The changes influenced the *quality of movement* as I had never seen, and I saw significant postural reactions, in some cases literally within a single session. As word-of-mouth spread through my waiting room, we continued trialing with one very willing family after the next. Families were enamored over the changes they were seeing.

"The voice can only reproduce what the ear can hear."
Dr. Alfred A. Tomatis

After the first year of adding this work to my practice, what started as disbelief grew into a steady awakening of the mind. I now realized there was more to using sound as an additional catalyst for change than I ever imagined, and I started looking for more information about similar programs. On my knowledge quest, I found Dr. Alfred A. Tomatis and the *Tomatis Sound* training program. Dr. Tomatis started the entire movement of sound therapy as it is known today, and is quoted and revered in every program that includes sound training. Dr. Tomatis was born January 1, 1920, in Nice, France, and passed away on Christmas Day 2001. The son of an opera singer, Humberto Tomatis, he spent a good part of his childhood in opera houses throughout France. He received his M.D. from the Faculte de Paris before specializing in ear, nose, and throat, and speech therapy. He was first to describe the function of the structure of the bones of the inner ear to protect against loud noises.

In 1954, Dr. Tomatis developed the *Electronic Ear*, a gated system with two channels. The two channels allow for music to be filtered at a specific frequency and intensity to switch from lower to higher frequencies. In addition to this switching action, the Electronic Ear has an ability to delay bone and air conduction in order for the ear to be prepared for sound. In addition to the Electronic Ear, Dr. Tomatis developed a range of electronic instruments designed to measure and work with learning disabilities, speech and language issues, problems with lateral dominance (the different functions of the right and left ear), and behavioral difficulties including attention, memory, aggression, and hyperactivity. His first law, "the voice can only reproduce what the ear can distinguish," was made official by the Academy of Science and Medicine in Paris in 1957, and named the *Tomatis Effect* in his honor. Dr. Tomatis received numerous distinctions from 1951 through 1967; he founded the International Society of Audio-Psycho-Phonology, and a museum in Brussels is now devoted entirely to his work. Tomatis held seven patents and authored fifteen books and at least seventy-seven scholarly works.

During the time when I was researching Tomatis, I learned that the very first Tomatis consultant training was being held in the U.S. that year, after quite a while of no training being offered. After much deliberation with regard to this quite expensive and very time consuming commitment, I decided that I simply had to make this intervention available to the families at my center. I went on to attend the comprehensive training and graduated as a Certified Tomatis Consultant (CTC). I have never looked back. Tomatis has catapulted our ability to help children in new dimensions and in ways I would have never anticipated. To this day, I sometimes cannot believe the benefits I've seen from adding the Tomatis Sound training to our work. Even now, with a deep repository of success stories, I still sometimes find myself shaking my head in amazement.

Neurons that Fire Together, Wire Together

Although these wonderful changes are great to behold, it has been the science that swayed my opinion most of all. What ultimately influenced my belief in this type of therapy is that Tomatis Sound training builds upon much of what is indisputably known about the brain and neuro-physiology. I immersed myself in what was already known about auditory processing pathways and how they relate to other receiving systems in the brain such as the visual, vestibular, and somatosensory systems.

What the science of neurology believes, and is also the basic premise of Sensory Processing Disorder, is that *Neurons that fire together, wire together*. (A good reference for families and professionals to learn more about this, is *The Brain That Changes Itself* by Dr. Norman Doidge.) The developing brain is all about *action potentials* in the nervous system that are more strongly activated by unfamiliar, or new and novel stimulation. If the brain is alerted to something new to contend with, it sparks the action potential of different parts of the nervous system, and the nervous system essentially goes into a *firing* mode seeking to *wire* other connections in the brain. The more the nervous system fires, the more the nervous system wires. This does not happen as strongly as when stimulation has become familiar to the recipient. Tomatis Sound training uses this feature of new and novel changes through different aspects of programming in multiple different ways. The changes in the various filtering processes are unexpected and frequent, while also focusing strongly on the stimulating effect of high frequency music in the brain. It causes the brain to remain alert and attentive to the processing of incoming stimuli.

The Auditory System Gets More Focus

Occupational therapists work with stimulating the sensory systems to become integrated for application of functional and occupational use. We must look at *all* sensory systems, and it stands to reason that we would not disregard one system when working with a child struggling with a Sensory Processing Disorder, as all senses can experience differences in terms of arousal and response patterns. Yet it is only within the last ten years that the auditory system has become a prominent entity in the treatment of children with sensory processing challenges. Considering the neurology and that auditory and vestibular information move together along the vestibulo-cochlear nerve, we begin to understand that the influence of the auditory system on especially the vestibular system and vice versa, simply cannot be ignored.

Occupational therapists always knew that putting a child on a swing likely stimulates more vocalizations or language, but we mostly considered the vestibular system in order to explain this phenomenon. We thought the movement of the swing ignited the language area of the brain, causing more language to be produced. Whereas, what was really happening was that the synergy between the auditory and vestibular systems was being activated, assisting the child to process language and the oral motor system to produce language at a faster rate.

Another example of this reliance can be seen in the simple act of talking on the phone. When the auditory system is isolated with no additional sensory support to rely upon (such as the visual system which would provide supportive facial and non-verbal information), it reaches out to and relies upon its vestibular comrade to help sustain auditory focus. How often do you see people pace while on the phone? The science behind this typical behavior is simply that the vestibular system is being engaged to support the auditory information coming in through the ear since both types of information travel together through the same cranial nerve.

Current research tends to isolate the smallest parts of the brain to prove their existence and function, yet so often outcomes are driven less by the utility of the individual pieces of the neurological process than by the relatedness of one part to another, or the process of one through another. When considered together, it is this reliance and congruency that ultimately explains why a child enacts on his life through different behaviors. We need more science without a doubt, but it is equally important not to lose perspective on the impact of how different parts *rely on each other* and must *function together* to form the whole picture. Tomatis Sound training is a global program that affects the client in different ways. Children show varied responses in motor coordination, the ability to process sensory information, language changes, changes in attention, and also increased ability to cope with their strong emotions.

To isolate these global changes for the requirements of specific research is quite difficult, albeit not impossible.

More "Sound" Research Needed

Our own research now spans multiple years of pre- and post-testing that we hope to use to inspire researchers to support of this work. Sound training has not been approved by the FDA as a medical intervention in the U.S., and therefore families cannot obtain insurance reimbursement when they consider adding this methodology to their existing program. The Tomatis Method is no cure for anything, but should simply be seen as an adjunctive tool to typically known therapies and interventions. Sound training cannot and should not make any medical claims as it simply needs more rigorous research with rigid control study groups in order to be proven, although it certainly has stood the test of time since Dr. Tomatis created this work in the late fifties and sixties.

The Tomatis Approach

The Tomatis Method challenges the ear to listen with greater facility through the use of filtered and unfiltered sounds of Mozart, Gregorian chants, Strauss Waltzes, the client's own voice, and for the younger client—the mother's voice.

Dr. Tomatis believed in using mainly the work of Mozart in his program because Mozart composed many violin concertos (full of high frequency music), which create frequent bursts of high energy potential. Our brain is stimulated by high frequencies as much as lower frequencies are stated to calm our nervous system. Gregorian Chant is used mostly for calming and for its broad effect on the neuro-vegetative system (the autonomic system that regulates functions such as hunger and pain). The Vagus nerve (10th cranial nerve) considers our autonomic system (eat and sleep, etc.) and has short and long branches that interact directly with parts of the auditory system starting at the external parts of the ear. Strauss Waltzes are used for the timing capacity inherent to waltz music and mainly interact with the vestibular system.

It is important to again consider that the hearing process and the listening process are two different capacities of the human system. What you hear or cannot hear reflects the ability of the ear to physically register sound. Dr. Tomatis spoke much about the difference between hearing (the ability to discriminate a range of sounds) and listening (the active processing of the sounds through the brain). Listening is made effective by the speed at which a sound stimulus moves through the brain in order to cause the highest adaptive response, while analyzing content at the same time, which also involves the limbic system (emotional center). Sound training does not attempt to change the ability to physically hear; rather, it works to affect the *adaptive responses* in the brain neuronal systems. It would be overwhelming for me to detail the full Tomatis Effect for you, but I do hope to help you understand by highlighting just a few points to illustrate the different areas of its application and how it can affect change.

Hearing... But Not Listening

Parents frequently say they know their child knows and can respond to his or her name, but for some reason they sometimes need to call the child three or four times before getting a response. From the child's perspective, however, he may have registered the sound information, yet the process through the brain may be slower. The child may not have understood the tonal quality of the sounds or had difficulty interpreting it emotionally, and therefore did not respond. Or the child may have registered the information, but found it difficult to formulate an accurate response and, therefore, seemed to ignore it. Another possibility could be that the child had simply shut down his auditory system in order to focus on his preferred task, as background auditory information disturbs or distracts him.

The Elements of Tomatis

Bone/Air Conduction—Dr. Tomatis believed in using the body's natural adaptations to sound at all times, and for us as humans this is *air* and *bone conduction*. From the very first day of Tomatis Sound training, sound is processed through both air and bone conduction, including during vocal work when the participant listens to his own or his mother's voice.

Air conduction is what you use to listen when others are speaking, but when you listen to your own voice as you speak, you use a mixture of air and bone conduction. This is why your voice sounds different when you listen to it on a recording. You're accustomed to hearing the sound of your voice through air and bone conduction, yet your voicemail greeting may sound strange to you because you're hearing it only through air conduction. Bone conduction is what people with profound hearing loss use to give themselves some feedback as they speak. From the Electronic Ear, sound is transported via bone conduction through a conductor in the headphones at the top of the head, as well as air conduction through the headphones over the ears. Bone conduction travels ten times faster than air conduction and its vibratory effect very quickly stimulates the vestibular system. In fact, one of the first changes usually recognized by children and families is an improvement in body awareness, mainly due to the effects of bone conduction on the vestibular system. This increased body awareness is followed by increased calming experiences in the body, making the child or client more available to his surrounding environment.

Right/Left Ear—Whether you're right or left-handed, typically one hand serves as the dominant hand while the other serves in an assistive role. It surprises many people to know that our ears serve similar purposes. Dr. Tomatis (1991) wrote much about the fact that the left and right ears have different roles. The right ear is the *leading ear*. It has a defined preference for more high frequency sounds and has a more direct pathway to the larger language centers on the left side of the brain. The left ear is more directed to the sounds of the environment (the auditory space 360 degrees around us). Together the sound from the right and left ears form a unit of information regarding auditory space and focal attention, enabling us to register information in the background while maintaining focus on a person speaking. This aspect of *tuning* the integration of information from the right ear (focus) and left ear (background) is another strong feature of the Tomatis Sound training program.

Audio-Vocal Feedback—I remind the reader of the crucial component of *feedback*, a very important neurological foundation of development. It is through a neurological feedback loop that our bodies are enabled to complete an activity again. The audio-vocal work through a microphone is a very important feature of the feedback loop between the voice and the ear. A microphone is attached to the Electronic Ear, and not only are the music and words altered for the client to repeat, but the client's verbal feedback into the Electronic Ear is also altered. The child listens to his own voice in an altered state through his headphones. During the audio-vocal feedback portion of the program, younger clients may do back-and-forth nursery rhymes while others read, repeat phrases, or simply discuss a topic. The audio-vocal work is an important part of the Tomatis Effect as we steadily work through the different frequencies to be listened to, and therapeutically activate different channels of receiving and expressing verbal information.

Mother's Voice—From a developmental perspective, the ear and hearing mechanisms are mature by the third trimester of gestation (some books say as early as 4 to 5 months in utero), by which time the baby is able to listen to his mother's voice. Research has shown through many studies that a fetus is able to respond to sound, and more able to respond to high frequency sound rather than low frequency sound. Science has yet to explain why, but we do know that high frequencies correlate well with high energy; energy is certainly needed to complete the developmental process. There also is speculation that the high frequency preference may also be to drown out sounds from the mother's inner physical system, yet this has not been scientifically determined. At my center, I encourage this concept of listening to the mother's voice in listening sessions. Again, at first I allowed skepticism to win over the reasoning of Dr. Tomatis, and I completed most of the first year of work without the use of the mother's voice. But after more research, I started to include this process more fully.

For the mother's voice portion of therapy, the parent is asked to read the book *The Little Prince* for thirty minutes into a microphone while being recorded. The recording is then played to the child at a high frequency level of 8000Hz. In some cases, the effect on children with a diagnosis of pervasive developmental disorder has been quite amazing; yet in other cases we do not seen a recognizable difference. The outcome depends entirely on the individual, and I have not been able to pinpoint a specific profile that this work is most helpful for. The greatest and most rewarding effect is the intimacy and bonding experienced by the mother and child. Parents have reported on multiple occasions, that after the Tomatis sessions that included their voice, it was the first time their child spontaneously hugged them or asked to be hugged. The children exhibited a need for increased closeness and parents were awed by the experience. This does not happen consistently in all cases, but since we do not have exact science on every child's individual path of development, I err on the side of caution and add this component whenever I can.

Adding Tomatis Sound Training to Intervention

The Tomatis process is time intensive, very complicated, and entails a certain level of expertise to administer. The center-based Tomatis program at my center is a sixty-two-hour training period. Clients come to my center for three sets of sessions called *intensives*, which could vary in length from 15 days to 8-10 days. Between each set of sessions, families usually take a four-week break with no intervention. The break is built into each intensive to allow the child to internalize and adjust to the changes. This is referred to as *consolidation*. After the sixty-two hours is concluded, families can elect to take a two-to-three month break, and then return for a full re-assessment.

During their two-hour listening periods, clients also participate in an occupational therapy intervention program. The therapy component of the center-based approach is of great importance. Complementing auditory therapy with targeted sensory and occupational therapy strengthens the *quality* and *feedback* potential of the therapy and also supports the *relatedness* of the auditory system to the other processes being addressed. It does make the program more resource intensive as children work one-on-one with a therapist dedicated to them, but it has proven to be well worth it. Some might question that it may be the therapy rather than the Tomatis that makes all the difference, but we also complete therapy intensives without the Tomatis component and find lesser degrees of integration. Additionally, we do not do any speech language therapy as part of Tomatis Sound training, yet we observe increases in communication and verbal expression as regular outcomes.

In addition to center-based programs, a Tomatis Sound training home program called *Solisten*® is also enabling many families to access Tomatis in a long-distance way, no longer hampered by distance to a treatment center. At this time, the home Solisten program is completed over two fifteen-day intensives (sixty hours), also with a break of four weeks in-between. The Solisten home program is completed with no direct therapy intervention and has also yielded great results. Solisten has also made the Tomatis Method available to countries with fewer resources, as training and equipment continue to become more cost effective.

Matt's Journey Through Tomatis

Matt's sensory profile made him a good candidate for an occupational therapy program that included Tomatis Sound training. His body awareness was impacted by the difficulties he was experiencing in his auditory, vestibular, and visual systems; and since these are the foundational building blocks of development, we knew to start with a bottom-up approach. Every environment Matt was finding himself in was a situation of stress in the making. If we were going to expect participation in learning tasks or social reciprocity with peers, we were going to have to start with how his central nervous system was adapting to the different environments he participated in. His adaptation abilities needed to become a comfort zone so he could use his full attention to face the changing expectations of his learning and social environments.

It was difficult to see Matt retreat in his mind when his body was in a place of challenge, and this was a pattern no one wanted to see become a habit for him. We also knew that we did not want the fight, fright, and flight posture he erected in facing new situations to become a part of his social-emotional identity. Matt needed to be available to his learning environment, to us, and to every peer and adult he encountered in his life. If he continued to judge every situation with only two options—withdrawing or fighting—he would not be available for the richness of the emotional experiences that would enhance his self-identity, his ability to define himself, and his role in his family and the community at large.

He needed his stage to be reset. As we saw with the Twister mat experience, Matt had so much potential, and I was confident he would continue to lead the way for us to follow. But as expectations rise with each passing year, it would become increasingly difficult for him to lead at the pace required if he continued to be constricted by the threat of every environmental experience he encountered. Through the occupational therapy intensive with Tomatis Sound training, we would be working to give Matt a stronger connection to his own development by establishing a stronger foundation of body awareness, adaptation, and feedback. The goal was to enable him to experience life, not from a place of defensiveness, but from a place of comfort within himself (through improved body awareness) and his environment (through improved capacities for feedback and adaptation).

Headphone Adjustment

Lauren was concerned about Matt being able to keep the headphones on, a common concern shared by many families. Many children become overly vigilant in their ability to use their ears for the slightest change in their environmental space. The idea of something covering their ears and potentially taking away their protection is a threatening experience. Families often think the dislike of headphones or hats is due to a physical adaptation, but more frequently it's that they need to keep their ears open and geared to constantly take in the environment.

Some children go into overdrive with their sensitivity, so much so that they start to shut down their auditory system when they cannot keep constant surveillance. Other children are truly tactile defensive in terms of their heads being touched, and the use of headphones holds potential threat to this system as well. But the headphones we use are large, they sit comfortably over the ears, and children usually adapt within one or two days. Children soon learn that they can still gauge the environment and continue to hear everything they need to hear, even with the headphones on. The gated music also starts to work very quickly and the child begins to more easily attend to the new and novel changes, while a good dose of low frequency music adds a further calming effect.

When I explained to Lauren that this was a direction I thought we should go, she had many questions. Up until that point, she only had experience with the traditional mode of clinical therapy once or twice a week. I explained the facts of how I saw Matt's progress and potential, and tried to help her put her own emotions in perspective. This program was not a cure, it was not going to bring utopia, and it was not going to heal. We were basically going to attempt to set up a new foundation for central nervous system adaptation that would enhance all of Matt's future experiences, learning, and enjoyment of life. Though Lauren had no experience with this type of approach, she decided to go ahead with it; and when Matt was four years, two months old, he started his first day in Tomatis Sound training. Matt completed the Tomatis Sound training center-based program, as this was what was available at the time of his treatment. Following is a description of some of the progress he made.

Postural Control/Balance

Prone extension and supine flexion are the two muscle systems essential to maintaining efficient trunk control and all kinds of motor activities, including simply remaining seated. When Matt started the program, his ability to execute a prone extension response (Superman pose) was limited. He was able to lift his thighs for three seconds and his arms separately for twenty seconds, but he was not able to lift them both against gravity simultaneously. He was also unable to assume the supine flexion position (crunch) independently. During his second intensive, it was reported that he was then able to assume the supine flexion position, but still experienced difficulty planning the prone extension position. Both prone extension and supine flexion positions resolved by his last day of therapy, though he still needed to work on increasing his strength to sustain these positions suspended against gravity for age-appropriate levels of time. This enabled Matt to not need to use his T-stool anymore when he re-entered school in the Fall.

From the perspective of balance, initially Matt's one-foot standing balance was one second on each foot with his eyes closed. On the sixth day of the first intensive, Lauren reported that Matt rode a two-wheel scooter for the first time and maintained his balance all the way down the driveway. This was celebrated by his family as a big milestone for Matt, and quite rightly so. The improvements in postural control and balance would foster his ability to attend for longer periods, as well as his motivation to participate in class and join in more games with peers on the playground.

Eye-Hand Coordination

Upon initiation of his program, Matt was unable to catch a ball; he would shut his eyes and turn away from it. By the end of the first intensive, he was able to catch a medium-sized ball, and by the end of the third intensive, Matt was able to catch a ball ten times standing on both feet.

The reader is reminded that ocular motility is also an important consideration when considering a task that includes vision. In order to catch a ball, we need to use both eyes together to gauge depth perception as the ball comes toward us in space. In order to know when a ball is going to reach you, and how fast you should move in order to catch it, you have to develop a certain sense of grading. This grading guides your ability to correspond with the right amount of response to a stimulus given. Though it was difficult to assess this level of function formally with Matt, this was a fairly good indicator that his visual skills were steadily improving along with his motor skills. Matt's improvement in this area, tested by seemingly simple tasks such as catching a ball, boded well in setting up the foundation for visual-motor skills such as drawing and writing, as well as his ability to visually perceive his environment with the correct perception in terms of visual orientation. It also opened new possibilities in terms of participating in family sporting events and participating with peers on the playground.

Motor Planning/Praxis

One indicator of motor planning/sequencing is to ask a child to touch each finger to the thumb one at a time in both directions, starting with the index finger, progressing to the pinky and back to the index finger. In the beginning of his program Matt was unable to differentiate his fingers in sequential movement and would use his whole fist when modeled to use one finger or fingers in sequence. By the end of the third intensive, Matt's fine motor and bi-manual skills had improved significantly and he was able to manipulate each finger individually in a sequential way. This was quite exciting, as so many learning and school experiences in early life depend on the use of the hands in different craft and learning tasks. He would now be better able to use his hands in a nimble way, and not shy away from participating in these types of activities. Another hindrance to school performance was being removed.

On day twelve of the first intensive, it was reported that Matt was showing significant improvement in his swimming skills with notably decreased anxiety during his swimming lessons. He held onto the side of the pool, kicked independently, put his face into the water, and blew bubbles for the first time at the instructor's request. This increased physical ability is a frequent occurrence and often clearly visible in functional activities during the first intensive. This is mostly due to increased body awareness and the ability of the body to give itself feedback through each movement. The body literally starts to *feel* better as the improved ability to perceive how it is working enables it to become more fluid and increasingly more flexible. The interaction between the vestibular, touch (somatosensory), visual, and auditory systems in therapy enacts on how the body is perceived by the individual as a whole, and this is the true purpose of being integrated.

Matt was becoming able to feel secure about where his body was in space and this increased his ability to plan motor movements more effectively. These initial improvements continued to increase throughout the three intensives and resulted in a period of increased physical risk-taking behavior. He was not engaging in extreme or unsafe risk-taking, but he was attempting to do physical activities he had never tried before or would have avoided in the past. He also became much more tolerant of bathing and having his hair washed. All of these changes were joyful observations, because once a child is able to apply himself to new and novel experiences, he is actually indicating that the environment is no longer being perceived as threatening.

Speech, Language, and Emotional/Social Processing

Lauren wrote in her feedback that on the first day of therapy, Matt was serene after arriving at home and happy the rest of the day. But during the morning before his second day, Matt experienced a major meltdown. He lay on the floor, screaming, and pounding his feet on the wall. He was not prone to outbursts like this, but when they did happen, it was usually later in the day due to being tired. He recovered quickly though, and after some cuddling with Mom, he was ready for another day.

On day seven, Matt experienced another meltdown and could not regulate himself into calmness at the swimming pool. On day eight, he became more irritable and was not as talkative as before; and on day eleven, he became crankier and even a little aggressive toward his younger sister. Matt was making significant physical gains, though he remained somewhat aggressive toward his younger sister. In retrospect, we concluded that the increased energy resulting from therapy was somewhat pent up and he had not yet matured a way to expend it. He was frustrated, he needed something or somebody to take it out on, and his younger sister was the easiest target.

It is also of note to remember that children invest in their systems being a certain way, even if it is not at the highest level of adaptivity. Matt was making strong leaps forward in many directions, feeling the effects of change in his body, and he needed to find a place of reset so he could effectively use it as his new comfort zone—*his new normal*. This is an unsettling process for many, and as much as we celebrate the positive changes, we have to be very supportive of the child and family as this point in progress is reached.

At the initial interview of his third intensive, Lauren reported that Matt showed an increased ability to socialize with his sisters and an increased initiation of play. His play interests were diversifying and he was more *with the family* in the moment. He experienced no meltdowns during this intensive. Matt was coming together in his sensory adaptation to the world which enabled him to want to experience life more fully. Though the emotional circumstance of fright and flight are with us our entire lives, Matt was in a better position to deal with the environment and be more open to the learning and social situations of his daily experiences. The emotionality and fluctuations in irritability levels Matt experienced are quite consistent, and occur frequently when both children and adults go through the program.

While a child is working through a growth leap in one area, another area often shows the effect of stress as the child tries to hold it together while allowing the maturation to take place. When these intensive programs diffuse barriers that long stood in the way of development, a child often experiences a rush of growth in several areas at once. With the roadblocks removed, the child can feel stress initially and turn to (or return to) things that make him feel safe. This return to safe habits is sometimes viewed as regression. Without understanding that this is a normal reaction, parents misinterpret this occurrence as if the child has lost something that was previously gained. What looks like regression is only the child's way of retreating and grounding himself in a place of safety (according to his perception), while changes occur in other developmental areas.

I have never witnessed a true regression, though people do tend to use this phrase as soon as they see anything that might look like it. Parents are especially prone to use the term mostly because of their fear of it. I always ask families to remember that the process of development is a very complex and multi-faceted phenomenon. Systems are bound to affect one another at different rates of speed and progress. Once parents realize what they are looking at, and when they look at the whole picture, they are more relaxed about the changes they see. In turn, letting go of their fear also helps the child in his experience of his own anxiety.

Autonomic Functions

During the first intensive, Matt struggled with some sleeping difficulties, decreased appetite, and bowel changes. He would sometimes awake in the early hours of the morning, laughing aloud in his bed. These autonomic experiences are not unusual. Autonomic functions are frequently affected during the stimulation period because of adjustments in the cranial nerve, more specifically, the Vagus nerve, which is responsible for these functions. These difficulties are typically short, temporary, and mostly only occur during the stimulation period. Other than experiencing some nausea on the first day of his third intensive, we did not see the autonomic symptoms as intensely as during the first intensive, and all was well by the end of the third intensive.

Repetitive Behavior

During the first intensive especially, Matt insisted on wanting to go outside to the same spot in his yard and repetitively pushed a two-foot aluminum pole into the ground, step back, and scan it visually up and down. This troubled Lauren, as she had seen him do this before but not to such an extent. Most repetitive behaviors that may puzzle us do have a calming effect on the child exhibiting the behavior; and just because they don't make sense to us doesn't mean they have no function for the child.

Lauren noted that in Matt's early years, he was inexplicably drawn to circles and round objects. This attraction seemed to then change from circular objects to vertical lines. Even as he became school age, Matt would visually focus on vertical lines in the environment such as the corner of a wall or the frame of a window or door. He would find a vertical line and follow it up and down with his eyes.

It took us several years to figure out that this visual tracking was his way of regulating himself when trying to focus and concentrate in multisensory environments, and this was why he scanned the bar during his first Tomatis intensive. There was also a period during the first intensive when Matt kept asking his sister the same question over and over. This was another expression of wanting *sameness* to quell the anxiety caused by the changes he was experiencing inside his body. Sameness equals comfort zone for all of us, but most especially for children who have difficulty dealing with how their bodies are feeling and experiencing their environments.

Communication

During Matt's first intensive, he became more talkative and entertained himself with much singing and humming. He became babbly for a period of time, and sometimes spoke in half-sentences that did not make sense. This loss of sentence structure is another occurrence observed from time to time, and is usually followed by an increased ability to use language more spontaneously and fluently. His Floortime practitioner at home reported increased language during their sessions with lots of chattiness during this first intensive.

At the initial interview of the second intensive, Lauren reported that the physical gains remained in place as they were at the end of the first intensive. He had calmed down considerably and was talking incessantly. On the first day of his second intensive, he showed a definite increased use of language as observed by his therapist. Though we do not do speech and language therapy in these intensive programs, we frequently observe these communication/language bursts in children. We are not sure if the language was already there and was simply unveiled by removing the hindrances posed by the environmental adaptation, or if the rhythmicity and timing caused by the inherent aspects of the music supported new language development. It could also be a combination of both; sufficient to say, Matt really lurched forward in this regard.

By the third intensive, Matt was exhibiting much improvement in his command over language, initiating conversation spontaneously, even introducing himself in speech on multiple occasions. He ended the intensive program happy and talkative, and there were no re-occurrences of the aggressive tendencies toward his sister as noted during his first intensive.

All in all, Matt emerged from his three-month program a fluidly verbal, spontaneous little boy who wanted to be more connected to play, school, and family activities. He still had work to do to increase his postural control, motor planning, execution, play, and social-emotional skills, but Matt was now a happier boy, ready to engage with the world and more able to deal with the influx of incoming information through his sensory systems. We were now poised to really start working on further solidifying the different levels of DIR. More importantly, Matt was now ready to move toward working on his social-emotional identity as his body identity had become more defined. With this progress, an enormous bridge had been built for Matt to begin working on the emotional and symbolic capacities needed to solidify levels four, five, and six of the comprehensive DIR work.

"Dealing with Life" with a Lighter Spirit

In follow up consultations with parents, I hear one consistent theme with regard to Tomatis Sound training. Yes, parents are quite happy with all of the physical changes Tomatis brings, but what I hear parents say most is that their child "is just able to *deal* with life more easily." Parents often describe their child as simply having a "lighter spirit" after Tomatis Sound training, and with this lighter spirit comes the confidence and agility to move through development with more motivation and purpose. Tomatis may not be a miracle cure, but parents agree, its by-products are a beautiful thing to behold.

I encourage you to go to www.tomatis.com and to www.tomatisorganization.org to read more about research that has been completed over the years. Yes, we do need more research, and hopefully our data will inspire a researcher to take it on as a project of interest. Until that time, I am thankful to the many families who have placed their trust in me over the years, and I am hopeful to continue this important work of merging different modalities into one program to give the child a stronger foothold in all the richness life has to offer. This was certainly the case for Matt.

"Level five is a place where children really need to experience all the emotional stops—including and especially the negative ones."

Chapter 11

Cultivating Emotional Growth and Self-Concept

Now four years old and with a full year of preschool under his belt, Matty began his second year of preschool after a great summer of summer camp, sound therapy at Maude's center, and continued Floortime sessions with Karen. As August came to an end, I was starting to see new sparks of confidence and curiosity, and he had become much more agile in general. Buckling him into his seatbelt on the bus that first day of school, I was nervous about what the first weeks would bring with a new teacher in a new classroom, but I also knew he was returning to a well-focused IEP and Maude's guidance. Looking back, I now see what an exceptional situation Matty really had that year. He literally lived in a DIR bubble at home and at school. I truly believe that this early intervention focus on *development* as much as academics was key to allowing him to shape himself into the more complete child he has ultimately become.

Embracing a Process Culture

Matty and his younger sister were now in preschool, and I was working just a few miles away. Work continued to give me the self-time I needed and the connections I drew from a business perspective kept me tethered to logic when my emotions and frustrations took off. The *process over product* connection is a perfect example of one of these frustrations that can just make me nuts if I let myself dwell on it for too long.

When it comes to education and the raising of our children, we as a society have become alarmingly imbalanced. Parents and the education system have a distressing addiction to *product*. Mine is a generation of *product parents* who want to see their children as glossy-covered annual reports spouting top grades and extracurricular highlights—but parents and educators could learn a thing or two from business.

When the *balanced scorecard* methodology became popular in the 1990s, corporate executives were encouraged to lead with a more balanced view of goals by taking strategic and non-financial performance into consideration as factors of success. Learning from the balanced scorecard approach, companies immediately started adding non-financial categories to their lists of performance measurements—things such as "customer, process, learning, and growth." *(Balanced Scorecard Institute)* It strikes me that, almost verbatim, I was striving for those same goals for Matty. Just substitute "purpose" for customer (after all, the customer really is sole purpose for a company's existence), and there you have it—purpose, process, learning, and growth. If corporate America can right itself toward a more balanced focus, why can't our education system? Oh, how our children would thrive if we could create a culture of process rather than our infatuation with product. If we did, we'd probably see that it's not nearly as hard as we think. Fortunately, children possess an intrinsic magic the corporate world does not. It's called childhood development. When you cultivate a child's connection to *purpose and process*, learning and growth flourish naturally.

One thing I've learned is that embracing process in a product world is an art. Like an artist, you need a mix of defiance, passion, patience, and courage to dismiss the socially expected products (the test scores, the Ws in the win column, or the number of friends and followers). Teachers know the value of process. They just get too little time to work on it given the warp speed of today's curriculums. It's a reality I can't change, but hopefully, a broader understanding of how this unbalanced perspective is impacting our children's development will begin to redefine and redirect our expectations.

The Value of One Word... How

In just about all of Matty's early IEPs, there was always an objective that read something like: "Matty will improve his ability to answer '*Wh*' questions pertaining to stories and other classroom content." Everyone's inclination when assessing a child's understanding is to begin asking who, what, where, and when questions related to the subject being taught. These '*Wh*' questions are important, but not nearly as important as the *how* questions that should be asked.

Who, what, where, and when questions assess recall; *how* questions invoke processing and problem-solving. When you ask a child *how* he is going to make a bridge between two parts of his landscape, he has to explain the steps he needs to follow, involving a beginning, middle, and end. This is the more concrete building block of subsequent *why* questions which involve abstract thinking.

In those early IEPs, I always made it a point to change the "*wh*" questions goal to read "*how and 'wh' questions.*" It's a small change but it's an easy way to keep the focus on process.

No Express Lane to Level Five

Matty had a great first day of school and never looked back. In mid-September, Maude hosted another group training session where she explained that our focus would be solidifying level three (circles of communication), scaffolding level four (elaborating on ideas and building bridges between ideas), and preparing for level five (emotional ideas). We discussed how as Matty's ability to regulate himself improved, so too would his ability to open and close circles of communication reciprocally during play. For now, it was a fairly easy formula. We should create opportunities for Matty to initiate and close circles of communication while fostering opportunities for new ideas and building bridges between ideas, and carefully expose him to new novel situations that would allow him to practice the problem-solving process.

I remember Maude saying how there is no express lane through level five, and that it would be vitally important to allow Matty to take his time through this level. "Level five is a place where children really need to experience all the emotional stops—including and especially the negative ones," she said. We talked about how Matty had started to show anger and frustration in Floortime sessions. Maude asked us to just watch Matty for the next couple of weeks to see exactly how he dealt with negative emotion.

"What I want you to observe is how Matt physically reacts to emotion, not just his own, but the emotions of others. What does he do when his sisters or classmates squabble or when someone gets disciplined? What does he say if anything? What does he do with his eyes, his face, his body? I'm not as interested in his own emotional reactions as I am in his reaction to others' emotions."

This fly-on-the-wall approach had taught me so much about Matty's sensory world a couple of years earlier, and I had no doubt this would now be a real eye-opener into his emotional world. As time would soon tell, going through the emotional realities of level five would turn out to be a bumpier ride than I expected, but one well worth it.

At our next meeting, Maude started us on a path to prepare for the emotional level. I had been watching Matty for a few weeks with some interesting revelations. I saw that when it came to anger and sadness, Matty would physically turn his body away from the emotions of others. Admittedly, there were a few times when I allowed things to escalate between his sisters just to see what his reaction would be. I saw that Matty would physically orient his body so he was never directly facing the situation. I probably never noticed it before because it was so subtle, yet it was absolutely consistent. Without exception, every time a tide of emotion would start to roll in, his first reaction was purely physical and almost instinctual. He literally *could not face* negative emotion.

Without Question

As I explained my observations to the team, Karen mentioned seeing the same reactions during play and his classroom teacher noted similar observations in class and circle time when reading stories with emotional content. In school activities, when the class would sit on the floor at circle time he would position his body at an angle, almost like a door ajar, prepared for easy retreat. I half expected Maude and Karen to detour off into one of their Floortime strategy discussions on how to foster emotional growth through play, but Maude's next recommendation took us all by surprise.

"No more questions," she said as we all looked at her with a bit of a blank stare. "When Matt physically turns away from emotion, he is literally using his body as a wall. It is a wall of anxiety. Anxiety means dysregulation, and dysregulation means he's right back at level one. All children have anxiety and they retreat a little as they embark on new developmental levels. Matt is no different," Maude explained, "our goal now has to be to reduce his anxiety, keep him regulated, and allow him to begin to experience emotional concepts more fully because he will be doing so from a more regulated place."

Maude explained that an effective way to keep anxiety in check is to simply stop asking questions. "Questions equal anxiety, not just for Matt, but for many children. They are laden with a host of difficult processing skills," she said. "At the very least, a single question involves receptive language and auditory processing, problem-solving, sequencing, and the communication skills to verbalize a response." We left the meeting with one immediate goal in mind. We were to simply try to reduce anxiety so Matty didn't retreat back to level one when faced with challenging emotional situations.

So for the next month or two we all tried to live life in the question-free zone. In the beginning it was much harder than I expected. It made me realize just how much of the communicating we do with children is in the form of a question. I found that I was as guilty as anyone of pummeling my kids with questions that I soon realized were really just a rapid fire waste of oxygen. I asked questions to obtain information when 90 percent of the time the answer was, "I don't know." I asked questions because I thought it was helping them process something they were trying to learn, when 90 percent of the time I was doing nothing more than interrupting their own processing abilities. I also found that most of the questions I asked were purely for my benefit to make me feel good that I was being listened to and understood.

"Questions are habitual and you just may be surprised how hard of a habit it is to break," Maude warned, "but you don't have to go cold-turkey, just start with *commenting*. When you are tempted to ask a question, stop yourself, and replace the question with a simple comment." She suggested that when there is a natural pause and we feel we must say something, just say "hmm" or "wow" and leave it at that. "And if you don't know what to say, say nothing at all. Everything else about your body language and physical presence will convey your connection in the moment."

She explained that Matty would not interpret our silence as a lack of interest. "Actually the opposite is true," she said, "I think you'll find fewer questions will actually increase your unspoken connection." And she was right.

Not asking questions helped me see how my verbal share of our interactions was actually more of a distraction and detraction than any kind of contribution. Silence really was golden. I became more comfortable with being silent and simply saying nothing. And I found that the more I kept quiet, the more Matty started to fill in the gaps. I found that in many of our conversations, he really did have more to say, and that my verbal interruptions got in the way of him expressing his entire thought.

But it didn't all happen at once. Days and weeks of replacing questions with silence and comments began to pay off in ways I hadn't expected. Matty was physically orienting his body in a more direct way. He began to face himself more square-shouldered with the whole front of his body exposed. It also seemed to up the level of respect and trust in his relationships—at least I know it did with me. There was a spark of esteem I hadn't seen, and a connection of respect I hadn't known was missing. I started to see a tender closeness that simply said, "thank you for dignifying who I am."

Shaking the Wire

Matty lives on a tightrope and I learned that for him, asking questions is like shaking the wire he so tenuously clings to for balance. During this time, I also learned that not all questions were inherently bad for him. I learned the nuances between the type of questions that create stress and the questions that give him power when challenged by a new process or environment.

For example, rather that asking, "Are you ready to go get a haircut?" which was definitely not a preferred activity and would typically do nothing more than elicit total silence or an emphatic, "No," followed by a lot of anxiety, I found that establishing the dreaded fact up front and using simple this or that questions to baby step him through the activity actually helped reduce his anxiety.

I would say something like, "We're going to get a haircut in a little while; do you want to wear a jacket or a sweatshirt?" followed by, "Do you want to bring juice or water? Do you think you'll pick a red lollipop or an orange one when you're done?" and so on all the way to the barber shop and through the haircut. I didn't bombard him, but as I saw the stress beginning to build I would give him simple limited choice questions to help him feel in control of how the activity was experienced. By helping him feel more in control of the process, his anxiety over the experience began to fade.

Opening the Door to Emotional Processing

Along with a more relaxed spirit, Matty was also feeling the benefits of a new level of postural control, physical balance, and motor skills. Days of belly rides on a scooter board through the school halls were paying off as he was more able to physically attend to the demands of sitting in circle and engaging in table-top activities for longer periods of time. With better body awareness, postural control, and balance, his body positioning was more direct and confident, and he was beginning to seem less fragile in his relationship with the emotional environment.

I wasn't the only one to notice changes, Karen and his whole team were seeing good things too. As Matty's anxiety began to decrease, Maude recommended we slowly begin exposing Matty to all types of emotions in all aspects of his life. Books read in circle time, Floortime play schemes, and home conversations were injected with emotional content of all types. Fear, anger, frustration, disappointment, sadness, surprise, and loneliness were woven into the fabric of his day just as much as happiness. Negative emotions definitely got as much air play, if not more than positive ones. In the realm of human emotions, there are simply more negative ones than positive ones, and there are more words to describe the nuances between negative emotions. They all make you feel bad, but in different ways. Negative emotions are also typically the result of circumstances beyond one's control. For kids whose connection to the environment is so dependent on control, dwelling in the unpleasant feelings caused by something you can't control is not something welcomed with open arms.

Throughout the fall of Matty's final year of preschool, we were able to help foster a decrease in Matty's anxiety level. Floortime focus was now on level four, where Matty was opening and closing circles of communication, practicing problem-solving and process understanding, elaborating on new ideas, and building bridges between ideas, all the while being thoughtfully exposed to all types of emotions to build the foundation for level five and six work on emotional ideas.

As with all children, you just never know when and where development is going to hit. It would be so much easier if a child's developmental milestones were as easy to read as some of the physical ones. If only kids would start drooling and get rashes on their cheeks and chins as they are about to enter a new developmental level. The eruption of first emotions are just not as easy to predict as the eruption of a first tooth. But what I've learned from Matty is that the value of the bond and nurturing we give our six- month-olds as we rock them in our laps while they gnaw on a teething toy doesn't begin to compare to the emotional connection of holding their hand and walking them through the most difficult emotional experiences of their development.

One Sad and Scary Load of Laundry

Doing laundry was always my place of peace, a place for me to regroup emotionally from the stress of the day. It's ironic that our laundry room would also become the place for Matty to deal with his first throes of negative emotion. One Saturday in late fall, when Matty was four and a half, one of my kids spilled juice on his bed. I threw his sheets in to be washed and went back to doing whatever I was doing. I walked by our laundry room a couple of times and noticed Matty sitting there watching the front-load washer. At first I thought he was mesmerized by the spinning laundry, but as I looked closer—I saw he was crying.

The emotion I saw on his face was the same I had seen a few years earlier when he so deeply reacted to the classical music. It was the type of moment I knew just shouldn't be hindered. I stood behind him for a minute or two; he didn't know I was there. I watched him as he watched his sheets and pillow cases turning and tangling in the suds. Standing in the doorway behind him, it dawned on me that Matty had probably never seen his bed stripped without sheets, as I usually did the sheets while he was at school. And he certainly had never seen his sheets being mangled in the washing machine.

Not sure what to do, I relied on what I had practiced so much in recent months—the art of saying nothing. Matty sat like a pretzel, leaning forward with his elbows resting on his knees. As the washer stopped to soak for a bit, he must have sensed my presence. He didn't turn to look at me, but just lowered his head. As he looked down a giant tear fell from his eye, hitting his jeans, never touching his cheek. I slowly sat to his left. I said nothing, and although my first instinct was to put my arm around him, I didn't. Somehow I wanted to respect his independence in dealing with the moment. I followed his lead, sitting like a pretzel, elbows to knees. We watched. Seconds turned into a minute and I could sense him getting more upset. I wasn't sure whether he was sad or scared—I think it was a little of both. To you and me, they were linens. To Matty, they were a sense of sameness and tactile comfort, a familiar place for quiet and regulation. And now they were under assault.

I felt myself overwhelmed with the same power of his emotions, just as I had felt when I saw the sadness the Mozart music stirred in him a few years earlier. I don't know why, but tears filled my eyes. Maybe, as a mother, I was overcome seeing my child so gripped by emotion, but my reaction was real. Matty sensed my genuine empathy. We sat together in silence. I wondered how long we would sit, but I was determined to allow him whatever time he needed to get himself through it. I found myself wanting to jump in with an end game, some diversionary suggestion like "the sheets are almost done, they will be okay; do you want to come downstairs and have some pretzels?" It was really hard to forfeit control of the situation to Matty, but the longer we sat, the stronger I felt that that he needed to go the distance of this emotional experience on his own.

I didn't know how long it would go on. The silence, the tears, and the look of fear. With every minute that passed, I couldn't sense if the tide of his emotions was coming in or going out. It was very unsettling. As a parent, isn't my role to comfort and protect? But I somehow knew in that moment, Matty needed something different. He needed me to be his strength in helping him navigate this scary, somber moment on his own. And my presence and my silence were enough.

After about five minutes of washing and a few more minutes of soaking, Matty looked closer, trying to find the sheets as they disappeared during the spin cycle.

"Where are they?" he asked with a scared, yet curious tone.

"They're up on the walls. They stick to the walls while the water drains. Then when they're done spinning, I'll put them in the dryer," I said.

Another minute passed.

Will they be warm in the dryer?" he asked.

"They sure will," was all I said, and he said nothing else until the machine beeped.

"That means they're done," I said, "I'll put them in the dryer and then back on your bed."

"Okay," he said.

"Do you want to help me put them in the dryer?" I asked.

"Not today," he replied.

We both stood up so I could open the washer door. As I bent over to reach for the sheets, he snuck behind me and was gone. He went downstairs and didn't come back up until later that night. I was curious to see what he would say when he walked back into his room to see his bed all made—but he said nothing. He went to bed as if nothing had happened. Had I not wandered past the laundry room and noticed him sitting in front of the washer that day, I likely would never have known of the depth of that experience for him. I wonder how many other moments I haven't happened upon… moments he's chartered alone.

Of all the laundry I've done in my life, I never dreamed one load could teach me so much. I saw the depth of Matty's emotional capacities and understood why he worked so hard to avoid them. It didn't matter what the trigger was, it only mattered that he had experienced something that unleashed a rush of genuine sadness and fear, and that he had the courage to take himself through it. I learned that sometimes it comes down to courage, his and mine, to make emotional moments matter most. We were both charting through unfamiliar and uncomfortable territory that day. Matty felt emotions he'd never felt, and I felt inadequate in not knowing how to handle it or when it would end. I felt the depth of the vulnerability he lives with every day, wanting to control the environment and the outcome, yet not having the capacity to do so. Even now, it's still unnerving for me to relinquish control of the end game and not know how or when a situation like this will end. But I now know the value of doing so.

This is but one moment that helped Matty cultivate a deeper range of experience with negative emotions. Through the years there have been other moments like this—always unpredictable and sometimes inconvenient. Without a doubt, turning an emotional moment over to Matty or any one of my children means not knowing how or when they'll get to the other side of it. It can be two minutes away or twenty minutes away. I can always spare the two, but only sometimes can I afford the twenty. I can't accommodate every opportunity that crops up and I sometimes have to take control, cut it short and define an end game. At first I thought it wasn't right to be erratic. After all, consistency is the golden rule of parenting, isn't it? And consistency and predictability are the things Matty clings to so dearly. But I realized that the value of ushering these emotional experiences whenever I can far outweighs the consistency of doing so at every opportunity. And frankly, I've learned that I burdened myself more than necessary with my sensitivity to being inconsistent. In time I realized—my kids never really noticed anyway.

As I reflect now, I understand how empowering it has been to allow Matty to fully experience negative emotions. Of all the time I give to my kids, no time is more painful and meaningful than the time I spend taking them through the many negative emotions they face during childhood. Whether it's with Matty or my girls, it never gets any easier to suppress my instincts to end the game and stop the pain. That's the quickest road to an easy resolution. But when the time and opportunity are there, I'm there. I sit with them, usually saying very little. It may sound unkind to allow children to feel sadness, frustration, and disappointment without saying a word, but I've learned that saying nothing is ultimately more acknowledging than any hollow response ever could be.

Terrible Twos with a Twist

Through the end of fall and winter break, Matty was cruising. His daily log described play where he brought emotion into play schemes and he was doing better at problem-solving involving the emotions of others during play. He would comfort the therapists when they were sad and negotiate when they were angry. Since returning to school in September, he seemed to change from within. He was just better able to deal with the environment. He was now more open, literally. He was now facing life with shoulders squared, not at an angle always prepared for the retreat. His face was lighter and he smiled more. He reminded me of a typical young toddler with not a care in the world.

He handled the rush of the Christmas holiday more easily than I'd ever seen and he had new interest in things he hadn't shown interest in before. He was starting to get into things in ways he hadn't before; but he wasn't just getting into things for the sake of it, he now had a purpose. Most times he was trying to help around the house. He would take wet clothes out of the dryer and put them on my bed, he would take clean clothes out of drawers and put them into the dryer, or he would turn the oven off while dinner was still cooking. He even organized a home fire drill, making everyone get their coats on, line up behind him, and walk quietly while he held an electric toothbrush to simulate the fire alarm.

At our first meeting with Maude in February, I had much to share. I described how Matty had become the two-year-old he never was. Only now he was a two-year-old with a purpose. We talked and laughed about how patience will be in high order while he works out the whole *connecting purpose to intent* thing. I shared the laundry room story and Karen shared some emotional successes he'd had during school. I mentioned that although Matty was worlds' happier, he had also started screaming in anger and frustration, much like a two-year-old. "He mostly just screams in the direction of whoever he is annoyed by at the time," I shared. "Sometimes he will say, 'I want to scream inside,' or 'I want to kick the wall.'"

Maude explained that he was now allowing himself to feel these emotions but he didn't quite know what do with them, and that any anger he was now feeling was being compounded by the frustration of not knowing how to channel it. We talked about how I couldn't allow Matty to express his emotions in ways that were inappropriate or unacceptable for my other children to deal with them. I couldn't allow Matty to scream and kick the wall when his sisters were not permitted to do the same. I tried to get him to jump on the trampoline but it didn't seem to do the trick. I had to help Matty release his anger in a way that worked within the structure of our household.

"I wish I had a punching bag hanging from the ceiling," I said jokingly, "then he could just smash away at the thing until he got it all out of his system."

"Well," Maude said, "why don't you improvise with a pillow? Find a special pillow he can use to release his anger. Not his regular pillow that he sleeps with, but a special *angry pillow*. It's very important for him to know he can exhaust those feelings and that he has the ability to do it on his own."

I took that suggestion and the next time Matty was overwhelmed with anger and frustration I took him up to his bedroom and closed the door. I grabbed a spare pillow, sat on his bed, held it in front of me, and told him he was allowed to hit the pillow to get the angry feelings out. I explained that he wouldn't be hurting me and that I wanted him to do it. He reluctantly hit the pillow a few times, but after a few good blows he really started to let fists fly. After he tired himself out, I explained to him that it's okay to feel angry and frustrated sometimes, and that it's good to find a way to let the anger out of your body. After he calmed down, I told him we can find a special pillow that he can keep in his room to use whenever he wants. We went to Target and he picked out a blue suede pillow that he creatively named, "Blue Pillow." We still have Blue Pillow. Although it's now stained, mended, and has lost some of its filling, Blue Pillow is still a dependable place for venting and comfort when Matty's emotions get the best of him.

Stuck on the Platform

I sometimes feel like the train carrying the typical school experience will forever elude Matty. Just when he seems to catch up and get close to climbing aboard, expectations rise and the train starts to pull away again. Matty always seems to be left standing on the platform.

I started to feel this way in the spring when Matty was turning five. He had done so much work and made so much progress in all the areas we'd hoped, especially in the area of emotional growth—but then came *homework*. Just after Spring break, Matty began to get homework assignments. They were no big deal, inconsequential busy work for other preschoolers, but Matty was adamant about not doing it. I was still living with a two-year-old in some ways and now we were upping the expectations to those of a five-year-old. Matty decided he wanted no part of it. With a combination of his two-year-old obstinance and his newfound approaches to anger management, Matty simply refused to have any part of doing schoolwork at home.

I soon found myself in a corner I am now all too familiar with. I was stuck in the position of having to ask something of my child that in my gut I knew was the wrong thing to demand. You see, I don't think homework for four-year-olds (or even five-, six-, and seven-year-olds) is necessary. As a matter of fact, I think it can sometimes do more harm than good when children aren't developmentally ready for it. This was the case with Matty and I struggled with how to deal with it. I know the homework being assigned was just part of the curriculum and I know the teacher had every honest intention of developing good habits going into kindergarten. But what I think is often missed is that young children still need the compartmentalization of home and school. I found myself between a rock and a hard place because I was being asked to encourage a behavior in my child that I disagreed with. I was also frustrated by the fact that some of the developmental momentum Matty had recently gained would be wasted on priorities I didn't buy into. This would be the beginning of an internal battle I would struggle with for years to come.

Homework is Not for "Home"

I very often find myself stuck in the dilemma of deciding how to handle certain expectations; sometimes the expectation is entirely wrong, but mostly it's that the timing is not right. Homework is just one example. From preschool and well into second grade, Matty adamantly rejected the notion of homework. He would pull out every trick in the book—diversion, negotiation, sabotage—to avoid bringing school work into our home. I knew he wasn't ready for it. I appreciate early intervention and promoting good habits, I really do. But I just knew in my gut that his evasion was rooted in avoidance, not deviance. He just did not want to bring school into the safe harbor of home until he was ready for it. He had taught me that the walls he builds are temporary, and he proved it as I watched him dismantle the fortress he built against negative emotions. All he needed was time. I knew this too was developmental and that he would put the pieces together to one day allow his two worlds to coexist, just not yet. But curriculum and classroom behavior plans think differently. They want it done on their terms and on their schedule.

What I knew in my gut was that it came down to security and motivation. Matty was simply not ready to allow school to invade his home for some reason. I didn't know the reason, but I had to trust and respect it as a need, not a behavior. It was sometimes difficult to blindly protect this wall until he decided to let it fall. I had other children who were very cooperative in getting homework done, and I often had to create the illusion that Matty was doing more homework than he really was just for their benefit. It wasn't until well into second grade that Matty started to come to the place where he was ready to disarm himself against homework. And on the third day of third grade he came home from school, told me had homework, took out his books and did his work with pride. Poof! The wall had disappeared.

"Factor Parenting" vs. "Product Parenting"

I parent by a factor of five. I have no other choice. Every demand placed on me gets multiplied by a factor of five as soon as it crosses my threshold. The thirty minutes of homework assigned to my elementary schoolers is 150 minutes the moment it comes out of our backpacks, and the $10 donation to the fundraiser is $50 before I reach for my checkbook. By definition, I am set up for failure every day. Every demand gets cranked through the factor of five algorithm and the result is always the same. At best, I'm half engaged with any one of my children's homework, and not a day goes by when I don't miss something or someone entirely.

In many ways, factor parenting is the antithesis of product parenting. Product parenting can afford the luxury of the time and attention needed to create the best *whatever* in the entire class. I don't have that extra overhead to spare. I am forced to triage expectations to focus on only the most critical, highest value aspect of a demand, and let the rest go. I barely have the bandwidth to get through nightly homework, and I don't have the time to devote to constructing award-winning dioramas. So I focus on process. I target the *how* in homework. I help my kids step through how they are going to break an assignment into steps and let the end product be what it is.

It's actually quite simple... give them the *how* and get out of their way.

On to the Big Leagues

In June, Matty graduated from preschool. What a ride so far. At five years old, he had already taught me so much. He taught me about sensory, the developmental perspective, and the depth of his emotional courage. He gave me the courage to trust my gut, and the patience to trust his ability to grow. So much learned from a child who said so little. But now we needed to start getting ready for the big leagues. Kindergarten was three months away and I was about to make a drastic decision. At the time, I wanted to be right, yet it would only take weeks to realize I was wrong, and it would take months for Matty to get back on course. Matty would go through a lot during this first year of school, most of it by my doing. But it would be his courage that would get him through this time, not mine.

Matty had lived a sheltered life in preschool with a safety net of teachers and therapists who understood him, respected him, and knew how to help him grow. He had made such great strides over the past two years, but now we were being thrown into the big and scary world of kindergarten, with much higher expectations, much less support, and all new peers. My instinct to protect went into high gear. Matty's three older sisters were now in Catholic school, and I wanted him to have the opportunity to learn and grow alongside them. And I didn't want to sell him short by assuming he couldn't. Matty thrived on structure and I convinced myself that the soft-soled environment of Catholic school and protection of his sisters would be enough to meet his needs. So in August, just weeks before his first day of kindergarten, we moved Matty from public school to join his sisters in Catholic school.

Come September, I put him in a uniform and put him on a bus to be with his sisters. We weren't totally severed from working with Karen, as Matty would still have sessions with her in the afternoons. But he would be completely on his own for morning kindergarten at the Catholic school in a class with twenty students, one teacher, and no educational assistants. I knew to expect anxiety, but was I blindsided by how fragile he almost instantly became. I felt like I sent my five-year-old off to school in the morning and a three-year-old came home in the afternoon. He was stressed. A year earlier, it had taken him just one day to adjust. Now, over a month into school, he was still worrying about going to school every waking moment of every day. He was not cooperating to do homework, telling me "I don't want to listen to directions," and "This book is for school; this is not for home." When he did capitulate, it was never completely. For writing homework, he would deliberately write his letters twice the size of the lines, or so tiny you couldn't even read them. He would do math sheets with every answer being purposely off by one.

His stress level was off the charts and there was no one to blame but me. He was constantly dysregulated, and any momentum he'd gained in the past year seemed to come to a grinding halt. In school he was a lingerer, always at the back of the line, always last to come out of the bathroom, and always lagging behind. Every day he would tell me he didn't want to go to school, saying, "I don't feel good," and he talked constantly about being a baby.

"I want to be a one-year-old," he would say as he grabbed a water bottle, wanting to sit in my lap. Several times a day he would tell me, "I want to be a baby bird," and made chirping sounds in his room at night.

I'd always told myself that it would be my responsibility to raise the bar and Matty would be the one to tell me when I had raised it too high. I just wasn't prepared for that to actually happen. It was painful.

By the end of October, I was almost there in my decision to move him back to public school when one conversation with Matty sealed the deal. On a Saturday morning just before Halloween, we were at home in the kitchen. Matty wrote on his sister's pumpkin drawing and she was upset. I showed Matty the drawing and told him his sister was feeling sad and angry because he wrote on her pumpkin picture. Matty looked instantly and deeply wounded. He suddenly became very sad, his eyes filled with tears and his whole body slumped. He looked down and said in a whisper, "I just can't go to school anymore." I think he got a rush of emotion, a *feeling bad about himself emotion*, and he immediately connected it to how school made him feel.

He asked me to go upstairs with him because he wanted to go to bed—it was 9:30 a.m. He wanted to build a nest on his bed. He made a circle out of pillows and sat in the middle. "Can you come in my nest with me?" he asked. I sat in the nest with him, saying nothing. He sat in my lap and I hugged him from behind. After a while he said, "I just can't go to school anymore. Not on Monday or Tuesday or Wednesday or Thursday or Friday."

"Can you tell me why you don't want to be at school?" I asked.

After a minute he replied, "I don't want to go to school. It makes me feel bad."

And after another very long moment, Matty looked down, almost ashamed, and said, "I need help."

"What do you need help with, Bud?" I asked.

After another long moment of silence he looked down again and said, "… with me." He actually said *"with me."*

I was stunned. I mumbled something like "I will always help you with school… and I will help you with you."

And after a few more minutes of silence he perked up and asked to play hide-and-seek—Mama bird finding baby bird, then baby bird finding Mama bird. I hid in the room where we have a swing and when he found me I asked if he wanted to make the cocoon swing into our nest. He said yes, and I gently pushed him until he was more regulated. We then went on a walk to pick up fall leaves.

In a note to Maude, I wrote: "It may sound crazy, but I think that when Matty tells me, 'I can't go to school because I don't feel good,' which he does often, he's really saying '*I don't feel good about myself.*'"

Self-Concept

The whole experience of seeing Matty flounder in an environment unsuited to meet his needs was distressing, but it was also a gift in that it started to weave a new thread in my understanding of another dimension of him. Had we not gone through those few painful months, I don't know that I would have learned the lesson of *self-concept* as deeply as I did. It surfaced a new connection in the complexity of anxiety, regulation, and motivation. Somewhere in the roots of Matty's anxiety and intrinsic motivation lies his sense of self. I didn't know exactly where and I still don't. All I know is that it's a piece of the puzzle—and for Matty, it was a missing piece.

Being thrown into an environment of higher expectations without adequate support for his needs exposed the fact that, although Matty now had many of the cognitive and physical tools for learning, one thing he still lacked was the self-concept to participate in the higher expectations of school. He had slammed the door to new experiences, gone into self-protection mode, and retreated to his fight, fright, and flight instincts.

The work of the past year brought down the walls that protected him from emotional thinking, only to expose a very raw and vulnerable sense of self. The Catholic school had limited resources and I knew that from the start. There were no opportunities for small group instruction, sensory intervention, or help with processing. I knew it couldn't provide the additional resources to support Matty's need for regulation and his approach to learning. It was my decision to take the risk and now he had nothing to cling to. I had moved him from one tightrope to another. Only now he had no balance bar or safety net. And like trying to walk a tightrope without a sense of balance, he was now trying to inch his way through each school day without a sense of self.

He was going through the motions of the school day without self-esteem or connection to purpose. I didn't fully understand the role of self-concept in fostering a deeper connection to motivation; I just knew it was part of the picture, and when it came to growing a sense of self, I was clueless. It was something I knew absolutely nothing about, but one thing my gut told me was that it wouldn't be done through an endless rash of *"good jobs"* and *"atta boys."* When it came to fostering the growth of Matty's self-concept, I knew I had to help him from a place of honesty. I knew I couldn't just throw out empty platitudes like sprinkling wildflower seeds, hoping something would eventually sprout.

Matty had shown me how deep his roots of emotion reached and I knew his sense of self wouldn't be any easier to cultivate. For Matty to begin to construct his *self,* I had to begin by helping him sense his value to the world, and I had to accept that it wouldn't be me who found or defined the things that would make him feel valued. As I had learned through our walks down the path of negative emotions, my role was only to give him time, recognize the opportunities that would allow him to journey forward, and hold his hand along the way.

Homeward Bound

It's such a poetic gift that many children with developmental deficits have extraordinary abilities in other areas. For Matty, one of those areas is a visual sense of direction. Although he may sometimes seem lost on the journey of childhood development, put him in a car and he's like no GPS you've ever had. From a very young age, Matty had an unusually vivid memory for mapping the routes we traveled in the car. Not only could he hover a half mile above town in his head, he could reverse engineer any set of directions to get you home from new and complex routes he'd never taken before.

We live in a town filled with roads laid out in ways that defy logic. Visitors definitely go home feeling, "It's a nice place to visit, but I wouldn't want to drive there." Having grown up here, I know most of the twists and turns, but one day I thought I'd take a shortcut home through a neighboring town. I was pressed for time as usual, and I came to a place where I wasn't sure which direction I needed to turn in order to get back to the street

I was familiar with. Matty was the only one in the car with me. I called a friend who lived in the area for directions but there was no answer, so I left a quick message. After hanging up from leaving a message saying I was a little lost and needed help finding Chatwick Road,

I heard Matty say, "It's over there."

"What Buddy?" I asked.

"It's over there," he repeated.

"What is?" I asked.

"Chatwick," he replied. Without hesitation, I followed his directions and after a few turns, he had me back on track. Even though I soon knew where I was, I let him continue giving me directions to get us the rest of the way home.

That ride home was the start of the *Get Us Home* game. Playing Get Us Home was an opportunity to help Matty relax and get regulated during the trying times of that kindergarten school year. It was also something that had meaning and gave him purpose. Although the purpose was simply to get us home, he connected to that purpose, he saw his value in reaching the goal and was therefore internally motivated achieve it. After making the mistake of sending him to Catholic school, the Get Us Home game was one of the first things I did right in getting him on the road to finding his sense of self.

"Hey Bud, up for a little Get Us Home?" I'd ask.

He'd be out the door sitting in the car like a shot. I would drive him somewhere he'd never been before and he loved the challenge of getting us home. I would make every turn he suggested, whether I thought it was right or wrong, and he always got us home. I never said "good job" or "you're good at this." That was not something he needed to hear. What he needed was to *feel* good at it. It was a game but I never said, "Betcha can't get us home," although I know he sensed the challenge. Pulling into the driveway his pride was palpable.

We celebrated with a simple high five and together we'd say, "Yay, we're home!" That was it. There were no prizes or treats for success in getting us home. I think they would have only diluted his genuine feeling of self-esteem. He now knew he was better at something than anyone else, and that gave him value—that was all he needed to feel.

Every episode of Get Us Home was filled with pure lagniappe for Matty. He delighted in his connection to purpose and was intrinsically motivated to map his way home every time we got in the car. In the process, he was mapping a meaningful and emotional route to his own sense of self. It taught me the value of a child's connection to his own worth, no matter what his contribution may be. Matty so rarely experienced feedback about his value to the world and it was beautiful to see how even a blip of genuine pride could turn up the volume on his self-worth. We sure wasted a lot of gas during the Get Us Home period and I extend my apologies to the environment for that. Yet, in doing so, we planted the seeds of a self-concept to help a child's journey become more complete. For that, I'm sure the environment will forgive.

The Strength of the "R"

Along with all the emotional work we'd done, what got Matty through this fragile time was the "R" in DIR. It was the strength of Matty's relationships with me and Karen that opened the door to turning the tumult into a time of growth. During the time Matty spent in morning kindergarten at the Catholic school, he was also spending the afternoons in Floortime sessions with

Karen. Thank goodness. Matty was stressed and Karen was a daily outlet and escape. A November DIR consultation report noted:

> *Matt has begun to display and talk about his emotions throughout his play and conversations with Mrs. O'Malley at home. Some of the emotions he is having are dealing with confidence issues in his school environment. This can be difficult to deal with, especially if he is distressed about his school day. This is also a great gain from where we saw him last month in that he tended to avoid emotional play and worked more on problem-solving. He is now able to add these emotions into his play and even talk about them in a candid manner with his mother. By keeping the play at this level and continuing to add emotions to his play, it will help him get a solid handle on level five and help him use his already established problem-solving strategies to cope with these emotions.*

Karen was seeing the same stress I saw and she was helping Matty deal with it through play. Matty spent a lot of time drawing and working in 2-D. He wanted to draw rather than visualize or verbalize. He wanted to depict through marker to paper rather than with 3-D figures and toys. Karen incorporated emotional content through pictures to encourage Matty to weave his feelings into the scenes on the paper. One bright light amidst all the stress was that Matty's sense of compassion continued to flourish. In a Floortime session note Karen wrote:

> *The biggest highlight of all was when he came over out of the blue and gave me a very soft kiss on the cheek about ten minutes after our session was over. It totally*

shocked me. It was just such a kind and caring gesture that it still touches me deeply even as I write this. I had been feeling under the weather this past week and maybe I discussed it in conversation or maybe he sensed the way I truly felt. Matt definitely knows when we are pretending to be sad or sick and thinks of it as a joke, but this was definitely genuine compassion. We have to continue to show more true emotion when the opportunity presents itself to give Matt more experience with the real thing.

He wanted help with himself and projected that by wanting to help others. He may have been a real bugger at home during that time, but he was also having more moments like this too. Not only was his range of negative emotions flourishing, but positive ones as well. As often as he'd tell me he didn't feel good about school, he would also tell me he loved me. For every moment of homework defiance came a moment of newfound tenderness. He certainly helped me learn that true growth always comes in packages of good with bad; but however it's wrapped, I always remember it for what it is. Genuine growth is always a gift.

Flying Solo

By Thanksgiving recess I'd already met with the public school IEP team to begin the process of transferring Matty into public school kindergarten. With school breaks and the IEP process being what it is, the move didn't happen until February, but the wait actually turned out to be a bit of a blessing. We lightened up on the homework pressure and it allowed time to really concentrate on his emotional growth and self-esteem. He had been through a rough ride, but we all came out stronger.

On a cold day in February, I drove Matty for his first day of kindergarten at his new school. I arranged for us to arrive a little late so he wouldn't be overwhelmed by the masses piling in at 9:00 a.m. He knew he was starting at a new school that day as we had gone in to see his new classroom and meet his teachers the week before. I put the prindle in park and the car was quiet. I turned around to see Matty looking out the window at the bright blue front door of the school. He seemed a little less worried than he'd been the month before, now more able to feel his feelings, talk about them, and process through them. He had been talking a lot in the recent weeks and seemed to have a more relaxed sense of maturity—even when talking about being a baby bird.

I fumbled to put my keys in my pocket while he sat quietly, staring at what lay ahead of him. As I turned around to grab his backpack, I heard a sigh of words that I will never forget.

"I'm scared to fly alone," he whispered through a long exhale. Few times in my life have I ever felt a stronger rush of emotion than I did at that moment. If I had opened my mouth, it would have released the floodgates of all my composure. It was so hard to let him feel what he was feeling, but I knew I had to. So I sat quietly and said nothing.

Something about his demeanor now spoke of harmony. He now had the beginning of a self-concept and was ready to embark on his first solo flight. He was no longer facing life with his head down, watching his own footsteps, afraid to look beyond the horizon. The past months were the humble beginning of his full emotional life and he was now able to face new challenges from a place of experience, not avoidance. He had walked through fear and the anxiety of emotional experiences, and he now had the beginnings of the sense of self to step him through it again. He was afraid—but he wasn't cowering.

Walking away from the car we held hands. I remember taking a few steps then checking to make sure I had my keys. Feeling my pocket empty I let go of Matty's hand to peek back into my car window, only to see that I had dropped them on my seat. I left them there, caught up to Matty and walked him to the school door. His teacher was waiting for us in the foyer... I quickly kissed him goodbye and apologetically backed out the door so I could finally breathe.

My baby bird had taken flight.

- *It is not about social targets. It's about bull's-eye intervention. It's about intervening at the root cause at the right time in the child's development.*

- *It is not as much about frequency of repetition, but about quality of the time spent in intervention.*

- *It is about maintaining the family structure so the child can learn from a typical family environment.*

- *It is about equipping the parent to intervene in a way that does not turn the relationship away from being a mother or father and into becoming a teacher or therapist.*

- *It is about twenty-four-hour intervention in as much a typical environment as possible, doing everyday activities through which every typically developing child is learning.*

Chapter 12

The Child Makes the Journey Happen

The Security Line

I stand behind Matt and his family. They have come to see the ceremony of my United States citizenship. My husband and I embarked down the path to U.S. citizenship many years ago—and today the day has arrived. There is a certain amount of excitement in the air as we finally take this important step in our lives. I met Lauren, Matt, and his sisters outside the Courthouse on this cold December day. We stood in line and chatted, then filed into the building to go through security.

Now in fourth grade, Matt quietly stood in front of the security doorway, hands shoved deep in his pockets, like so many other boys his age. His attention was locked with full eye contact on the officer explaining the steps of the security process. He waits his turn and complies with the instructions under the ever-watchful eye of his mother, always ready to support. As I watched, I felt a surge of warmth in my heart. I wished I could just go over to him and hug him so very closely to my chest. But I too must to follow his example, behave appropriately, and stay in line.

One by one, as Matt's sisters go through security, memories rush through my head. I reflect back on Matt's progress over the years, and the common denominators he shares with so many others. In many ways, he was like that teacher we've all had in our lives, that person who challenged you to new heights simply by believing in you. In his gentle, unassuming way, Matt challenged us as a team to remain committed to his needs, and, in doing so, we learned to trust his lead.

One of my first recollections of Matt was his insistence on playing with a Twister mat virtually every day for months. We had so much anxiety over this, just as so many caregivers would. Because of the pervasive element of a global media highlighted disorder, repetitious activities loom large, as something to be disapproved of—and almost taboo. But with Matt, we found the opposite to be more true in every single case. Like the child gleefully dropping her spoon over and over, each time learning something new or building on what was learned from the last drop, we never lost sight of this in Matt. Though sometimes frustrated, we always considered his *need* to remain on the Twister mat. We respected how the mat was feeding his system in some way, and it was his only realm of communicating those needs at that moment.

We always kept perspective on our expectations and used our expertise to strengthen each foundational building block by working through his needs in a functional way. How can we join him? How can we make him feel safe with us so he wants us to be with him? How can we use a particular interest to expand his repertoire of ideas, play, and emotional connection? When we respected what Matt was prepared to give us, when we understood that he knew best where he was in each moment in time, we earned his trust and he allowed us to move him forward. This is the same trust we value in our relationships as typically developing children and adults—and we should never lose sight of this. We want people to respect us, to value our opinion, and to understand our apprehension to being pushed out of our comfort zone. Yet, painfully, I fear we do not always observe the same consideration for many children with special needs.

I am fortunate. My journey to citizenship can end with a sole act. With a single oath, I can acquire the full rights and privileges other Americans were born into. I wish it were so easy for children like Matt. I wish I could just stand up and speak some alienable truth to magically embellish them with the childhood journey their peers were born into. If I could, you'd find me shouting from the mountaintops. If typical early development is good enough for a typically developing child, it is good enough for the child with developmental needs.

The Right Team... the Right Intervention... the Right Time

A big factor in our intervention plan with Matt was a solid team approach. It is important for every family to realize that it's not any one professional they should be seeking; rather, they should look to surround themselves with a team of people who are well-versed in their particular field. I've seen so many families go from one therapist to another, from one intervention to another, never feeling satisfied, and quite frankly, being exhausted of time, energy, and funding. At a recent consultation, parents shared an entirely packed schedule of interventions for a child who is barely two and a half years old. I truly believe in early intervention and want it to occur as much and as soon as possible, but the answer lies not in *more* intervention, but the *right intervention* at the *right time*. This precious toddler's parents' jaws dropped when I explained that the therapy intervention plan we were recommending was not even one-third of what they were planning.

The basis of any learning is valuing caregiver relationships and working from a mutual platform of enjoyment. This does not mean we don't intervene; rather, we target therapeutic intervention for periods of time, while equipping and empowering parents to understand their child and reinvest that understanding into creating a natural scaffold for learning. Turning the family home into a revolving door of therapies may be necessary to temporarily cope with difficult situations, but what really trains the mind is the provision of a typical home structure where learning is safe, accepting, and warm.

The Story of So Many Others

Some days, it seems, fate speaks more loudly than others. Today was one of those days, as more warm memories flashed through my mind. As we sat together in the courtroom, time stood still for a moment as I wondered, "Is this why we're here?" It certainly feels good to have played a small part in Matt's intervention team, and I have no reason to overstate my particular involvement. As far as I am concerned, it was, and still is a team effort that brings any child to this place of being. It's just that in this moment of seeing Matt turning into a young man, he personifies the countless others who I never get to see completely grow up. I don't get to see the many successes of their lives outside my clinical sphere.

Seeing Matt today is a real reminder that there are so many others traveling this road with him; those who have shared their lives with me for just a short space in time—and who are moving on, pressing forward. It's as if they have graced my presence for a short while just long enough so I can learn from them and be part of the absolute pleasure of helping them engage in this world filled with so many sensory riches and relationship strengths to enjoy.

Starfish Children

Children have an inborn resilience; they are created to adapt and cope. But many children retreat to their coping mechanisms far too early, and are too soon constrained by personal traits that tie them to a life path of tightly structured boundaries. We must commit ourselves to helping each and every child find their unique course of development, as only this will allow them to shoot for and reach their highest potential. We need to know typical development so we can analyze where development is not completing the correct wiring, and then intervene with a treatment plan aimed at the most basic level of developmental support. From there, we work our way up the typical ladder to the best ability we can.

Human development from utero until adulthood has not changed in recent decades, but unfortunately our expectations have. In general, we have become an impatient, product-oriented society that focuses only on the face of an issue. Some of this was born out of a sense of necessity, as the number of children with all kinds of traumatic experiences and developmental delays has increased dramatically. The thinking is: If we could only find some common ways to help this growing population of children in the shortest possible time, while also keeping expenses down. But since development is individual to each child, this looms as an almost impossible feat.

But does this mean that no one is achieving success? Absolutely not. In my work I remind myself of the story of the boy picking up beached starfishes, throwing them back into the ocean one by one. When asked why he was doing so… what good would it do since he could not possibly save all of the starfishes, he simply replied, "But it is good enough for those I can save." It is simply our obligation to honor the starfish lives we touch every day.

Social Development Depends on all of the Building Blocks

I also want to add a word on social skills and teaching social development. I do believe social skills training serves a purpose and is important for many children. But as soon as a child receives a certain diagnosis, such as on the pervasive spectrum, social skills training becomes an automatic referral. Social skill is built on a foundation of human relationships and the exercise of mutual affective engagement. This begins even before a baby is born through mommy's continual voice presence while in utero, and further builds on the child's understanding of himself, his ability to perceive and make sense of his environment, and his sense of self-identity. This is all strongly dependent upon his emotional experiences of early life, and developing the theory of mind to understand that others have needs different from him. Social communication further relies on an innate understanding of social reciprocity and having the ability to wait, take turns, and speak in a rhythmical manner. The very nature of social skills lies in the spontaneity that only comes with automaticity. This is but the tip of the iceberg of skills necessary for us to be social; but sufficient to say, it encompasses every single building block in our physical and emotional systems. Yet we insist on putting children in social skills training groups where, at best, they must cope and accommodate with cognitive strategies with little regard for the cost imposed on their developing systems.

Every child has a spirit and a sense of himself in his world, and as professionals and caregivers, we have enormous power in channeling that spirit. Many well-meaning therapists, caregivers, and teachers exercise a will on children that says, "I know better than you," as the child's needs go unheard.

I recently sat at an IEP meeting where a social worker stated that we did not need to find out *why* the child was behaving a certain way. "It would only be speculation," she interjected, "so we just need to figure out a behavior plan to stop it."

This attitude never ceases to amaze me. We would not even think to approach problems this way in our adult lives, yet it is perfectly acceptable for children with special needs because "we know better than them." We must also be extremely careful about the message we send children behind our words and intentions. If we bucket children according to certain behaviors or diagnoses, they learn that this is the expectation of them, and it is soon embodied in their sense of self-identity. If we understand that we ourselves need to be loved and understood, then we should afford the same respect to any child, especially the child with special needs.

Out with the "Time-outs"... In with the "Time-ins"

More than anything else, it's love and discipline that counts. I see many families struggle with how and when to discipline children with special needs. It is certainly a tough situation and there is no easy answer. If we look only at *behavior* and succumb to the fear that a child will become a behavior difficulty, we too quickly and too often resort to a system of negative consequences or time outs. But if we can step beyond our own anxiety, we will more easily see the underlying need for the behavior. We must always allow ourselves to find different ways of valuing a child's emotions and expression, even during a heated moment, and deal with the rules after all has calmed down. All children, typically developing or not, need the same boundaries as their siblings to feed their sense of self-identity. Children have an amazing sense of resilience and acceptance in understanding that one child may need a different path of order to adhere to house rules. Having regular house meetings to reinforce rules in a warm way becomes a good platform to also discuss each child's differences in needing to deal with issues in different ways.

In the height of a heated moment between adults, we all say things we do not mean, and it really is not the time to engage in any form of logic. Yet so many intervention plans enforce ignoring a child's behavior (and what he might be communicating through that behavior), breaking any form of engagement, and putting the child in his chaotic, over-aroused state alone in a time-out environment far-removed from any emotional stability. This is so contrary to what we expect for ourselves. We want to be understood and valued, we want to be heard, and we want to be supported, albeit in our own way. In speaking with children who can verbalize their emotions, they talk of how scared they feel when they get out of control, and how it is a downward spiral that leaves a lasting feeling of vulnerability. Children need caregivers to be an external anchor in times of need and this is certainly not the time to leave them alone. Is this not when they need us most?

I firmly believe in the concept of *time-in*. With this approach we do remove the child to a designated safe spot, but we stay with him, give him distance, yet stay near. We remain calm, quiet, and use few words while he is in a state of chaos, as logic does not compute at that time. We assure him with short sentences that we know he is mad and upset, but we also know that he can gain calmness himself. We let him know we will stay with him until he is ready. We do not take over the job of comfort and regulating; we give him the responsibility, and trust that he can overcome it himself. This always takes longer the first number of times, but the child soon learns that he is understood and he has the ability to gain control himself. Time-ins soon become shorter in duration. By approaching these situations from a place of respect, and by targeting the reasons why a child's frustration and anger have reached the level of tantrum or meltdown, the child's dignity is preserved and his trust in relationships are strengthened.

"Be the Change You Wish to See in the World"
–Mahatma Gandhi

Without a doubt, intervention programs can be costly for families, school systems, and our entire social structure, and I do not pretend to have a solution for the community at large. But I do know the answer must start from within. We need to understand the whole child and be responsible for knowing when the level of expectation exceeds the level of development. Missing this crucial starting point for learning sets the stage for the most predictable outcome of increased task and social avoidance. Just as we would avoid situations that hold little potential for a sense of accomplishment, children quickly shut down and shut out learning and social situations that hold little real value to them. My hope is for professionals and caregivers to embrace a personal commitment to consciously ask themselves whether they would like to be the recipient of every treatment plan, every behavior plan, and every consequence they impose on the children in their care. "Do unto others as you would like done unto you." This single notion can create a whole a new level of understanding and new heights of respect.

An Approach of Dignity

The journey of Matt O'Malley highlights the essential elements of what he needed to complete his development. My hope is that the road I traveled with Matt and Lauren will leave you with something more than you expected, and give you much to take with you. I hope that our experience becomes a part of your journey, and that the O'Malley's joy becomes your joy.

Through Matt's example, I leave you something from my heart. A simple approach of dignity…

> *Stepping through the layers*
> *Building the foundation*
> *Of typical development*
> *Over a process of years*
> *With a team-oriented approach*
> *Always respecting him*
> *Always raising the bar*
> *In a way that he could lead*
> *And we support…*

My wish is for every child to grow to their fullest potential, to shine the light of being and knowing themselves, and to grace us with their laughter as they choose to join us in making the journey happen.

Maude Le Roux

"Allies of respect, understanding, and the security of close relationships have become the threads that have allowed Matty to weave himself into who he is today."

Chapter 13

Our Greatest Allies

Matt's journey has been defined by the breadcrumb trail of allies he has found along the way. Allies of respect, understanding, and the security of close relationships have become the threads that have allowed him to weave himself into who he is today.

For typical children, it seems respect is an entitlement. But for Matt, it is something he wakes up each day having to earn from his peers and the countless others who don't understand him. As the whisperer of children with needs unheard, Maude has had an uncompromising respect for the dignity Matt deserves in this world. And with every layer she peeled back of my sweet little onion, I have been blessed with even more admiration for who he has become.

Every child writes his own book of development. For some children, their first chapters may be scribbled and scrambled in ways that don't make sense, ultimately leaving them disconnected to the meaning of their own story. That's how Matt's tale began. But with unwavering respect, Maude escorted him back to his beginning to allow him to recompose the pages of his own development, and allow me to relive his journey with the respect that he and other children like him so rightly deserve.

Maude has paramount respect for each and every child's potential and motivation to connect to their own development. She's like the Glinda of intrinsic motivation. Glinda, as any good *Wizard of Oz* fan knows, appears at the end of Dorothy's journey to tell her she has always had the power within her to return home.

To Maude, every child holds motivation intrinsically within, but physical kinks may prevent some children from fully tapping into it. Maude sees every child's glass of intrinsic motivation as half full, but rather than filling it using external factors such as behavioral rewards or consequences, she addresses the root causes and lets the child top it off themselves.

Matt also has an ally in understanding. Through his story and through you, at least one more person in this world will now understand the depth and the beauty of Matt and other children like him. Understanding children with developmental differences is rooted in appreciating the connections that define how they interact with the world.

- It all begins with knowing that our sensory systems are at the foundation of development, and that a child's developmental capacities are the infrastructure of all learning.

- It's knowing that even the slightest dysfunction in sensory processing can ripple through all areas of learning and development.

- It's developing a new read on the many ways a child communicates, including through behavior, to understand more about his needs and where he is in his development.

- It's understanding the sensory systems and physiological foundations of execution that impact a child's ability to learn and participate in a classroom environment.

- It's realizing that drivers of development such as intrinsic motivation and emotional development are gained not through earlier academics but from the richness of early play.

- It's grasping some of the physical roots of intangible things such as control, avoidance, and motivation, and for this understanding to empower you with more patience and respect.

- It's seeing peer interaction for the complexity it is, and understanding that your child's real BFFs are *process*, *self-concept*, and feeling his *sense of value* to the world.

There is no greater gift we can give our children than to learn about them, appreciate what's at the heart of their development, and allow them to shape their own sense self-respect and understanding of others. With these gifts a child will soar.

For Matt, I think his best ally along this journey has been me, and I have been honored to have that place in his life. I look forward to the day when he has developed the fullest sense of himself, and takes my place as his own strongest ally. Until then, I will be patient. I will understand him. I will respect him.

Gut & Guts—Time and Timing

As I look back I now see that my experience was defined not by my deepest fears, but by my own greatest allies, the *gut and guts—time and timing* I now appreciate more fully than I could have imagined. Even now, in every minute of doubt and moment of vulnerability, I continue to look to these allies as my source of strength, my beacon for direction.

Trust Your Gut

My story begins and ends at home. I began this journey with little more than a gut feeling that something wasn't quite right. Over time, I learned to trust in, and more importantly, act on my instincts. Every time I sensed something that bothered me, following my gut led me to a deeper understanding of the foundations of development. Learning about your child from a sensory and developmental perspective will foster your intuition for knowing when to be patient and when to intervene. Understanding sensory connections will also hone your instincts in identifying the *whys* of your child's behavior, and what he is trying to communicate through that behavior. Know that nothing pays itself forward more than intervention targeted at normalizing a child's sensory and developmental capacities. Listen to your gut as attentively as you do your child's cries... as it will be your instincts that are the first to hear his cry for help.

Have the Guts

Gut feelings hold no value unless you have the courage to follow them. You know your child better than anyone else on the planet. Offer your observations and thoughtful viewpoint; you'll soon find that your input and intuition are valued as much as any medical opinion or artifact that goes into developing a course of action for your child.

Have the courage to respect all that your child is—and don't let him be defined by what he's not. Let go of your need to control outcomes; throw the ball in his court and be patient to see how he plays it. Rely on a developmental frame of reference for setting expectations and never underestimate your child's potential. Stand as the agent of your child's needs and have the courage to protect them. Put external expectations in perspective and always be prepared to put yourself between those expectations and your child's real needs.

Parenting today seems to come with an endless need for random acts of courage. This journey has unleashed moments of emotional endurance I never thought possible in myself. Know that the strength to endure is within you too.

Give them Time

Time is a child's greatest steward of development, please respect its value. Ignore society's overly aggressive and miscalibrated clock, and be at peace in knowing your child as the clockmaker of his own development. Trust your gut to intervene early, but have the patience to wait for the developmental journey to catch up. Find the courage to wait for your child's intrinsic motivation to sprout and, when it does, put all other expectations aside to cultivate it. Know that time invested in developing *process* will never be time wasted.

Know the Timing

Understanding your child's sensory and developmental profile brings the gifts of timing and patience. When development and learning are in sync, learning is more integrative and has more meaning. When you know where your child is developmentally you will be better equipped to know when the timing is right (or not right) for intervention or curriculum. Know that timing is opportunity and the value of opportunity can never be underestimated when it comes to fostering meaningful moments in your child's development. Recognize opportunities when your child shows you he has amassed developmental leverage, and use that timing to harness his intrinsic motivation. Don't be afraid to throw consistency to the wind and seize a powerful moment; and don't feel guilty when you can't.

Resign yourself to accept that need trumps guilt, and that your child needs to learn from opportunities to foster emotional growth much more than he needs absolute consistency from you. Follow opportunities even if they lead you down a path of reacting outside the norm of your typical family harmony. Model genuine anger, frustration, fear, and disappointment, and let your child see how even the most powerful emotions are only temporary, and that they always bring you back to who you really are. Let your child see this in you and experience it in himself. Children develop the security of knowing they can circle through emotion and back again only by living it. Please give them the opportunity to learn this for themselves.

Time Flies

My baby bird is now ten. He is happy. He is peaceful. He has grace. The image of his childhood journey remains etched in my mind. I see a trail making its way through the forest. A footpath paved with darkened dirt bending into a horizon of green. The trail is not too wide and looks narrow up ahead. A group of tweens and teens walk ahead of me, my daughters included, leaving just enough distance between me and their conversation.

To my right, about two feet ahead, I see Matt. At any moment, I can reach out to feel the tickle in my palm as I run my hand up the back of his buzz cut. His gait is less rhythmic than mine as he walks with one foot on the path, the other rustling through the tangled ivy. The laces of his left shoe look speckled with coffee grinds as he scrapes it along the path. His right knee bends and straightens like an oil rig drill, revealing a clean white shoelace with each careful step. His childhood journey continues with one stride on the typical beaten path, and the other stepping slowly through the forest floor, always a little cautious of the unknown lingering beneath the green.

In our family, we call Matt "Bud." He's our buddy and we're his buddies. For now, we are his closest friends.

Matt's story is told for two people in this world—a parent and a child whom I don't know and I will never meet. For that child, I will never know your beauty; but through Matt's journey, I hope the rest of the world will. For that parent, should you find yourself traveling a journey similar to mine, my hope is that you find just one connection in my story to give you a richer sense of yourself as you write yours. I wish you the intuition to know your child, the courage to follow your gut, and for your experience, like mine, to be defined not by your greatest fears but by your greatest allies. In return I ask this of you. Promise me that you will live every day of your life with an unwavering respect for your child, and demand that the world *follow your lead.*

To you... that parent, that child... the journey of Matty O'Malley is now yours. Please respect its legacy, wherever you take it.

Lauren O'Malley

Lauren O'Malley

Resources

Biel, Lindsey and Nancy Peske. *Raising a Sensory Smart Child: The Definitive Handbook for Helping Your Child with Sensory Processing Issues.* New York, NY: Penguin Books, 2005.

Brazelton, M.D., T. Berry and Joshua D. Sparrow, M.D. *Touchpoints: 3 to 6.* Cambridge, MA: Perseus Publishing, 2001.

Brazelton, M.D., T. Berry and Joshua D. Sparrow, M.D. *Touchpoints: Birth to Three.* Cambridge, MA: Da Capo Press, 2006. Goddard, Sally. *Reflexes, Learning, and Behavior: A Window into the Child's Mind.* Eugene,
Oregon: Fern Ridge Press, 1957.

Greenspan, M.D., Stanley I. and Nancy B. Lewis. *Building Healthy Minds: The Six Experiences that Create Intelligence and Emotional Growth in Babies and Young Children.* New York, NY: Perseus Publishing, 1999.

Greenspan, M.D., Stanley I. and Jacqueline Salmon. *The Challenging Child: Understanding, Raising, and Enjoying the Five "Difficult" Types of Children.* New York, NY: Perseus Publishing, 1995.

Greenspan, M.D., Stanley I. and Serena Wieder, Ph.D. *Engaging Autism: Using the Floortime Approach to Help Children Relate, Communicate, and Think.* Cambridge, MA: Da Capo Press, 2006.

Greenspan, M.D., Stanley I., Serena Wieder, Ph.D., and Robin Simons. *The Child With Special Needs: Encouraging Intellectual and Emotional Growth.* Cambridge, MA: Perseus Publishing, 1998.

Heller, Ph.D., Sharon. *Too Loud, Too Bright, Too Fast, Too Tight: What to Do If You Are Sensory Defensive in an Overstimulating World.* New York, NY: HarperCollins Publishers, Inc., 2002.

Irlen, Helen. *Reading by the Colors (Rev.).* New York, NY: Penguin Group, 2005.

Levine, M.D., Mel D. *All Kinds of Minds: A Young Student's Book About Learning Abilities and Learning Disorders.* Cambridge, MA: Educators Publishing Service, Inc., 1992.

Masgutova, Ph.D., Svetlana. *Integration of Infant Dynamic and Postural Reflex Patterns – MNRI Neurosensorimotor Reflex Integration.* United States, 1998.

Michnick Golinkoff, Ph.D., Robert and Kathy Hirsh-Pasek, Ph.D. *How Babies Talk: The Magic and Mystery of Language in the First 3 Years of Life.* New York, NY: Plume, 2000.

Miller, Ph.D. OTR, Lucy J. and Doris A. Fuller. *Sensational Kids: Hope and Help for Children with Sensory Processing Disorder.* New York, NY: Penguin Books, 2006.

Nicoli, Francois and Maude Le Roux. *The Listening Journey for Children: Boosting learning, communication, and confidence through sound.* Australia: Hear and Now Publishing, 2011.

Schneider McClure, Vimala. *Infant Massage: A Handbook for Loving Parents (Rev. Ed.).* New York, NY: Bantam Books, 2000.

Siegel, M.D., Daniel J. and Tina P. Bryson, Ph.D. *The Whole-Brain Child: 12 Revolutionary Strategies to Nurture Your Child's Developing Mind.* New York: Delacorte Press, 2011.

Sollier, Pierre. *Listening for Wellness: An Introduction to the Tomatis Method.* Yaug Tong, Kowloon, Hong Kong: Everbest Printing C, Ltd., 2005.

References

Balanced Scorecard Institute. "Balanced Scorecard Basics", "Why Implement a Balanced Scorecard?" June 11, 2010. http://www.balancedscorecard.org/bscresources/aboutthebalancedscorecard/tabid/55/default.aspx

Begley, S. (2007). The puzzle of hidden ability. *Newsweek, Aug 20-27; 150* (8-9), 50.

Braun, E. M. & Davis, R. D. (2010). *The gift of Dyslexia.* New York, NY: Perigee Trade.

Brazelton, T. B., & Sparrow, J.D. (2006). *Touchpoints—Birth to three.* Jackson, TN: Da Capo Press.

Centers for Disease Control and Prevention. *New Data on Autism Spectrum Disorders.* Retrieved from http://www.cdc.gov/Features/CountingAutism (accessed October 16, 2012)

Dunn OTR, FAOTA, Winnie. Sensory Profile. The Psychological Corporation, USA: A Harcourt Assessment Company, 1999

Greenspan, S. (2001). Affect Diathesis Hypothesis. The Role of Emotions in the Core Deficit in Autism and in the Development of Intelligence and Social Skills— The Journal of Developmental and Learning Disorders, special edition, Vol. 5, N. 1., Interdisciplinary Council on developmental and Learning Disorders (ICDL), Bethesda, Maryland. http://www.icdl.com/bookstore/journal/documents/2001_v5_1_.pdf

Greenspan, M.D., Stanley I., Serena Wieder, Ph.D., and Robin Simons. *The Child With Special Needs: Encouraging Intellectual and Emotional Growth.* Cambridge, MA: Perseus Publishing, 1998.

The Parent Review Report Volume 6, Number 2 (Summer 2008. What's the Point of Infant Gestures? http://www.viacord.com/cord-blood-news/summer-2008/_assets/pdf/TPR-Vol6No2-2008.pdf

Perceptual Development Corp, & Irlen , H. (1998). Light sensitivity, fluorescent lights and Irlen. Retrieved from http://irlen.com/index.php?id=56

Pert, C. B. (1999). *Molecules of emotion.* New York, NY: Simon and Schuster, Inc.

Tronick, E. (2007). *The neurobehavioral and social-emotional development of children.* New York, NY: W.W. Norton & Company, Inc.

Wilbarger, J. & Wilbarger, P. (2002). Wilbarger approach to treating sensory defensiveness and clinical application of the sensory diet. Sections in alternative and complementary programs for intervention, In Bundy, A.C., Murray, E.A., & Lane, S. (Eds.). *Sensory Integration: Theory and Practice*, 2nd Ed. F.A. Davis, Philadelphia, PA.

Wurzburg, G. (Producer & Director). (2004). *Autism is a world.* [Motion picture]. United States: CNN.

End Notes

1   Greenspan and Wieder, The Child with Special Needs, p. 34.
2   Stanley Greenspan. *Affect Diathesis Hypothesis.*" http://www.icdl.com/bookstore/journal/documents/2001_v5_1_.pdf, page 5 (accessed October 8, 2012).
3   Affect Diathesis Hypothesis, page 1.
4   Affect Diathesis Hypothesis, page 3.
5   "What's the Point of Infant Gestures?" *The Parent Review Report, Volume 6, Number 2 (Summer 2008)*: page 1. http://www.viacord.com/cord-blood-news/summer-2008/_assets/pdf/TPR-Vol6No2-2008.pdf (accessed September 9, 2011.)

Maude Le Roux

Maude Le Roux was born and raised in South Africa. She completed her degree in Occupational Therapy in Stellenbosch, South Africa and moved to the United States in 1993. In 2001 she opened her private practice, which is now in Glen Mills, Pennsylvania.

Maude has extensive experience working with children who struggle with diagnoses such as developmental delay, Sensory Processing Disorder, autism spectrum disorder, learning disabilities, and reading disabilities. She is steadfast in continuing her own education to always gain more knowledge, learn new approaches, and shed more light on the development of children. Her particular affinity is attempting to "see" in the mind of a child, and read the child's cues to determine the message beneath the behavior.

Among multiple certifications, Maude is an international trainer for Tomatis® Sound training and holds a certificate in DIR®/Floortime™. She develops her own courses, speaks at several international conferences, and is co-author of the book: "The Listening Journey for Children" with Francoise Nicoloff.

Her wish is for all to understand that it is a child's motivation to be understood, to please, to be accepted, and to be respected. Her team-oriented approach is built upon the foundations of sensory/physical and emotional building blocks in child development. Read more about her work at www.atotalapproach.com.

Made in the USA
Lexington, KY
29 March 2018